Searching for Life's Water

Traveling the World to Find the Source

Sita Mitchell

Oasis Publishing
San Diego
2009

First Edition
Printed in the United States

Library of Congress Catalog Control Number: 2009921670

Publisher's Cataloging-in-Publication Data
Mitchell, Sita.
Searching for Life's Water: Traveling the World to Find the Source
ISBN: 978-0-9823340-0-3
Cover design and book layout by Michael Mitchell
Cover photo by Zahoor Ahmed, Pakistan

For Michael, who understood

Contents

Foreword

How cool that little symbols on a page can transport us to an inner realm inside ourselves! And even more so is the effect of another person's passion rubbing against ours until sparks fly and a fire breaks out. This is the test of a book, or of any work of art—to touch us and move us so that we aspire to be better persons. And that is exactly what I believe Sita has done with this book. She wants you to live the fullest life possible, and so she has worked hard to give you a little bit of her soul. And if it expands you in some way, then her efforts will have paid off.

I have to say how much I enjoyed watching Sita write her book and work through all the creative stages to bring her passion to a reality. Creating is something we all do, and adventure is something we all want. This act of creating adventure is something we do even if mostly in our head. But at the end of the day or, more importantly, at the end of our own story, what have we learned, felt, and experienced?

We have been given a body with a mind to use, feelings to be felt, and guts and legs to get us there. But where is 'there'? Where have our beliefs come from and how have they shaped our outlook on life? Sita takes us, her friends and readers, on a journey to consider these questions. One amazing thing about humans is that we can observe the journey even in the moment of the journey. This awareness can lead us to new places. And really, isn't gaining awareness what traveling is all about?

To examine Sita's life for a few hours is really an invitation to examine our own. We are all unique and have our own path to travel, but without relationships to mirror who we are, how could we ever find our way? In allowing yourself to travel through Sita's eyes, you will definitely have a meaningful journey and walk away with a few insights. And if some fear overtakes you along the journey, just tighten your seat belt and breathe. Because what is fear anyway? Just excitement without breath.

Words are powerful, but still just words. Any meaning they have depends upon you. Words cannot fully convey the meaning of a trip or a life well lived. So if we are going to fly, we must give up taxiing around the runway. Sita asks us to pack our bags with a smart thinking cap, a questioning spirit, and don't forget the spiritual underwear. And if you hit a little turbulence in your psyche—just roll with it.

MICHAEL MITCHELL

Preface

When I was growing up, I was intrigued by what a Persian poet wrote: "Everything has to do with loving and not loving." His thought had an effect on me and helped me give voice to a part of myself. For it is true that human beings have a unique relationship with love because we have an ability to love and reflect on love like no other creature can. When I first realized this, I felt so much sadness since my parents lived and talked as atheists. To them and their friends, love wasn't a spiritual quality.

Though I enjoyed traveling with my family as my father conducted scientific studies in foreign lands, I felt lost. I couldn't trust science the way my parents did. It caused me agony because I loved my parents and naturally wanted to follow in their footsteps. But I came to see more and more clearly that science couldn't explain the meaning of life to me. For even though it has made great strides in understanding the physical laws, it can't understand the spiritual laws.

Science's proclaimed mastery of nature has led many people to believe that it can adequately explain the origin of life, including love. But it can't. For though science can accurately predict the planets' path around the sun, it can't say, without controversy, how they formed in the first place. Neither can it say where love came from and why so many believe that it has a divine source.

Though I could understand the physical level of life as a spectacular molecular phenomenon, it wasn't enough for me. I was constantly drawn to see it in a broader context, as an expression of an immense spiritual dynamic. That way I could focus on the beauty of life and the gratitude I felt for it. I couldn't bear to think of life only in terms of the nuts and bolts of physical forms.

When I looked at cactus flowers growing in the desert, I was awed by their magnificence. Their petals were delicate, purple, and papery thin even though they were surrounded by dangerous thorns. How could those flowers be so beautiful? The relationship of the flower to the thorns was indelibly stamped on my mind and imagination. I conceived a metaphor that shaped my thoughts thereafter. It was that the cactus flower, like the spiritual essence in all of us, could blossom in spite of the hostile world around it.

Science, sadly, became to me the thorny part of the cactus because it seemed to prevent people from recognizing something essential: that we all have the capacity to understand both the physical and spiritual sides of our lives even if we have convinced ourselves otherwise. Also, I noticed that scientists, more than most people, are afraid of love and deny the power that it has. In fact, most of them claim that love is just the result of an accident, thrown out by the forces of a blind and dumb nature. But love is purposeful, a willed intention on the part of those who practice it consciously in their spiritual life.

Inevitably, my desire to love and be loved in a spiritual way caused me to leave my family and all that I knew in the Western world. I called myself a seeker, searching for meaning as if for an oasis in a dry, barren land. My search lasted for decades and, after many adventures, I finally found the water of life.

My travels along the way immersed me in the religions of the world and I saw many strange and curious sights. I felt I had to share what I learned through all my efforts. I wanted to explain, especially to my father and mother and two sisters, that love truly is the essence of life. That Persian poet was right. Everything is about loving and not loving.

SITA MITCHELL
Encinitas, California

The voyage of discovery is not in seeking new landscapes but in having new eyes.

Marcel Proust (1871-1922), French Novelist

CHAPTER ONE

Desert Nomad

My first spiritual teacher was a desert nomad. He pointed south into the deep silence of the Sahara, the biggest desert in the world. My eyes strained to see where he pointed beyond the shimmering heat waves. There was supposed to be an oasis out there, like a tiny island in a sea of sand. But all I could see was the barren desert plain that was so dry that even an insect couldn't survive. I imagined that the oasis was a magical place where sweet water flowed in the shade of fragrant flowers.

Still, the reality was that the gravel outline of our road was gone, either blown away or buried. Whatever had happened, it disappeared somewhere south of In Guezzam and beyond the Algerian border. Our Land Rover was stopped in its tracks, the only rise and the only shade as far as I could see. We had to trust that the nomad could show us the way to the oasis called "Arlit." He was a Tuareg, one of the desert people who run camel caravans and live in tents. He must have known exactly where we were, some thousand miles from the north coast of Africa.

To me, he wasn't an ordinary man even if the desert seemed ordinary to him. He didn't climb into our Land Rover and show us the way to Arlit just for money or whatever it was we gave him. He stood for something new out beyond the last palm tree, beyond the shade of the comfort zone.

The comfort zone is a useful way to illustrate how we protect our self-made boundaries and beliefs. And even though we constantly have new opportunities to learn about ourselves, it doesn't mean we will expand our self-understanding. Our comfort zone won't let us. It stubbornly shields us from seeing through our blind spots so we sink into a fixed way of thinking, into a mind-set that is usually prejudiced. But opening our mind and heart to see ourselves more clearly involves a special effort. And we usually have to be affected by some influence, like the Tuareg was on me.

He was covered in blue cotton swirling around him in the wind. Only his black eyes and dark hands were exposed. In contrast, I was scantily dressed wearing shorts, a short-sleeved shirt, and a straw sun hat over my neck-length hair. Thin and muscular, I claimed the strength and courage of a boy, and I wanted people to think I was a boy, as a way to hide my inner sensitivity.

But even though the Tuareg and I were also different in age and cultural outlook, we could still share the most basic similarity. We could be conscious of having a spiritual need, a need that couldn't be satisfied by anything anyone could give us no matter where we lived, unless it was true spiritual knowledge.

I wanted to drink the water of life. I wanted to find the fountain of truth that bubbled up through the parched places of the earth which were, for me, the arid stretches of atheistic science. I felt terribly thirsty knowing that my parents expected me to be an atheist like them. They avoided any search for God, or any meaningful discussion of the concept of God, maybe because they were afraid of where it could take them. They considered the confusion that blew out of religion and its choking dogma to be like a perilous sandstorm. They weren't willing to risk that religion might hold some truth, especially organized religion. But they didn't know about spiritual longing because they didn't recognize that they had a spiritual need.

My dream was that there was a spiritual oasis, and that I would have the courage to find out where it was. But I knew that meant having to cross the vast loneliness of believing in myself in spite of what others would say to discourage me. The oasis couldn't be found by science, because its tools couldn't point out the way across the sands. Though I appreciated how science had improved many aspects of our physical lives, I was aware that it couldn't bring contentment to our hearts.

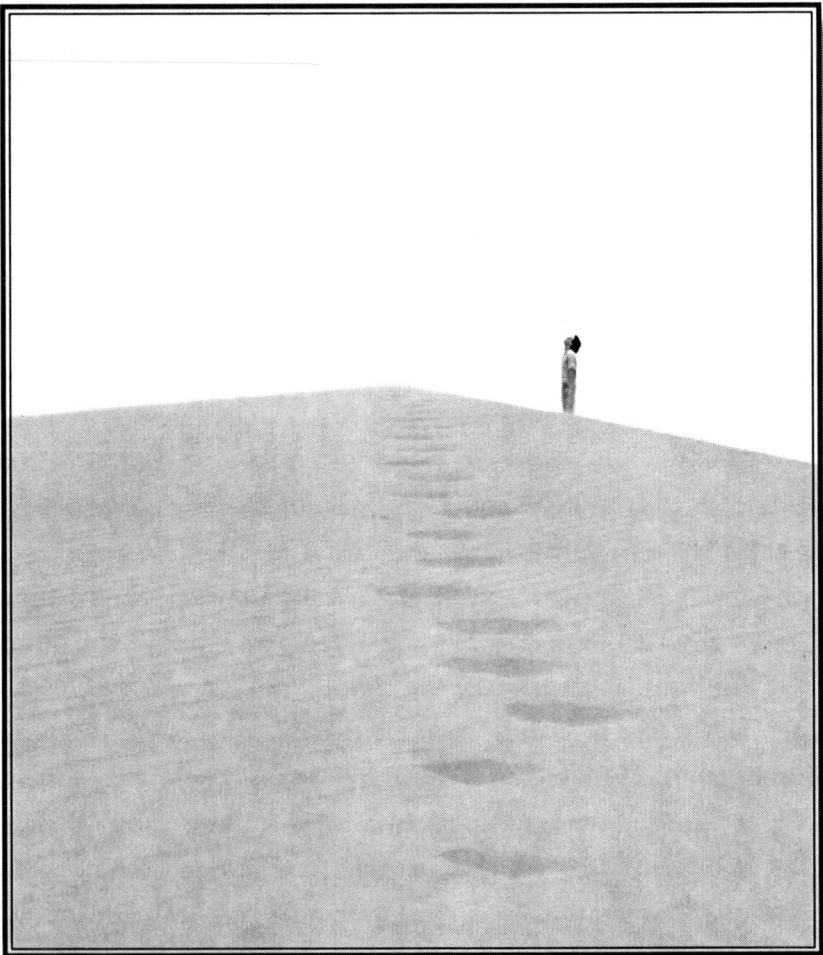

Meeting the Tuareg was a special experience in my early life and a memory that I always built on. I wanted to believe that he was a spiritual teacher, like a guide to the oasis we couldn't find by ourselves. But in my parents way of thinking, we only bumped into the Tuareg because we were trying to cross the Sahara to get to plants that lived on the other side.

As a world-class biologist and professor of botany, my father was seeking to contribute new knowledge to the annals of plant morphology and the journals of *Science* and *Nature*. He was funded by grants from the National Science Foundation to collect and photograph the mistletoe plants that he studied. His primary interests included learning about their taxonomic classifications, pollination systems, and genetic peculiarities.

Besides collecting data for science, he had to keep his wife and three young daughters safe from the hazards we could encounter. Driving the length of Africa, which is the second largest continent in the world, we faced many challenges due to changing climates, cultures, and countries. We had to be wary of getting lost or stuck in sand or mud, and flat tires, which happened often. And there were the concerns of running out of food, water, or gas, and being stopped or robbed at border crossings or somewhere else. There were also other visible and invisible dangers like ticks, venomous snakes, hyenas, malaria, leprosy, and river blindness.

We drove a white four-door Land Rover south from England, through France, Andorra, and Spain. When we reached the Mediterranean Sea, we crossed by ferry at the Strait of Gibraltar and entered Africa on the north coast of Morocco. Our destination was the Cape of Good Hope, the southern tip of Africa. Our route to South Africa was through the central Sahara and the desert countries of Morocco, Algeria, and Niger. Then south through sub-

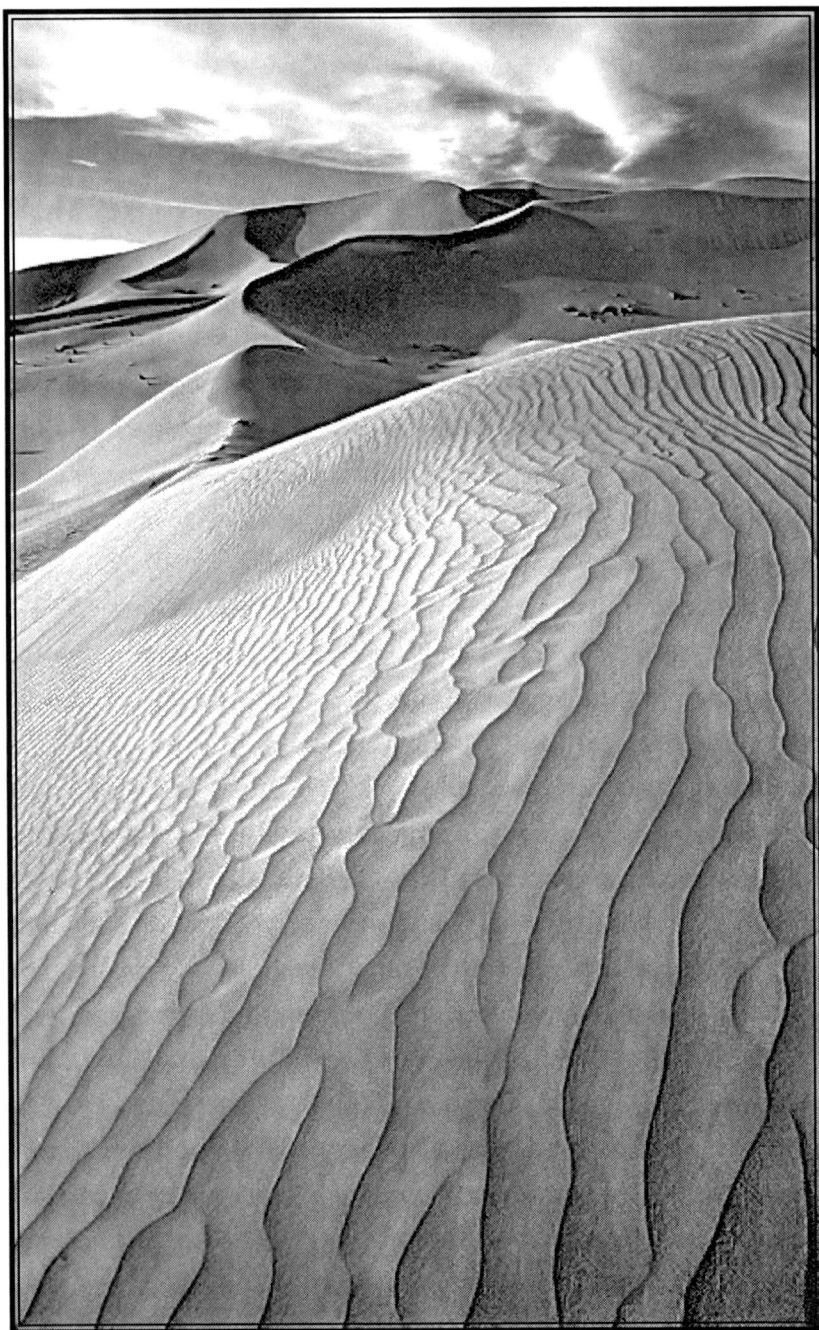

Saharan Africa and the countries of Nigeria, Cameroon, Central African Republic, and down into Zaire, Congo, Uganda, Kenya, and Tanzania. After passing through Zambia, Malawi, Zimbabwe, and Botswana, we would finally reach South Africa.

The Sahara, which means "desert" in Arabic, is only 25 percent of Africa's land mass, but it is almost the size of the United States with a sand dune as big as France. Most of the Sahara is not sand seas, as many people imagine, but vast windswept plains covered with black, red, and white gravel. As one of the most sparsely populated places on earth, it can be a treacherous place to travel. Temperatures reach up to 140°F, and oases are few and scattered.

Around 350 miles south of Algiers, the seacoast capital of Algeria, we encountered a huge white sign on the roadside. Written in Arabic, French, and poor English, with typos, it warned travelers heading south into the central Sahara:

> **TRAVELERS VIA THE GREAT SOUTH FROM EL GOLEA AND AT EVERY FOLLOWING STEP. YOU SHOULD STATE AT THE DIARA YOUR ARRIVAL AND DEPARTURE. YOU WILL BE PROVIDED WITH TRAVELING PERMIT. ANY INFRACTION OF THIS RULE IS PUNISHED BY LAW. YOUR SECURITY AND YOUR LIFE DEPENDE ONE THIS.**

Someone had tried to correct one of the typos on the sign and had blackened out the "**E**" on the end of "**ONE**" to make it read "**ON**." We stopped for a while to ponder the sign. English-speaking people who headed out across "**THE GREAT SOUTH**" were probably more likely to encounter problems than those who spoke Arabic and French.

I thought the "The Great South" on the sign would be better called "The Great Deep" because of the great silence of the Sahara. The impact of so much silent space was enhanced by the absence of people. Since much of the Sahara's 3.5 million square miles is without any reliable rain, few people find a way to live there.

On our Land Rover we had roof racks, side racks, and bumper racks. On the roof racks we carried a tent, sleeping bags, plant presses, and various other gear. On the side racks we had jerry cans of extra gas and water. In Morocco, we slung a black-hair goat-skin bag tied with a rope on top of the jerry cans. Though the water inside stayed amazingly cool, it tasted bitter and strange so we used it mostly for washing our hands. The bumper racks carried our sand tracks, two long metal strips about five feet long and two feet wide that were grooved with circular holes. We would put them under our wheels for traction whenever we got stuck in the sand.

Behind the back seats, we stored food in a large blue trunk. It mostly contained powdered milk, oatmeal, pasta, rice, and what seemed like an endless supply of cans of corned beef and sardines. We also had many packets of dried peas, which were available in Morocco and northern Algeria. We could also get bread, jam, and peanut butter. But south of Algiers, it wasn't easy to find food.

There were only six main oases through which the sandy-gravel road passed, heading south for over a thousand miles into sub-Saharan Africa and the tropics. The roadside was a grave-yard for vehicles not able to manage the heat, bumpy terrain, or whatever it was that stopped them. Partially buried by sand and stripped of their parts, they were bleached like bones.

The country of Algeria alone is more than three times as big as Texas and 90 percent desert. South of Algeria is the country of Niger, which is about twice the size of Texas. In this vast space of Algeria and Niger, the oases on our route were Ghardaia, El Golea, In Salah, Tamanrasset, In Guezzam, and Arlit. We could sing them like a song and we all knew where they were on the map, a tiny blue dot that meant there was water.

The word "oasis" is believed to come from an ancient Egyptian word meaning something like a fertile place in endless sand. Ghardaia, which was closest to the Mediterranean coast, had a colorful outdoor market. There were piles of dates, figs, melons, peaches, oranges, wheat and barley, and many other fruits and vegetables.

South of Ghardaia, food became more scarce. In El Golea we purchased six melons, a kilo of cucumbers, and we also found fresh meat, which was a rare treat. We watched the butcher hack up unidentifiable chunks of a goat with an ax on his tree-stump chopping block. Then he ate grapes with his bloody fingers between customers and flies. When we cooked the meat on our camping stove, it was so tough that we could only chew a few pieces.

The oasis of In Salah looked like a movie set with Arabian-style architecture. The buildings were freshly coated with red mud striped by finger marks. There was almost nothing for sale in the market there, just some fodder for animals, some onions, a few grapes, and sandals.

South of In Salah and all the way to Kenya, we had trouble finding food, though occasionally we got bread, marmalade, couscous, and an egg or two. We usually had food enough for a week or a little more at a time. In Nigeria we were able to buy bananas, papayas, and pineapples. We could eat a few pineapples at a time along the roadside, and we called these feasts "pineapple pig-outs." In the Congo we found oranges, coconuts, and enormous avocados and mangos. It was my first experience eating mangos and dealing with their strange, flat seeds.

Besides food, clothes, and our camp gear, which included the folding table, folding stools, and cooking utensils, we carried shovels, a first aid kit with malaria pills, plus cameras with telephoto and wide angle lenses, and an endless supply of film. We even had a movie camera, a tape recorder, a microscope, and a BB gun for collecting the darling little sunbirds with their long curved beaks for whatever reason science could conjure.

We also had boxes of cigarettes, though my dad and mom didn't smoke. My dad gave them to the border officials as gifts, but maybe they were more like bribes. They loved them and were in a better mood when he led my younger sister, Alison, in by the hand to charm them with her bright blonde hair. Little white girls were rare travelers, especially in the central Sahara. They always loved her hair and sometimes wanted to run their fingers through it. Then they would wave us through their barbed wire fences staked in the sand.

My dad could always get us through any border, as tough as it might seem. He was clever with people and worldly-wise and knew how to get what he needed. Whether it was information about the road, a stamp in our passport, or where to trade money on the black market for local currency, he always came through. He was friendly too, and played the tape recorder back to the African people who had never heard their voices taped before. They would yell into the tape recorder and then laugh hysterically when they heard how they sounded.

But my dad couldn't really trust their laughter. He called Africa "the bloody continent" because of the tribal warfare of the African peoples. He always said that Africa's wildlife would probably survive because humans were so busy killing each other that the land would never become too populated. From his comments, I always thought he had more hope for the future of African animals than for African people.

But it seemed such a bleak outcome for intelligent people capable of love. It was a sad commentary on the potential of people no different from us, even if their lifestyles didn't include travel to foreign lands like ours did.

I wondered what it was about humans that made us so unpredictable when we were supposed to be so smart compared to all the animals. Just like the Africans, everyone everywhere had to make basic choices about how to deal with each other and especially to those not related to them. I noticed that unlike animals, only people could decide who they wanted to help or hinder. And only humans could change their minds about what they claimed they originally did or wanted to do for others, depending on who influenced them.

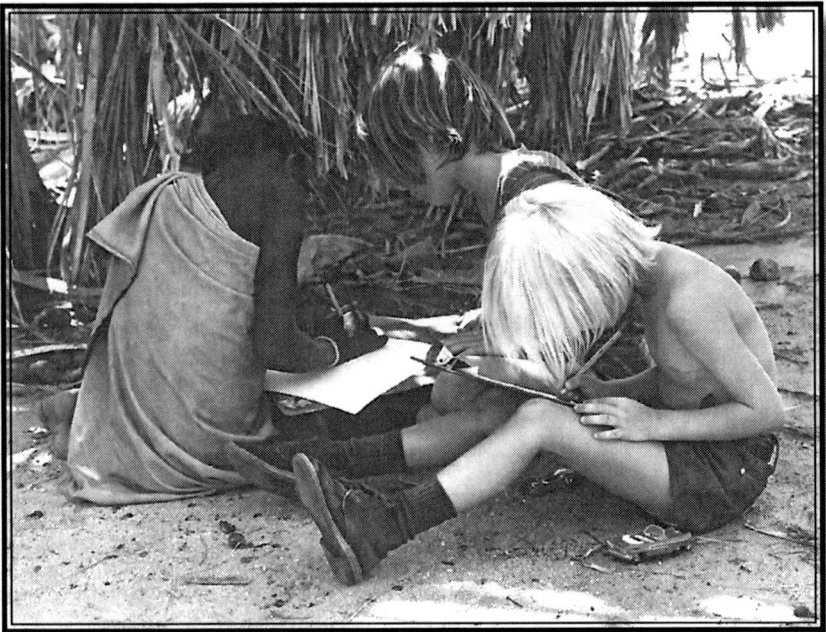

Good people could turn to doing bad and bad people could turn to doing good. But wild animals were never plagued with this problem. Their behavior was usually steady. Everyone knew that lions roared at dawn, leopards hunted at night, and monkeys slept in trees. Everyone also knew that animals never really trusted man because he wasn't like any one of them. People were strangely irreconcilable with the rest of the animal world. For this reason, I couldn't believe that humans could be accurately classified as another kind of animal.

I began to wonder what it was that governed humans and our choices. Animals were governed by instinct, so they couldn't think about what they wanted to do in any situation. But people had to think all the time. Even though my family didn't talk much about what it meant to have and cultivate a conscience, I knew that being human had to do with learning what is right and wrong, and making choices to do what is good for ourselves and others. People had a responsibility that animals could never understand.

As we left the Sahara and entered into the Saharan fringe, plants and trees began to reappear. And with the plants and trees came new kinds of animals and many more people. But they looked different from those we had seen. Their skin was darker, the breadth of their noses was wider, and they didn't wear many clothes. In fact, we often saw women on the road who wore only a colorful cloth around their waists. Children were often naked or wearing tattered shorts, and sometimes sandals.

White travelers probably didn't pass all that often through their villages made of clay and grass huts. Whenever children heard us coming, they sang and shouted and ran alongside our Land Rover waving to us and clapping. When we stopped, dozens of arms would come through our windows and everyone's hands would be on our heads and touching us wherever and however they could. Slowly their arms would disappear as we closed our windows, but not their smiles pressed up against the glass.

Even if people lived close to the land, I couldn't believe that it proved their ancestors were animals. I realized that people made decisions about what they wanted to do based on their background, opportunities, and preferences. And though little African children constantly rode on the hips of their big brothers and sisters, who sometimes weren't that much older than them, they were constantly learning new things. They had to acquire an understanding about who they were in their world based on the choices that they made. But animals, by contrast, had a small capacity to learn new things because their knowledge was mostly instinctual.

More than anything else, I wanted to know what made a person who he was, though I didn't care so much about outward appearance. I cared about inner inclinations, and what it was that could influence someone to change besides a payment or punishment. I wondered what would make one person kind and helpful and another person mean and cruel, especially if they were born into the same family.

I knew science couldn't give me the answers to my questions because it wasn't equipped to deal with feelings. I never met a scientist for that matter, and especially the atheist kind, who was really comfortable with feelings. Even my own mother and father never once told me "I love you" when I was a child that I can remember.

One day we stopped on the roadside to collect a mistletoe that we saw growing in a tree. A young African man was sitting nearby, but no one else was around. His posture was strange and slouched. With one hand he braced the ground, and with the other he held a long thin stick horizontally in front of his face. I realized that he was sick. He was using the stick like tissue and was blowing his nose onto it. Slowly he pulled the mucus away in long drooping strands. I felt so sad to see him there sick by himself, but I wasn't permitted to go near him.

It occurred to me as I stood some distance away, that there was a huge rift between the scientific mind that wanted to know impersonal things about physical life, and another kind of compassionate mind that didn't care so much about gathering facts and figures. The scientific mind, as I then thought from the perspective of a kid, could treat sick people like animals but the compassionate mind would treat sick animals like people. There was a big difference.

It was as if science forced people, especially those who wanted to be scientists, to ignore their feelings. But that was impossible for me, and not just because I was young. Having to ignore feelings was like being told to put on an itchy woolen hat in the scorching heat and having to wear it all day. I had a strange thing happen to me that was sort of like having to wear such a hat. It was an uncomfortable obsession which forced itself on me and established in my mind, with the greatest conviction, that the scientific outlook on life could be cruel to the heart.

The obsession was like a pestering voice that insisted that I had to count every single sand grain where I stood, and as far as I could reach. It brought on a feeling of endless frustration and weariness because I knew it wasn't by counting sand that I could find real meaning and joy in my life. I suppose my bad vision of the sand counting didn't come from nowhere. My dad and mom often counted mistletoe buds, and then took what they called a "sex ratio" to determine how many plants in the population were male or female. This always seemed pointless to me, but it wasn't because I was mean-hearted. It just didn't satisfy my need to communicate about feelings, especially loving feelings.

I wanted to discover the inner secrets of people, and not plants. I needed to know what made people the way they were, and why some people were kind while others weren't. I noticed that outer cultural differences and the color of our skin didn't make a difference when it came to being helpful, angry, or hungry. Everyone too, I decided, must want to find out what gives us purpose and happiness beyond having enough to eat and a decent way to live.

I decided to try my own experiments. But mine were with people, not plants. The first one was to see how it felt to give something valuable to someone whose name I didn't even know. I found a boy around my age near a village where we camped

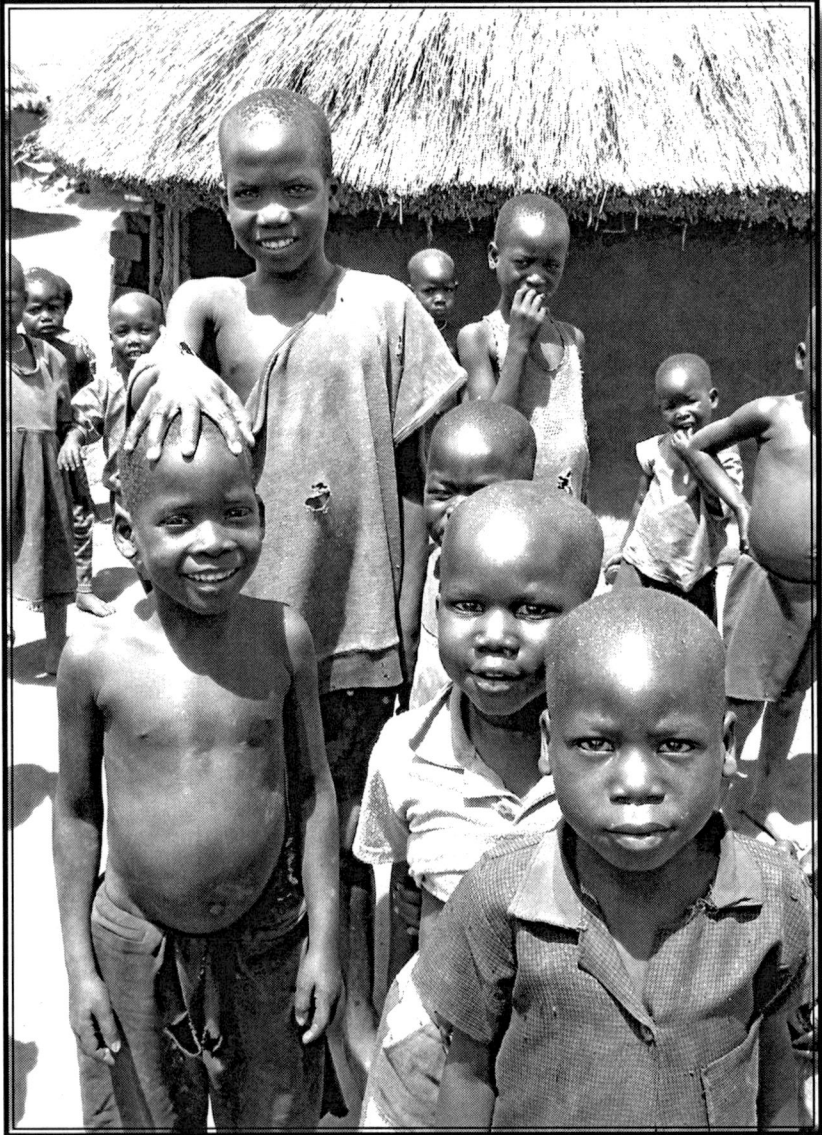

one night. After we played together, I took his hands and put some beautiful coins in them. They were my special treasures and I always kept them in my pocket. I was sure the boy had never seen them before because I had collected them in Europe. They were from different countries and were shiny and new. He looked them over, carefully turning them many times. When he smiled, his eyes danced. He was so happy. I decided I would give him the coins that he liked the best.

After that experiment, I always thought about why it feels so good to give, and especially to people who didn't have what I had. With the wind in my face and my chin on my arm, I tried to think out more experiments as we bumped along the road passing people who carried heavy loads of bananas, water, and wood on their heads. I always wondered who the people were, where they lived, and how many were willing to share what they had with strangers.

Another experiment I worked out was watching how long people would smile at me when I smiled at them. Once, we stayed with a nun for a few days in the Cherangani Hills of Kenya, where she ran a hospital. Her name was Sister Rosa. When I smiled at her, her eyes never smiled back. Her lips would seem to smile, but I think she just pretended. She'd turn her lips up in the corners like a real smile, but then they'd instantly fall flat. It was so strange to watch her. I tried many times to see if I could get her eyes to smile, but they never did.

That experiment led to another, that of trying to feel how a person felt inside themselves even if they didn't say anything or said very little. I looked at their eyes and how they moved their feet and learned a lot about them. My encounters with strangers were usually interesting, and, as far as I knew, my family never encountered any serious or life-threatening problems with the African people. But maybe my parents never told me.

We were searched at the border in Malawi by the Red Pioneers and I was so distraught that I kicked the chain link fence with my boot, and they thought that was funny and laughed. But they didn't harm us or confiscate our things, and we were fortunate that they didn't find our BB gun as they might have thought it was a weapon we were planning to use on people.

We were robbed in Kenya, but not when we were around. One night when we stayed in the Ainsworth hotel in Nairobi, a child (as we were told the next day), must have entered our Land Rover from some place under the floor in the front where a metal plate could be lifted out and a small body could squeeze inside. A lot of our gear was stolen. But we were never robbed when we camped along the road where it seemed we would have been easy prey because we were easily outnumbered.

I had two frightening encounters with people, but not because they were angry. The first one was with an African woman who actually laughed at me when I screamed. My mom and I wanted to buy a stalk of bananas (that we liked to hang in the Land Rover) from her little roadside stand. As she lifted a stalk from the pile where my mom pointed, an enormous black spider jumped out at us, biting the air. Its legs were longer than my fingers. When it hit the ground, it ran for cover up between the woman's legs and disappeared. I was horrified for her and couldn't help but yell, "look out!" But with just a giggle and a vigorous swoosh of her skirt, she knocked it down and it took off running towards the jungle.

The other time was late at night. We were camped somewhere just off the road because the vegetation was so thick. There was no town or village that we could see from where we camped among tall trees. As my sisters and I slept in the Land Rover, and my parents slept in a tent outside nearby us, there was always someone getting up to go to the bathroom in the night. And as we never had a toilet, unless we had the rare convenience of a campground, we had to go wherever we could find a place. Most of the time that was easy.

But that night it was more difficult, as I had been having some sort of intestinal problem. It was so cloudy and dark that I woke up my mother and asked her to accompany me. She held the flashlight as I dug a hole with my heel on the edge of a field where it looked like some crop was growing. We were scanning the ground for snakes when suddenly a man came out of nowhere. The whites of his eyes seemed huge because his skin was so dark. I was so scared that I felt like I was going to faint. But when my mom shined the light fully on him he almost seemed to smile. He understood the urgent nature of our visit to his field and backed away without a word, though he stood and watched us for a while before he disappeared.

Most African people seemed friendly, especially the children. On many occasions, my sisters and I taught them how to play jump rope where we stopped to camp. They caught on quickly and we would pal around with them for a few hours, and sometimes a few days, depending on where we were. Sometimes we played with their animals and rode on their donkeys. My sisters and I were never bothered by any adults, and it never crossed our minds that we could be kidnapped.

But there were times when we were unnerved by the interest that the Africans took in us. It often happened that when we started eating breakfast early in the morning, one or two people walking along the road would stop and stare at us. We must have looked so odd sitting at our folding table on the edge of the road, and sometimes in the road because it was the only open area, eating cooked white rice with cinnamon and powdered milk.

One morning was especially memorable. A man passed along like usual, and he stopped to watch us. Then as others came along and word got out that we were there, more and more people

stopped to observe us eating. Eventually, a group of men, women and children stood together whispering, giggling, and pointing at us.

They were so curious about how we looked, what we ate, the utensils we used to eat with, and the items that made up our camp, that they inched nearer to us, step by step. They came as close as they could, a thick wall of arms and legs and smiles, until my dad stood up to sweep them back. They politely retreated, but then they came forward again. Little by little they came closer than the previous time until at last we left.

It was the same way when we stopped to collect plants. My dad could always spot mistletoes in the trees even when he was driving. He had a quick eye that could discern their shape and color. We'd park where we could, and haul out our long metal pole-like contraptions for pulling the mistletoe out of the tree. The pole seemed fifty feet tall when it was assembled. Coming out of the side of the pole near the top was a long straight nail which my dad tried to hook over one of the main stems of the mistletoe so that he could pull down a sizeable piece of the plant. Then we collected its buds, berries, and leaves. After the mistletoe was photographed, we'd press it in our plant press made of wood, cardboard and newspaper tightly strapped together.

When the mistletoe was up too high to reach, my dad would drive the Land Rover as close to the tree as possible, and then stand on the hood or roof-racks with the pole extended upward while trying not to lose his balance. When he hooked the plant, he'd give a strong pull on the pole and the clump would fall with a "whoosh." When we heard it coming down, my sisters and I would run. We had to be careful not to have the plant come down on top of us because a poisonous snake could be pulled down too.

Mistletoes in Africa are classified into two plant families. The first is the kind that we know of as Christmas mistletoe, though in Africa there are many different species. One species grows on a succulent right on the ground and another grows on a cactus-like Euphorbia. Most people don't know that mistletoes are parasites that suck out the nutrients from their host plant by means of little root hairs.

The other kind of mistletoe family that lives in Africa is completely unlike the one that we know in North America. Though it, too, is a parasite, it has long colorful flower buds that pop open explosively when probed by sun birds seeking nectar.

After we brought down to the ground whatever kind of mistletoe we found, we prepared for what must have looked like a fascinating ritual.

The Africans were always curious and stopped to watch us carefully. First we'd take out big brown jars of acetic acid and alcohol, and mix them in a special ratio. We were making a preserving potion called "fixative," which we'd pour into little clear vials with black screw-on tops. Then we'd all sit cross-legged in a circle, plucking off mistletoe buds and dropping them into our vials, along with the ticks that we sometimes found on ourselves. We had to treat the vials with the greatest care so that we wouldn't knock them over. We must have looked so bizarre picking at the buds with our heads bent down and sitting very still.

We only had one strict rule that we followed with African people who spoke English, especially border officials. We never told them where we were really going. When they questioned our route we couldn't say that our destination was South Africa. We had been warned by other white travelers that if they had known we were headed to South Africa they probably wouldn't have let us through their borders. Most African countries were steaming mad at South Africa because of its political policies. At that time, its government was run by whites who practiced racial segregation called "apartheid."

Under apartheid, which was justified for commercial benefit to the whites, everyone in South Africa was legally classified into racial groups: black, white, colored, and Asian. People were forcibly separated from each other on the basis of this classification. The black majority were treated terribly. They were forced to become citizens of particular homelands like Native Americans on Indian reservations. So, naturally, the whites had it coming to them by all the blacks in Africa. White policies were so hateful. They prevented non-white people, even if they were resident in white South Africa, from having a vote or influence except in their homelands. Their rights were restricted to these homelands that they may never have visited. Education, medical care, and other public services were segregated too, and those services available to blacks were greatly inferior to whites.

My parents always seemed to be practical and matter-of-fact about travel no matter where we were. They couldn't get involved in other people's problems, like apartheid issues and other difficulties, because of their scientific commitments and goals. But it must have been hard for them sometimes. One time was when we pulled up to camp for the night in what looked like a gravel pit with a few large pipes lying on the ground. Out of one pipe clambered a boy about ten years old. He was all alone and came to meet us with pleading eyes. He was so hungry.

We shared our dinner with him and he gulped it down like he was drinking water. That night he slept under our Land Rover to get out of the rain, though he probably still got wet. In the morning he had another big meal before we left him there alone. My dad and mom talked to us about how he deserved a better life, but that they weren't in a position to give him one. I always wished that we had taken him home and I could have had a brother. I used to think that if we had made him a part of our family, then he would have understood me like none of the others did. He knew how it felt to be alone.

It always pleased me that my dad and mom had such a flexible willingness to confront constantly changing conditions. They weren't afraid of physical challenges, and they didn't worry too much about the risks of travel in such a wild place as Africa. I always thought they were probably among the first people from the western world to take a five year old, their youngest daughter, across the Sahara and down the length of Africa in a Land

Rover. But, by contrast, it always surprised me that my parents didn't have a similar flexibility to explore themselves, including the foundation of the concepts that shaped their beliefs.

For example, they believed that life was propelled by an accidental evolutionary force and this belief entirely shaped their outlook. It defined the contours of their mind and controlled their emotions, just like the road defined the contour of the land and where we could go. But I always wondered one thing: How could they believe that they evolved from nature when they were so much more intelligent than nature? This bothered me because they always said that nature wasn't intelligent. But they couldn't deny that we and the Africans were intelligent.

My parents seemed so strong about their priorities. I never heard them doubt their abilities to be safe, and somehow free, from the unknown dangers of unexpected situations. After all, we children were still quite young. Even so, I never heard them talk about going home because they were tired of uncertainties like not knowing where we would camp, what the road conditions would be like, or when we would be able to wash our hair and clothes. And there was always the uncertainty of what would happen if our Land Rover broke down in questionable places and we had to split up for some reason. There was an unspoken awareness of things that might go wrong, and though they usually never did, my dad would tease us from time to time that the Land Rover broke a spring. It was the favorite April Fool's joke.

As we bumped along the red-clay roads of central Africa and the jungles of the Congo Basin, my mom's arm was a clever clothesline. She'd extend her arm out the window with clothes hanging on it, and then pull it in when we hit potholes full of water. Our underwear never seemed to fully dry. Unlike the desert, water was everywhere and so were the difficulties associated with having too much water around us. There were roads that were flooded and we heard stories of people crossing rivers with their cars on dugout canoes that the Africans steered for them.

There was also the story of a mud hole, a huge pit of oozing muddy clay, that supposedly stopped cars for days, or even for weeks. We heard that cars had to wait for a truck passing that way on the road to pull them from one side to the other. I envisioned a hole the size of an enormous swimming pool full of red mud where cars often drowned and sank to the bottom. I imagined that the jungle was too thick for a road to be cut around the hole and so we would have to wait our turn to be hauled through it.

I worried that the Land Rover might turn upside down and we'd have to swim up and be pulled out by our arms. But I guessed we had to take the risk of going through the hole because it happened to be on the only road. When the dreaded day came, we had an amazing sight to celebrate. The hole was almost dry.

There were other problems we had to face with water. When we reached the tropics, we couldn't touch it. Not any free-flowing water. And that was hard when we had to cross flooded roads or cross big rivers by small ferries because it was easy to get splashed. The water carried "schistosomes," a terrifying word for a worse reality. Schistosomes are microscopic parasitic worms that enter your blood through the pores of your skin whenever you touch water infected with them. They cause a deadly disease of the blood vessels called Bilharzia.

The problem with the worms is that they lay their eggs in your blood vessels. Millions and millions of Africans are infected every year and eventually they all will die. I always thought that the reason the African kids had bellies as big as watermelons was because they were full of worms, but I never knew for sure. We heard it said that even when medication to kill the worms could be found, it could still prove fatal to take it. The dead worms floating around in your blood could clog up your heart valves.

My mom and dad were always harping at my sisters and me not to touch the water. Thankfully, none of us got the schistosomes, but it was a risk we all took. There were other risks, besides schistosomes, that were floating or flying around us, like crocodiles, malaria mosquitoes, and tsetse flies. But we could usually avoid them, just like we tried to avoid risky places.

In one terrifying place we heard about, hyenas were known to claw through your tent at night and drag you out by your head. They were such scary-looking creatures and many people believe that they have the strongest jaws because they eat so many bones. But this is just a myth which emphasizes how much people fear them. The strongest jaws in the animal world, at least of those that live on the land, belong to the Tasmanian Devil which has a stronger jaw proportional to its size.

My parents were never weakened by the mind-set of complacency. They had a freedom to explore and a willingness to meet life and experience it out on muddy roads, or wherever we were in the wilds. They were not alarmists or complainers, but instead they were prepared to deal with whatever came along. We all learned to be especially watchful for snakes, even on the road. It was said that if you ran over a mamba, which is long and powerful, it could come up through the window swinging its head and still have the strength to bite you on the neck. Mambas, like cobras, have neurotoxic venoms that shut down your nervous system and so you stop breathing. In about ten minutes you'd be dead.

Besides the ground, we also watched the sky for bees, the aggressive African kind that can kill people as they hit like lightening in a fast dark cloud. If we were outside collecting plants when we heard them coming, we'd drop to the ground flat on our bellies, unconcerned for the moment with little crawling things. Giant millipedes didn't pose any problem besides their awkward ugliness, their writhing legs a bit sickening until we got used to them. At the base of Mount Kenya, Alison and I would collect them into heaps and see how long it took them to untangle themselves.

We also played with orphaned chimpanzee babies at a plantation in the Congo. They hung around our necks and sucked the buttons of our shirts. There were also mongooses to chase and phosphorescent butterflies to catch. Once, a mad chase led me to a viper. It was fat and short, so I just jumped high over it, which wasn't a good idea because it was too risky.

Sometimes creatures outside the Land Rover managed to find their way inside. There were times when someone didn't close the lid on the jam jar tight enough, and the Land Rover was invaded by ants. At one time, bugs that resembled earwigs seemed to hatch by the thousands in our clothes. And then there were also the times when tiny white wiggling worms came out of my own body, to my great astonishment.

But for all their ability to cope with the changing conditions of their physical environment, my parents had one big fear that I never could understand. They couldn't explore the possibility of life having a divine origin. They couldn't discuss whether all the amazing things we saw and experienced came from a source that had a purpose for life, something that was intelligent, ever so much more than they could ever be. But they didn't have the focus or maybe the courage for an inner inquiry. They wouldn't search their hearts to find out if there was a valid truth to why people everywhere believed in some kind of god.

They stamped the world with a definitive finality, the atheistic belief that allowed life only one intelligent urge, the urge to procreate and replicate the self. Whether one was a man, a bird, or an elephant, the only reason for life was the same, to pass on one's genes to the next generation.

My father used to say that heart disease wasn't a real menace to human life because it usually killed you after you had your children. Heart disease could stay established in the gene pool for this reason.

But there was a distinctly human feature when it came to how humans could plan to have their babies. I noticed that unlike any animals, people could usually control their breeding habits. That seemed significant to me, and was an important observation. Humans were completely different from animals that had their breeding habits hardwired into them.

Africa's million different colors, shapes, and sizes made my mind and heart explode. But I knew that accidents never made things beautiful. Somehow deep down, I knew there was a God. But it did confuse me that African people had so many diverse ideas when it came to claiming who was God.

Probably most African religions were a mixture of tribal beliefs (like animism, where natural objects have their own spirit) and some worldwide religion like what the Muslims or Christians taught. Many African countries had suffered the strain of being colonies of the English, French, and German at some point in their history and so the prevalent religions of those colonizing powers were exerted forcefully upon the African people. But there were still some people who seemed untouched by this outside influence because they were so isolated.

I wondered if the naked little pygmy man knew who God was. He appeared one morning with his primitive wood and twine bow and poison-tipped arrows. His bow was too small to kill monkeys or okapi, the elusive giraffe-like creature with dark stripes like shadows across its legs. He must have been hunting something small like birds. The mist was still rising off the jungle as he reached our camp and stood before us.

I wanted to believe that he wouldn't only see me as a white girl who came from far away, from a land across an ocean that he didn't even know existed. But there didn't seem to be anything special about the pygmy, even though he lived deep in the jungle. He traded his bow and arrows for something my dad gave him, though I don't remember now what it was. He pointed at the arrow tips and then at my sisters and me and shook his head and waved his hand. Not wanting to take any risk with that poison, my dad sawed off the tips of the arrows as the little man walked away.

My sisters and I were in a position to learn about life in a way that other children never did. Without a TV or a routine at school, we could experience life in an immediate way without the filters of walls, ceilings, and rote memorization that were remote from pygmies, monkeys, and snakes. As a result, our minds were not dulled by clutter or troubled by boredom. Our experience was powerfully stimulating and we had many unusual encounters.

One muddy, slippery day, as our Land Rover came to a sliding halt with almost two wheels hanging over a cliff, my mom immediately ordered my sisters and me out of the car. We didn't have our shoes on, but we jumped out scared. As we landed in wet red mud that oozed up and out between our toes, Alison said, "Now we are like the real people!" It wasn't a complaint or some kind of disappointment that she expressed as we watched my dad maneuver the Land Rover back onto the road. She was exultant and proud.

Though we eventually forgot about the incident, for years Alison's words were in my mind. I always wondered if there was a "real" people, and what gave them that qualification.

To Alison, the real people lived on the land. They were connected to the earth. As for me, I wasn't so sure. I knew that what was real dispelled superstition and false ideas, and so real people would be honest and kind. But I didn't know where to find the real people. I didn't know where they lived, or if they would recognize me as wanting to be one of them.

After we passed through the dense jungles of the Congo Basin, we dropped down into the Great Rift Valley and into the broad open plains of the savannah grasslands. There were immense herds of wildebeests, zebras, kudus, and impalas by the tens or hundreds of thousands. We saw leopards sleeping in trees and

huge colonies of weaver birds with their communal nests hanging like enormous baskets from the branches of acacia trees. We also observed flamingos and storks, hyenas and lions, vultures eating carcasses, fighting giraffes, and herds of elephants.

There were also baboons that would jump on the Land Rover if we stopped for any length of time. They would sit on the hood and climb up onto the roof racks. The little ones, not always knowing what we were, would make funny worried faces. But the adults were powerful and aggressive with big teeth and strong hands, so we had to be careful that our windows were tightly closed.

One day up by Lake Turkana, we were stopped along the dirt road and some Pokot women carrying loads of green bananas on their backs came running up to us. I was sitting in the back of the Land Rover, up on the foam pads that rode on top of our supplies and created a sleeping place during the day. I held a camera in my hands. But it wasn't real.

I made the lens from the cardboard center of an empty toilet paper roll, and the body from a small square box. The whole thing was carefully connected with black electrical tape that I found in one of our tool kits. I made various dials and buttons, and a mount for the flash from odds and ends that were always present in our traveling life. The cocker was a piece of metal from a corned beef can. As we had many cameras on board with us, including a wide angle and telephoto lens, my camera was just another one added to the collection.

When the Pokot women came near to us, I raised my fake camera and started taking pictures. I wanted to see if they would notice that it wasn't real. In those parts, the Pokot were used to seeing Caucasians as Kenya attracted many visitors, because it was not so remote as the jungle and desert countries to the north and south. The unspoken agreement for the Pokot, which was started by some traveler and his camera, was they would expect payment in exchange for being photographed. Usually this came in the form of money or goods, such as food and clothing, or pencils and paper.

When they saw me photographing them, the women dropped their loads and came running up to the rear window with their hands outstretched, demanding payment. Since I was in the back of the Land Rover, no one in my family saw me taking pictures and so no one understood what it was the women wanted. For a while my parents tried to understand their frustration, but they lacked common words to communicate the problem.

I watched the whole event knowing what each side didn't understand. I was too embarrassed to tell my parents that I was just playing because I didn't want the women to think I was making fun of them. From that experience, I learned how important it is to have a true perspective. That way you don't get lost in arguments that neither side understands.

In Oldavai Gorge, in Tanzania, we visited the sites where Richard Leaky was searching for missing links between apes and humans. He had a curious assortment of fossilized footprints, jaw bones, eye sockets, and bicuspid teeth. He felt he could use these to reconstruct man's evolutionary tree, meaning the theoretical lines of descent along which humans supposedly evolved. He, like my parents, seemed so sure about his understanding of our human nature and position in life, in Africa, and in the universe. But I wasn't so sure, and it wasn't just because I was young.

The Bushmen of the Kalahari Desert in the country of Botswana, have a saying that I learned when I was there. It went something like, "Heaven and earth meet in billowing clouds." I knew what that meant, or at least it had a special meaning to me. There is a point in life where you feel that the billowing clouds are an obscurity. If earth symbolizes all that is physical, and heaven, all that is spiritual, then we have to find out what is their true relationship. It wouldn't be right to deny one for the other.

The Bushmen must have known that only a few want to find their way through the clouds and see the marvelous truth. But this involves a journey more dangerous than walking with black-manned lions, and more beautiful than the double rainbows over the Serengeti plains.

Your task is not to seek for love, but merely to seek and find all the barriers within yourself that you have built up against it.

Rumi (1207-1273), Persian Poet

CHAPTER   TWO

Searching For Springs

Shambala is hidden from the world in a high Himalayan valley. Some say it's just a mythical city, but that's because they haven't found the way inside. The entrance is veiled by more than just a thick mist. Only a few can find the narrow gate.

It's like the story of the blind man stuck in a room with twelve doors. Only one of the doors leads him out of darkness to where his sight will be regained. But how can he find the right door being that he is blind? And what can he rely on to guide him to that door?

Metaphors like Shambala, with its narrow gate, and the blind man and his groping are useful for pointing out aspects of our life that deserve attention. They can help us to see what we might have missed before. Take the figurative blindness of the blind man, for example. What do you think it symbolizes? It is an ego-based blindness. Why an ego-based blindness? Because our ego blinds us to truths that are greater than our own making, and those of others whom we reply upon to tell us what is true.

Ego-based blindness is not as abstract as it sounds. It's simply a refusal to look more closely at ourselves and our cherished ideas about what we consider to be true. But if we're blinded by our ego, then we'll never know how much we're in the dark. There is a ancient saying that shows us the eventuality of confusing ignorance with insight: It says that if, in reality, the light that is in you is darkness, how immense will be your ignorance. It sums up the futility of playfully praising the words, "Ignorance is bliss."

Though we can all agree that there is something that equates with light and dark, like knowledge and ignorance, we might disagree on the details. Like one man said, "In real life, unlike in Shakespeare, the sweetness of the rose depends upon the name it bears. Things are not only what they are. They are, in very important respects, what they seem to be."[1]

Seeming and believing are often so mixed up that most people think that truth is only relative to a specific idea or set of circumstances. It might then seem that the question of whether there is an absolute truth regarding knowledge and ignorance is insoluble. For the history of philosophy shows that the lover of wisdom, which is the usual translation of the Greek term *philosophia*, can be found in any way he wants to spin his mind. Philosophers are the most masterful weavers of truth because they create meaning according to their preference and profit.

While I was searching for an infallible standard for knowing what is true and false, I studied science, philosophy, religion, and especially religious people. Once, I stayed with a Sikh family in London for a month to learn what they believed about God and the purpose of life. I had a tiny attic room and heard the pigeons clucking every evening outside on the roof. But every morning I was awakened by a mournful song.

It was a man singing in Punjabi, the language of the Punjab, the state in India where most Sikhs live. Opinder Singh, the grandfather of the family, played the song on his tape recorder, though at first I thought it was him singing. He sat in a high-backed wooden chair and listened with his eyes closed. He wore the traditional Sikh turban head cloth, called a *pagri*, wound around his head. His was blue and his hair was long, though I never saw it down. Like most Sikh men, he never cut his hair. It was a symbol of obedience to his conception of divine law.

"Opinderji," I said one morning as I approached him sitting in his wooden chair, "what is the man singing about?"

"Sitaji," he replied, as I sat down cross-legged on the floor beside his chair wrapped in my yellow shawl, called a *chuni*, "it is a song of surrender."

I knew that. "But tell me, what is happening in the song?"

Opinder's eyes, like most Sikh eyes, were stunning. They were dark and shaped like almonds, curving up at the corners.

"The man is waiting for Waheguru" (the Sikh name for God).

"What else, Opinderji?"

"The man is thin. He is starving. His ribs are sticking out. He falls down in an empty field because he is so tired. So then the crows come and flock around him and he cries out some words."

"What does he say?"

"'Oh Waheguru, Oh please don't let the crows peck out my eyes so when you come at last I can see you.'"

To most intellectuals this song will seem maudlin. But the search for truth doesn't draw its strength from the mind. It's like what Jesus said. The truth about light and dark is hidden from egotistical people whom he often associated with close-minded intellectuals.[2]

There was a special reason why he chose twelve ordinary and unlettered men to be his closest friends. He wanted us to recognize that those who want to be admired for their intellectual achievements aren't the ones to entrust with sacred secrets. They are too concerned with achieving a higher status among others like themselves.

When Jesus said that the truth is hidden from intellectuals but revealed to childlike ones, he wasn't deriding the mind or the value of gaining knowledge. He was making a simple contrast. He wanted to illustrate the quality of having an open heart. He was highlighting the fact that children constantly learn new things because they are open to learning them. They are also willing to apply what they learn.

The Sikh word for God, Waheguru, means "Wonderful Lord" or "Great Teacher." And though the Sikhs may seem a bit extreme in their portrayal of pain as an essential part of the search for truth, the exhausted seeker in the song is open-hearted and humble. He recognizes that his worth as a person is no longer determined by what his ego achieves for him. He knows he has to look beyond his own body and mind if he wants to discern truths greater than his own making, or the making of other men. His falling down in the field means he has surrendered himself.

This Punjabi song of surrender also points out the inevitable. When it comes to spiritual truths and finding satisfying answers to spiritual questions, we may have to search for a long time. If there is no spiritually wise one to guide us, then we will search for answers in the wrong places. But that is the way it goes sometimes. I know from my own experience.

When I was sixteen years old, my spiritual aspirations were eating a hole in my heart. But even years before I thought I had a heart problem because it ached with a strange kind of longing. I had to admit this to my mom one day when I was eleven years old. We were in Hawaii, hiking up to view Kilauea Crater and the fiery magma sloshing around inside. There was a sign on the trail that warned that anyone with heart problems shouldn't go close to the rim. The heat posed too much risk. Though it was an uncomfortable moment of reckoning, I knew I had to be courageous. "I guess I have to turn back," I said to her. When I pointed to the sign and explained about my heart, she was surprised. But she said in no uncertain terms that there was nothing wrong with me. But I knew better. My heart was hurt because I had feelings that I couldn't share with my family or our family friends.

I had no language or context to articulate what the feelings were because no one had taught me about them. They were hard for my mind to describe, though they were so familiar to my heart's desire. They made me want to search through life and find its secrets. But I knew these were secrets that my family didn't want to find because they were related to feelings that didn't fit the definition of my life as my parents had defined it for me.

I knew that I had a spiritual need, but I didn't know how to articulate what it was. My parents didn't speak in religious terms because they didn't associate with any religion. They didn't know religious language. As scientists, they derived meaning through observing the physical forms and functions of life, but as atheists, they denied that spiritual laws could apply to them. They must have accounted for people's spiritual pursuits as an arbitrary consequence of having a human form and a brain big enough to contemplate death.

For this reason, my dad and mom couldn't give me any spiritual inheritance, just the genome of my bloodline. In the gathering silence around spiritual subjects, I understood that they believed there was no spiritual being to ponder about or pray to. Spiritual things were seen to be defective, like the clipped wings of a whimsical subjectivity. But they would have science soar on an objective and truthful reality.

Still, I noticed the illogic of an apparently logical outlook. My parents worshipped chance as a causal agent, as the way to account for the complexity of life. They believed in quirks, mutations, and anything that came from nothing, but nobody that came from somewhere. They preferred uncertainty to certainty, unintelligence to intelligence, and purposelessness to purpose. Still, Chance was personified as king. As the Maker of life, they believed in his decree: "Change alone is changeless."

But I wanted to know what makes us love, and why love is so distinctly human. This need grew, and as it grew I became restless and frustrated, and no one ever knew why. I couldn't be open with my feelings because neither of my parents encouraged openness. They never taught me how to understand and manage my feelings, especially spiritual ones.

Not surprisingly, I couldn't turn to school to help me with my spiritual need. Though I was always a good student, I wanted to know what was the basis of math, English, and science. I wanted to know what was the spirit of life, but not in terms of a social or scientific explanation. The spirit of life spoke its secrets, but not at school. Nothing at school could fulfill my desire to love and be loved in a spiritual way. As time went by, it was like two parts of me were living together side by side. There was the hidden part, which was what I really wanted to live and express outwardly, but didn't know how, and the other part on the surface that was my routine with my family and friends.

I had no idea back then that there were people who lived in the world and could still outwardly identify themselves by their inner feelings. They didn't have to keep them hidden. They actually talked about their spiritual feelings, and nourished them too, because they had spiritual words and spiritual minds to understand them. They shared their spiritual feelings with others who felt the same way. They also knew what spiritual feelings were and where they came from and why they were important.

Long before I knew about how spiritual experience is awakened in us, I made up my own spiritual language. For years I called my spiritual feelings "the wind in my blood," "the fluttering leaves of my heart," and "the secret spring that's like a fountain." I used nature metaphors to describe my feelings because I loved the wilderness intensely. It was a natural spiritual guide for me in the absence of a human one.

As a family we hiked, backpacked, and white-water rafted beginning when I was younger than seven years old. I was constantly and happily exposed to the wilderness. As I grew older, I was more and more grateful for its beauty and I came to love the mountains and deserts as my best friends.

I noticed that, compared to nature and its self-revealing ways, most people locked up their hearts and didn't want to talk about how they felt inside, and what God would be like if they ever found out who he was. Instead, they seemed to fill their minds with distractions that prevented them from being in touch with what their heart wanted to understand. And since I was surrounded by a godless mind-set, in terms of my family dynamics and those of our family friends, there were always boundaries around expressions of love and expectations of how it should be shared. It wasn't that my parents and their friends were cold or heartless. They loved, but in a limited kind of way. They gave presents and were generous, especially to those who shared their outlook. But they couldn't cultivate trust in love as a spiritual quality and seemed to be wary of those who did.

Before I realized that I couldn't touch my parents' hearts and awaken their desires to be open in a spiritual way, I did try hard to tempt them. I often disguised my intentions through scientific questions.

"Dad," I asked one autumn evening as he put wood on the fire and I sat on the hearth in my nightgown, "what is the purpose of emotion in animal life?" But what I really wanted to know was what he thought was the purpose of love in our lives. And, of course, I wanted him to open his inner feelings to me.

"It is simply to help them survive," he said, standing.

"But animals don't laugh or cry, do they?"

"Well, animals can express pain and pleasure in the sounds they make." He poked the fire with the fire tongs and stared into the flames.

"But that isn't the same as laughing or crying is it?"

He stuck safely with science and said, "Positive emotions are expressed as altruistic traits which are essential for survival. Do you know what it means to be altruistic?"

"Yes." I knew.

His definition of altruism pointed out a helping instinct between animals that could be reciprocated. For example, rabbits thumping the ground and squirrels screeching to announce danger to those around them are considered altruistic. He further explained that the benefit of being altruistic came after an animal put itself in danger to protect its relatives. A time would come when some other individual of the group would do the same. Such positive emotions or instinctive behaviors would help the group survive.

"So, survival is key?"

"Yes, of course," he replied.

As an instinct in animals, altruism was harder for me to apply to people. For one thing, people have conscious awareness and free will. Their choices in difficult situations are variable, unlike rabbits, squirrels, and even more intelligent animals like birds, dogs, and apes. Though we all have basic survival instincts, we can choose what we will do in any circumstance depending on our age, experience, and inner inclinations.

I wanted to tell my dad that altruism as a law of physical love doesn't get far with people, but I couldn't find the words. Countless men and women have died for others unrelated to them. But I believed that love was a spiritual quality more than a physical one and I longed for spiritual relationships.

My first spiritual relationship was with Matt, my next door neighbor. We were both twelve years old, and he was a Mormon. I asked him what his religion taught about love. I meant the kind of love that wasn't tied up with genes or reproduction in animals. I meant love as the most essential attribute of intelligence and conscious choice. Matt knew more about love as a spiritual quality than anyone else I knew at that time. He was always willing to talk with me. He was gentle and kind and cared so much about people.

We had many discussions about spiritual subjects. We mostly talked about whether humans could evolve from apes by chance, or had to be created by God on purpose. I tried to explain as best as I could the evolutionary point of view, though it always seemed so shallow. I knew that was what my parents expected of me, just like Matt's parents expected him to repeat what they taught him when it came to defining life and its origins.

I often recorded our conversations on an old tape recorder, and then listened to them over and over when I was alone in my room. I was interested in how we came to be human, and if there was a way we could know for sure how it happened. I was intrigued by the questions Matt asked me about the probability of humans evolving from "stupid apes" as he called them, versus being created in the image of "pure intelligence," as he said. He had a spiritual vocabulary and a willing ability to talk about spiritual things that I hadn't experienced before talking to him.

Sometimes I'd ask my mom how she would have replied if Matt had asked her the same questions. She never hesitated in her answers. She was assertive and unwavering in her viewpoint that humans evolved from their ape-like ancestors. She was as certain that we evolved from apes as Matt was certain that we were created by God.

One day I asked her if she thought nature was intelligent. She said that it couldn't be intelligent, and I knew why she had to say so. By the rules of evolutionary science, evolution is not considered to be the result of any intelligent process or force. It is driven by chance, not by choice. Then I asked her if she thought Albert Einstein was intelligent. She had to agree that he was a very intelligent man. I asked her why she could say he was intelligent but nature wasn't, since, by her reasoning, that is where he had come from. She didn't know what to say, so she didn't say anything. I didn't want to hurt her feelings, so I kept to myself that her reasoning didn't make sense.

Besides our discussions about why humans seemed to be the only self-conscious life-form, Matt and I talked about what was sacred. We defined something as sacred according to how it made us feel. We agreed that what was sacred was loved in a special way because of its special qualities. For me, what was sacred was the wilderness. It was beautiful, and it wasn't contaminated

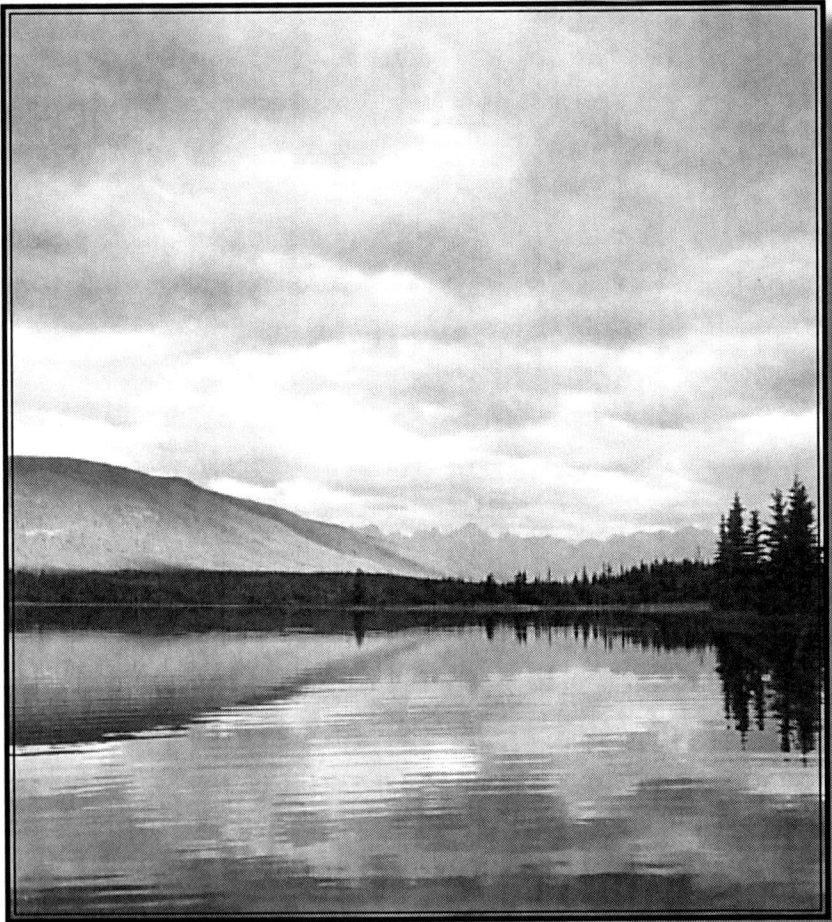

by people's noisy minds and their stingy, unloving ways. It was sacred, too, because when I was in nature I felt exhilarated and content. I didn't feel the restlessness of the world, but instead, so much vitality.

One evening we were sitting outside on the grass. Matt was trying to illustrate the meaning of faith, a concept that I didn't know much about, but understood involved something like being close to what felt sacred.

"Close your eyes," said Matt.

"Okay," I played along.

"Hold out your hand with your palm up."

He put something in my hand that was cool and round and connected to straps on both sides. I realized, as I touched it with my other hand, that it was his watch.[3]

"Now," he said, "how did the watch get into your hand?"

"That's a no-brainer," I laughed. But I knew he wasn't joking because his tone was serious.

"Really," he urged me, "how did it get there?"

"You put it there, of course."

"How do you know when you didn't see me do it?"

"Because I know you did it. I could hear you," I opened my eyes and made a silly face at him.

But Matt persisted to make his point. "Even if you can't see God or hear him breathe, you know he is there because of that sacred feeling that you have. You can feel his spirit, like you feel the watch in your hand with your eyes closed. It is faith to believe God is there, even if you can't see God with your eyes."

Matt's illustration was fascinating, but also confusing. I could understand the concept of there being a relationship between faith and what we consider to be sacred. In my experience, being in nature gave me faith in what was sacred. And loving what was sacred built the foundation for understanding faith. But his illustration didn't give me a way to know who God really was. In my travels I had been exposed to many strange ideas about how we should relate to God.

In the massive Christian cathedrals of Europe, I watched people worship a dying man nailed to an ugly, bloody cross. The Muslims in North Africa woke us up in the night crying out their prayers from their mosques to a God that seemed really hard of hearing. Tribal people believed that God lived in trees, rocks, and rivers. And Hindus worshiped cows. Buddhists prayed to a fat guy made of stone.

I knew all the gods out there couldn't be the same "God" unless God could have many different shapes and purposes all at the same time. But nothing in nature could morph like that, so how could something spiritual? Matt tried to convince me that there was only one God, and I believed him, but I didn't know how to decide which one was true.

I went with Matt to his church one Sunday. They passed around trays of tiny paper cups filled with red liquid that was probably punch as Mormons weren't allowed to drink wine or any alcohol. As everyone solemnly drank from their cups in silence, a platter of white bread cut into bite-sized squares was then passed to each person. I didn't join in the drinking and eating because I couldn't understand what it had to do with faith or God. I shook my head when the cups and bread squares came to me. I felt sure that the other kids didn't understand what was going on either, because after the meeting they couldn't explain what it was all about.

But Matt said that drinking the punch and eating the bread had to do with faith in Jesus because they were drinking his blood and eating his flesh. I wanted to tease him that Mormons seemed like cannibals, but I didn't want to hurt his feelings. I didn't know much about Jesus except what I had learned at a Unitarian church many years before where my mom took my sisters and me on a few occasions. I remembered that they taught that Jesus was just a regular man, and not the son of God. They stressed that point so much, and repeated it so often, that I gathered that most people thought he was God's son, whatever that meant. As for the Mormons and their way of worship, I was convinced that they didn't know the truth about God. At least their eyes didn't show that they were happy. I couldn't see beauty in their church or feel the sacred joy I always felt in nature.

After attending Matt's church, I decided to share a little of my own family's worship with him even though it didn't involve an elaborate ritual like his did. My parents worshiped the human mind, with the scientific mind-set as the savior. Unlike the Mormons, there was nothing in my parent's belief system that could conceive of an intelligent power greater than the human mind.

Even nature was considered stupid and blind though it did have, by their reckoning, some kind of miraculous ability to create intelligence by accident.

They must have thought that every concept involving God was just an expression of someone's playful, devious, or undisciplined brain waves. And then over time, these concepts would acquire shape and form in terms of habit and tradition. Then they would become religion.

I decided to tease Matt one afternoon. We were standing in my house, looking out the window and eating apple slices. I said to Matt that I would let him in on a family secret. His ears perked up. With as straight a face as I could make, I told him that the round white rock on the windowsill had secret power. The rock was the size of my fist and had probably come back from some desert trip. I picked up the rock and held it in my hands, closing my eyes and moving my lips like I was chanting something special. I peeked over at Matt, who was shaking his head, and we both laughed for a long time. It was ludicrous for us to think that people worshiped rocks. We both agreed that a lifeless rock, even if a face was carved into it, couldn't represent in any meaningful way the essence of conscious life that identified humans apart from every other life-form.

When I was in high school, I began to question the relationships that people had with their beliefs, like scientists with scientific methodology and religious people with their religions. I noticed that belief systems were a lot like corrals. They separated people and fenced them off into groups that learned to dislike and even hate each other. The cause of all wars was deceptively simple. It was just stubborn stupidity. People with clashing beliefs couldn't see through their own arrogance on either side of the conflict. They weren't wise enough to control their violent inclinations.

I couldn't pinpoint what was inherent in acquiring and upholding beliefs that made humans so dogmatic as to agree to organize themselves to kill each other. Of course I was aware that the human ego is the visible mechanism that ran conflict and war, but I didn't know at that time what could give it so much force. But I did know that whatever it was, it always had the effect on people of making them focus on their differences instead of their similarities.

I decided that beliefs severed trust between people because beliefs, especially the dogmatic kind, turned the mind into a bully with a hard and hoarding quality. Why a bully? Because a bully only cares about his own strength and how he can dominate others. He won't listen to anyone who tries to teach him something new, unless he is beaten up and forced to listen for a change. Like a bully with a strong ego, most belief systems encourage a cut-and-dried or black-and-white outlook on life. The bully-like mind makes itself, and those who support it, right while everyone else is wrong.

I also noticed that whenever a person accepted some belief, then his heart became subject to its dictates. Loving and feeling, and all the aspects of emotion, had to conform to the mind and its rules and expectations regarding life and its purpose. The mind established the limits and direction for how the heart should feel, love, and give. It demanded the heart's allegiance to support whatever form of prejudiced and bigoted beliefs it conceived to be true, regardless of how subtle or blatant they actually were.

I felt that most people's hearts had to be tormented deep down because they had been forced to submit to beliefs that were not kind to themselves or to others. I was sure that this was the reason why society was always so sad and sick with problems.

Large groups of people never seemed to radiate the beauty of nature because they were usually divided and angry.

In eleventh grade I saw a documentary about animal life in India and how a young elephant is tormented when it is time for it to be "trained." I couldn't get the images out of my mind. The poor thing was tied to stakes and couldn't move for days. Though it was starving and struggled and cried for its mother, she wasn't allowed to come. The young one had to accept the will of its new master or die if it didn't. Its natural loving instinct had to be destroyed, its spirit broken. I realized it was the same sort of thing that happened to people when they were being indoctrinated by their parents' beliefs, whether religious or scientific, and especially when they were young.

Even though indoctrination of people is generally more subtle than what the poor elephant had to endure, there is always some form of punishment for those who rebel. In Muslim cultures, for example, young women are killed just like the young elephants if they defy the order of their husbands, brothers, or fathers who believe they can treat them like slaves. If I had been born into a Muslim culture, I'm sure I would have died. I felt a fierce unwillingness to be indoctrinated by anyone or anything scientific or religious because I needed to find out what was true by myself. Though I wouldn't let my spirit be broken, I didn't realize that my heart would have to break.

I was so sad that my parents had submitted to science, especially the evolutionary kind. It was as harsh to them as the elephant trainer was to the elephant. But they didn't even know it. They didn't want to. They allowed the theory of evolution to destroy the true value and meaning of human love in their own lives. Why? Because the theory diminishes the power of love to an unconscious and accidental by-product of the evolutionary process. Only a mechanical unconscious force like genetic mutation is considered to be a true force powerful enough to create change.

When my dad and mom accepted that the mechanical and unconscious force of chance is a stronger agent for change than an intentional conscious one like love, they lost the ability to cultivate love as a spiritual quality. They had no reason to talk about how to cultivate love in their lives as a primary purpose of their existence. They couldn't show great interest in love because they had agreed to believe that human love is just a glorified animal love. And animal love is mostly instinctual. They couldn't focus on why humans are capable of amazing conscious acts of loving kindness, unlike animals.

I longed to find someone who had spiritual feelings, could admit them openly, and could explain how they were related to God. But I couldn't find anyone in those days who could help me, though I was always open to conversation.

One early morning I was walking to high school, feeling perplexed and staring down at the road. I often felt frustrated on account of how little my teachers seemed to know about life. They were a part of the mainstream, just wanting to pack my mind tight with things that didn't mean anything to me personally. They wanted me to forget the hidden voice that constantly clamored inside me.

I looked up to see a man approaching. "Good morning," he greeted me. "How are you today?"

"Okay, I guess, but I get tired of going to school."

"Why is that?"

"Because I want to know what is really true."

"You sound like a philosopher."

"I'm sure I'll be one someday."

"So," he smiled, "why not enjoy what you have for today? Why not be content?"

"I can see what you mean," I replied, "but you don't know what it is that I want to know and I can't learn it at school."

"Do you really know what you want to know?"

"I know, but I don't exactly know how to say what it is." I added, "Do you ever hike in the Wasatch mountains?"

"Once in a great while," was his sad reply.

"Well, I hike all the time. What I want to know has to do with silence and what I feel in silence."

"Oh," he laughed, "then you'll never know what you want to find out because you won't be able to talk to others about what it is." He wished me a good day and continued on his way. I could see his holy undergarment, that peculiar white, one-piece Mormon mystery under his shirt sleeves as he waved goodbye.

It made me mad how he left, though I didn't blame it on his being a Mormon. People everywhere were always afraid of deeper talk than the usual kinds of conversation. The minute you mentioned silence, oh my God, they'd think the sky was falling down! Or if you tried to talk about the truths inside silence, or inside nature, they looked terrified and changed the subject or ran away like the Mormon man. People seemed to me like a bunch of chickens living in different henhouses.

I began to think that belief systems were just a way for people to keep their minds satisfied with some kind of thought that gave them meaning, like a shifting anchor in the wide open sea of life. But I couldn't find anyone who wanted to look at life from the inside out, who would be willing to pull up the anchor and drift around and watch, from the little boat of their own awareness, what would happen to them. I thought there must be something deep down, maybe our ego, that was terrified of seeing itself when the mind was not held down to some identity that any belief system could provide.

For this reason, I decided that all belief systems had a lot in common, even if the beliefs that composed one belief system seemed to contradict the beliefs of another. If all belief systems were supposed to support some aspect of our human needs and desires, especially those of our egos, then all beliefs had to be more or less related to each other. It was as if beliefs were all cut from the collective human ego, just like facets are cut from one diamond.

I could see how political, philosophical, scientific, and religious belief systems were just different versions of themselves according to cultural temperaments and people in power. For example, there are socialist, democratic, and communist governments. There are pragmatist, existentialist, realist, and rationalist philosophies. There are the reductionist and compositionist methods of science. And there are the religious people who label themselves as monotheists, polytheists, and transtheists.[4]

I always wondered what would make a person become a Muslim, Hindu, Sufi, Buddhist, Christian, or any other religion besides cultural ties, family indoctrination, and peer pressure. If all religions were relative to each other in that they all satisfied some basic human need, then what was the point of believing in one over another? Was it just some special appeal to a person's own intellect, emotion, or background that made him decide what to believe if he had the freedom to decide?

Then there was the strange and unsettling part about how people viewed their own beliefs, regardless if these beliefs were religious, political, or scientific. They had a sort of unspoken emotional allegiance to the person who was credited with founding them, without even knowing who that person actually was.

I guessed that most people craved so much to label themselves by some identity, by some belief system, that they willingly took the colored glasses off someone else's eyes and put them on their own. They agreed, somehow too easily, to see the world through that person's particular shade of bias, regardless of how distorted that bias actually was. I observed that when it came to defending their beliefs, people gave up their basic discerning capacity because they blurred the distinction between what kind of person the founder of their beliefs really was in his or her daily life, and how that person was idolized by others over time.

I noticed that my parents trusted Charles Darwin the same way Matt's parents trusted Joseph Smith. But Darwin and Smith were exceedingly strange people. When it came down to finding out who they were and how they arrived at their particular brands of truth, I wouldn't have wanted to be friends with either of them. I wouldn't ever base my beliefs about life on what they said was true, or on anyone who said it was "right" to put my trust in them.

The one was a flamboyant narcissist and sex addict who, despite being married, conned other women into believing that God had revealed to him that He would sanction plural marriages

(as polygamy). The other was equally troubled, but in an opposite sort of way. He was racked with depression and suffered
from ailments commonly known to have a psychological origin. They included a long list of problems that included severe
anxiety, hysterical crying, vomiting spells, shaking, fainting,
and dying sensations.[5]

Even though the focus of Joseph Smith and Charles Darwin may seem entirely different in that one was focused on spiritual matters and the other on physical ones, they actually had a
lot in common. Both had a religious background and believed in
God. Both struggled with their own ideas about who God was and
their personal relationship with him and, based on this, their relationship with other religious people. And both also had devoutly
religious wives named Emma, and neither Emma approved of her
husband's iconoclastic ways.

Joseph Smith was born in 1805, in the state of Vermont, four
years before Darwin was born in England. Around 1820, the teenage Joseph claimed to have the first of three visions. Alone in the
woods, he saw a pillar of light above his head. Then two figures
descended. Guess who they were? None other than God and Jesus.
What do you suppose they told him? They told him not to join
either the Catholic or Protestant Churches, which were constantly
clashing, but to await words of truth from them. It was a good solution to young Joseph's religious disillusionment.

Whether consciously or unconsciously, Smith repeated
the usual historical pattern and created a new religion. He satisfied his own desires and avoided what he couldn't resolve just
like Buddha, Mohammed, and Guru Nanak (among many others) did before him. Buddha, who was tired of being a Hindu,
founded (or is credited to have founded) Buddhism. Around 500

B.C.E., he declared, after he became enlightened under the Bodhi tree, that there was no God.

Buddhism is based on the concept of *anatman*, meaning "no soul," in stark contrast to Hinduism. Buddha developed the four noble truths and the eight-fold path as a philosophy for a good life that didn't have to rely on God. He left out the pantheon of Hindu gods and goddesses, but in time they crept back in. It is important to notice this because it shows how human personalities often shape what is believed to be transcendent to them. Tibetan Buddhism, for example, is a religion based on the interplay of gods, demons, and other spirit forces, though Buddha had specifically created the new religion as a philosophy of life without including any concept of God as an omnipotent spiritual force.

Guru Nanak, also from Hindu roots, was weary of his people being persecuted by Muslims. He was also worn out by formalistic ritual and worshiping idols. So, early in the 1500s, he joined Hindu and Islamic elements to create the Sikh religion called Sikhism. Guru Nanak preached that there was only one indefinable, indescribable ultimate reality called Waheguru, who had no physical form like idols sought to portray, but could still include the names by which people wanted God to be called and known.

The origin of Islam arises from a similar kind of religious conflict with Arabs and Jews, but Mohammad's visions couldn't sort them all out. For example, the Qur'an, the sacred book of the Muslims, accepts that the Hebrew Torah (the first five books of the Bible), the Book of Psalms, and the Gospels of Jesus (Matthew, Mark, Luke, and John) are divinely inspired.[6] But then the Qur'an contradicts itself by denying that the Messiah would come through the line of Isaac as is stated in the Torah, in the book of Genesis 21:12.

In this verse of the Torah, it is written that the Jewish descendants of Isaac, and not the Arab descendants of Ishmael, would bear the seed of promise (the Messiah). But poor Mohammed was a descendant of Ishmael and so he was an Arab, not a Jew. Still, he insisted on being the Messiah. Wanting to prove that he was the Messiah on the basis of the holy books he believed in, he simply denied the detailed events of Jesus' death and resurrection as recorded in the Gospels, which the Qur'an states have a divine source.

Mohammad, who died about six hundred years after Jesus in 632 C.E., had the Qur'an rewrite the history of Jesus' death. He made it read that it only seemed to appear that Jesus died by being nailed to a stake: "They said (in boast), 'We killed Christ Jesus the son of Mary, the Messenger of Allah, but they killed him not, nor crucified him, but so it was made to appear to them, and those who differ therein are full of doubts, with no (certain) knowledge, but only conjecture to follow, for of a surety they killed him not.'"[7]

Around 610 C.E., Mohammed held out the Qur'an to whoever would believe that it contained the perfect words of God, regardless of its contradictions. And just like Mohammed, who claimed his prophecies were given to him by an angel called Gabriel, Joseph Smith claimed he had prophecies given to him. But his angel was named Moroni.

The angel, by Smith's account, gave him golden tablets in 1827 which he was inspired to translate into English and call the *Book of Mormon*. The book tells the story of a group of Hebrew people who left Jerusalem and migrated to the Americas some hundreds of years before Christ. A main goal of the book is to establish the Hebrew peoples as both the ancestors of the Mormons as well as of the Native Americans. But it is commonly known that DNA evidence shows how Native Americans are closely related to peoples of northeastern Asia and not the Middle East.

Smith claimed his last vision in 1829 in which John the Baptizer came to bestow upon him and his friend, Oliver Cowdery, the priesthood of Aaron. He convinced others that he had God's backing, that is, the God he created in his own mind. It was not the God of the Hebrew and Greek Scriptures that he touted to be the basis of his newfound sainthood because he contradicted what the Bible taught regarding the new priesthood that did away with the old priesthood under the Mosaic Law. The priesthood of Aaron ended when Jesus died.[8]

If Smith really based his knowledge of God from the Bible, then he would have known that he could not assume the role of prophet either. Luke, who wrote the Gospel of Luke in 58 C.E., explained: "The Law and the Prophets were until John [the baptizer]. From then on the kingdom of God is being declared as good news, and every sort of person is pressing forward toward it."[9] And John wrote some twenty-five years later in the book of Revelation, "The bearing witness to Jesus is what inspires prophesying."[10] This scripture shows that the basic purpose of Bible prophecy was to point forward to the role of Jesus as Messiah. When John (the last of the apostles) died, the time of the prophets was over.[11]

But Smith wanted to be a prophet like Mohammed wanted to be a messiah. When the *Book of Mormon* was published in March of 1830, the clergy of established churches didn't like the competition. They denounced the book's departure from traditional Biblical teachings and announced that he was a quack. But Smith appealed to people who were tired of hand-slapping, fire-and-brimstone type preachers who were out to get them to repent of their sins in exchange for a good sum of money.

Smith also extended to his would-be followers that they could be special. America's "fruited plain" would be linked to the Holy Land through the Native Americans as he explained in the *Book of Mormon*. Many liked the idea that the Native Americans were descendants of the legendary Ten Lost Tribes of Israel,[12] though it wasn't originally Smith's idea. Thomas Thorowgood, in 1650 (about 180 years before Smith) wrote a book about the probability that the Native Americans were really Jews.[13]

Some days after the publication of the *Book of Mormon*, the first congregation of the Mormon church was organized. Despite setbacks and persecutions from the established sects of traditional churches, Mormonism spread. It had its own divinely channeled scriptures through its own living prophet and flourished with phrases, like "and thus it came to pass," giving it an authentic ring. In addition, Smith threw carrots out to the congregation to feed the desires of those who believed in him. He preached that every good person (who followed him) could be transformed into a god or goddess and rule over a planet in the heavens. There were, of course, plenty of planets to go around.

Unfortunately for Smith, his wife Emma was reluctant to join his church and refused for six months until she was finally forced into becoming a member. Her qualms were due to the fact that her husband was adored by many attractive women. Apparently, Joseph wanted to make plural marriage a moral practice in the Mormon Church in 1831, just one year after it was founded. He tried to entice women who were already legally married to also marry him on the grounds that their marriage would be "celestial" and better than the usual "mundane" ones. Evidently he secretly married more than thirty women between the years of 1833 and 1844 though polygamy was never legal.

Things came to a head in 1844 when men in leadership positions in the Mormon church refused to let their wives marry their prophet even though such a marriage was supposed to be sanctified by God and spiritually elevated. The angry men felt betrayed, bought a printing press, and tried to expose Smith publicly as a morally degraded man. But he ordered his faithful remaining contingent to destroy the printing press. As a result, the governor of Illinois charged Smith with violating the First Amendment and ordered his arrest. He was jailed, but shot to death when he tried to escape. He was thirty-eight years old when he died and is considered a martyr by Mormons today.

Just four years after the birth of Joseph Smith, Charles

Darwin was born in 1809 to a wealthy family of intermarrying Darwins and Wedgwoods in England. Both families were Unitarians, though the Wedgwoods were adopting Anglican beliefs. Like young Joseph Smith who witnessed the religious conflicts between Catholics and Protestants, young Charles Darwin witnessed the conflict between Unitarians and Anglicans. Though Darwin's father had him baptized in an Anglican church as a baby, he was surrounded by Unitarians who did not believe in the doctrine of the Trinity or that religion should mix with politics.

When Charles was eighteen years old, he prepared for a career as an Anglican priest after he failed his course in medicine. He was admitted to Christ's College, University of Cambridge, to study theology. At Cambridge, he particularly enjoyed reading William Paley, a Christian philosopher who died in 1805. His favorite book by Paley was *Natural Theology; or, Evidences of the Existence and Attributes of the Deity*. Charles wrote in a letter that he "hardly ever admired a book more than Paley's Natural Theology" [14] (and almost knew it by heart), and that the careful study of Paley's works was the only part of his academic course at Cambridge that left a permanent impression on him. In fact, he did so well in the theology part of his finals that he came out tenth in his class of 178 even though he barely scraped through in classics, math, and physics.[15]

Paley's book explained natural theology as the belief that the attributes of God, especially his "beneficent quality," could be understood through his creation. Natural theology focused on the evidence of God's design in the natural world and so emphasized observing natural laws as proof of God's existence as much as, or more than, revelation and scripture. What had initially appealed to Darwin about Paley's writings, and perhaps especially after his voyage on the Beagle and his collections of many animals not then known to science, was that Paley wrote about the "fit," or special adaptive features, of animals to their environments.

Even as late as 1859, when Darwin was fifty, his belief in God was evident when he wrote in the conclusion to his most famous book, *The Origin of Species*,[16] about the magnificence of "the view of life, with its several powers, having been originally breathed by the Creator into a few forms or into one."[17]

In *The Origin*, he remarked about complex organs such as the eye. He said, "To suppose that the eye...could have been formed by natural selection, seems, I freely confess, absurd in the highest degree possible."[18] Darwin knew the improbability that the components of the eye could have evolved through "slight modifications," as he called them, because chance as a driving force was not sophisticated enough to meet the requirements of the eye's complexity.

He also wrote, "Many instincts are so wonderful that their development will probably appear to the reader a difficulty sufficient to overthrow my whole theory."[19] He evidently felt that instinct was too complex to evolve.

He further made clear his uncertainty when he wrote, "I may here premise that I have nothing to do with the origin of the mental powers, any more than I have with that of life itself."[20] He raised another doubt as to the credibility of his theory of evolution when he said, "I am well aware that scarcely a single point is discussed in this volume on which facts cannot be adduced, often apparently leading to conclusions directly opposite to those at which I have arrived."[21]

In his autobiography, which he began writing in 1876, he recalled that at the time of writing *The Origin* he should be called a "theist." His reason was based on, in his words, "The extreme difficulty or rather impossibility of conceiving this immense and wonderful universe, including man with his capacity of looking far backwards and far into futurity, as the result of blind chance or necessity...when thus reflecting I feel compelled to look to a First Cause having an intelligent mind in some degree analogous to that of man; and I deserve to be called a Theist."[22]

Even in 1879, three years before he died, he related in a letter that he had never been an atheist. After admitting confusion about his personal relationship with God he wrote, "What my own views may be is a question of no consequence to any one but myself. But, as you ask, I may state that my judgment often fluctuates. In my most extreme fluctuations I have never been an atheist in the sense of denying the existence of a God."[23]

Why Darwin sought a unifying principle for the diversity of life, which he called "evolution through natural selection," is questionable. If he believed in God until the end of his life, then he had to refute chance as a causal agent. By God's design, species could show variety, and go extinct, but could not "transmutate." Darwin tried to solve this difficulty just like Joseph Smith solved his. He decided to play God.

He remade God's purpose for the earth and man and especially himself. Though he kept God as Creator, as "first cause" as he affirmed in his book, he required that the "first cause" should breathe life into only one or two forms and then split the creative scene. This way "God" would support his theory of evolution and let chance evolve the rest of the natural world. In so doing, Darwin opposed the Biblical teaching that God created "kinds" that could not mutate into other life-forms.

Having set "God" straight, Darwin kept trying to find evidence for transmutation and transitional links in the fossil record. But he faced a perplexing problem. He didn't know whether the fossil record was complete enough for a fair test of his theory of evolution because he couldn't find any transitional links required to support it. He asked with perplexity: "Why then is not every geological formation and every stratum full of such intermediate links? Geology assuredly does not reveal any such finely-graduated organic chain; and this, perhaps, is the most obvious and serious objection which can be urged against the theory."[24]

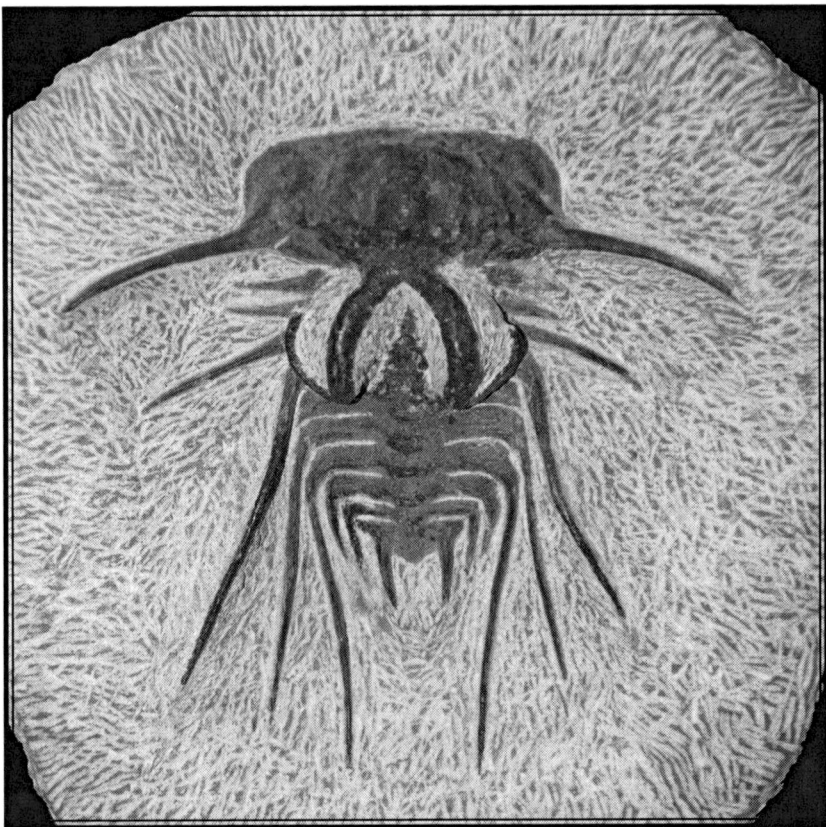

Darwin was aware that the fossil record did not confirm his theory of gradual evolution. He wrote, "The abrupt manner in which whole groups of species suddenly appear in certain formations has been urged by several paleontologists...as a fatal objection to the belief in the transmutation of species."[25]

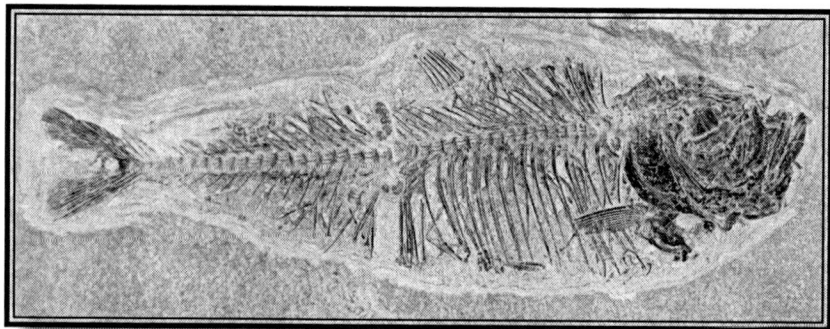

He knew that his theory had failed when he said: "There is another and allied difficulty, which is much more serious. I allude to the manner in which species belonging to several of the main divisions of the animal kingdom suddenly appear in the lowest known fossiliferous rocks...the case at present must remain inexplicable; and may be truly urged as a valid argument against the [evolutionary] views here entertained."[26] He conceded, "If numerous species...have really started into life at once, the fact would be fatal to the theory of evolution by natural selection."[27]

Darwin did try to get around the fact that the fossil record did not support his theory. He suggested that it was capricious: "I look at the geological record as a history of the world imperfectly kept...imperfect to an extreme degree."[28] But in the end, Darwin admitted that the fossil record did not support his ideas for evolution by natural selection. He said, "The distinctness of specific [living] forms and their not being blended together by innumerable transitional links is a very obvious difficulty."[29]

All those who today support the theory of evolution by natural selection consider Darwin to be a man of reason with great skill as a naturalist. But many don't realize that most of his only real time in the natural world was spent when he was in his twenties. He was an invalid most of his adult life.

Darwin frequently discussed his mental and physical problems in his letters and he also kept a diary about them.[30] His own description of his condition included the following: "I am forced to live...very quietly and am able to see scarcely anybody and cannot even talk long with my nearest relations."[31]

He once complained that speaking for only a few minutes to the Linnean Society "brought on 24 hours vomiting."[32] At another time, Darwin had a house full of guests and after he visited the parish church for a christening, he was "back to square one" and his health "had vanished like a flash of lightning" and sickness returned, including vomiting.[33] Due to the severity of his problems, he wrote in his autobiography about his life as a recluse. "Few persons can have lived a more retired life than we have done. Besides short visits to the houses of relations...we have gone nowhere. During the first part of our residence we went a little into society, and received a few friends here; but my health almost always suffered from the excitement, violent shivering and vomiting attacks being thus brought on."[34]

The sudden onset of his incapacitating illnesses, as illustrated by these incidents, indicates that Darwin's episodes had a strong psychological component. Maybe he was tortured by inner conflicts about how he wanted to make his theory fly. In the summer of 1881, he was downhearted and depressed. He wrote to his friend Wallace, "I am rather despondent about myself and life has become wearisome to me." Wallace explained that Darwin was gloomy "on the future of humanity on the ground that in our civilization natural selection had no play and the fittest did not survive."[35]

Darwin's theory always seemed to me to be lusterless, as a projection of his own lusterless life. He couldn't experience love in an open way, and hid from feelings. In a letter he expressed: "A scientific man ought to have no wishes, no affections, a mere heart of stone."[36] As a result, he relied too much on his own mind and drowned in his thoughts. He refused to find out the power of love and the source of its beauty. Since he turned away from feelings, he could not know the creative and healing force of love. Instead he tried to convince himself, and everyone else, that an unconscious mechanical force was behind life's astonishing variety.

He admitted that he lost feelings for people and the ability to connect with them. He wrote in his memoirs. "I have lost the power of becoming deeply attached to anyone, not even so deeply to my good and dear friends Hooker and Huxley, as I should formerly have been. As far as I can judge this grievous loss of feeling has gradually crept over me, from the expectation of much distress afterwards from exhaustion having become firmly associated in my mind with seeing and talking with anyone for an hour, except my wife and children."[37]

I began to wonder, as I learned more about Darwinists and Mormons, if the people who followed Charles Darwin and Joseph Smith really cared what they invested their time in believing. It seemed to me that most people didn't care what they believed, and weren't as concerned with what their belief systems amounted to, as long as it supported the lifestyle that they wanted to live.

For example, many Darwinists do not believe in God and are generally uncomfortable with expressing feelings. They are like Darwin was: afraid to jump into life and love and find out more about themselves. They would rather believe that love has no strength compared to genetic random mutations.

Richard Dawkins, British Zoologist and Fellow of the Royal Society and who treats Darwin's theory as fact, said that because of Darwin it is now possible to be an intellectually-fulfilled atheist.[38] But Dawkins doesn't know, or doesn't want to know, that Darwin never was an atheist. Like most people, Dawkins doesn't really know what he believes and why he wants to believe what he does.

If a man does not keep pace with his companions, perhaps it is because he hears a different drummer. Let him step to the music which he hears, however measured or far away.

Henry David Thoreau (1817-1862), American Naturalist

CHAPTER THREE

Ruins in the Sand

Percy Shelley, the English poet of the 1800s, wrote a poem about a traveler from an ancient land who saw "vast and trunkless legs of stone" standing in the desert sand.[1] And though the statue's head had fallen down, the face still bore a sneer of arrogant command. On the pedestal of this colossal ruin was written: "My name is Ozymandias, king of kings: Look on my works, ye mighty and despair!" But no one can look on his works because nothing remains of them. Shelley ends his poem with what seems a lament about the fate of Ozymandias: "The lone and level sands stretch far away." Perhaps Shelley wants us to think of stretching sand as a metaphor for passing time because time puts all of our pursuits in perspective.

As a poet of the Romantic movement of European literature, he was concerned with the theme that feelings, if they're used in the right way, can teach us more about ourselves than reason. The Romantic poets considered the faculty of reason to be a dangerous tool for gaining knowledge about ourselves and our purpose in life because too much focus on intellectual questions and answers can warp our ability to cultivate love for ourselves and others.

With this in mind, we can see that Shelley's poem involves much more than just a static visual of the collapsing statue of a once-important king. The point of his poem is not regret that time makes ruins of the strength of mighty men. And it isn't nostalgia for the past, as if the past gave a better life to people who lived before us. His intention is for us to encounter something more of ourselves through his poem.

First, we can realize that if we don't have the right perspective about who we are and what is important to understand about our lives, then our hard work may become just an embarrassing example to those who live beyond us. Like Ozymandias, we may be found screaming out our self-importance to a desert that cannot hear. And though his inscription still speaks as if he is a sovereign, no one believes what it says. He wouldn't have thought while he was alive that time could have proved to be greater than himself, but then he believed he was a god.

The name Ozymandias is thought to refer to Ramesses, the Pharaoh of the nineteenth dynasty of ancient Egypt. It represents a transliteration into Greek of a part of Ramesses' throne name, the tongue twister User-maatre Setepenre. According to ancient Egyptian religion, all of the Pharaohs were an incarnation of Horus, the god of the sky, sun, and moon. Horus was portrayed on earth as a man with a falcon head because he was so "high up" and "far off," but he was also connected to kingship in the physical life of the Pharaoh.

As for Shelley, he must have known the connection between the name Ozymandias and Pharaoh User-maatre Setepenre. But his poem isn't just about mocking false gods like Horus and all of us who want to have a similar kind of claim on fame. There is something else that Shelley expects to communicate to us. He offers us a challenge, a sort of test to our own integrity that involves more than just thinking about how others will view us after we die.

The challenge is for us to see ourselves as a ruin, but not from the future looking back. It is to see ourselves as a ruin from a present perspective. Though this may seem confusing at first, it really isn't hard to understand. Shelley wants us to recognize that there is wisdom in identifying parts of ourselves, like old beliefs and mental habits, that do not serve us in a positive way. He is pointing out that it is valuable to know that we can choose to detach our minds and hearts from false ideas and feelings. For when we cease to identify ourselves by them, then we can be more honest about what we've really gained in life.

We can squeeze past theories and beliefs that hold us hostage to a mind-set. We can have a broader and more truthful perspective about how we view ourselves and the world and where we find meaning. It's only useless habits and false beliefs that we let fall into ruin, like pieces of our ego breaking down. For when we drop old patterns of thinking and feeling that do not make us happy, then we can begin to experience what it means to be fulfilled.

I recognized the first ruin of my life. It was the totem of my family tribe. Totems were originally used in a tribal setting and referred to an animal, plant, or natural object that had some special meaning to a specific group of people. Totems provided a way for families to distinguish themselves from each other, and gave the structure for their religious lives as well. But in modern usage, a totem is an emblem or a symbol that defines an outlook or identity.

My family totem was the idea that life, and humans too, evolved by accident in progressive steps over long stretches of time. And, by implication, that only physical aspects of life are real. Most evolutionists believe that the only human attributes worth thinking about are the physical ones. But to me, the most important attribute of human life was not physical, like having an opposable thumb, being bipedal, or having a brain that allows us to speak. It was spiritual. Why spiritual? Because only a spiritual attribute can explain why we have a conscience.

Only humans can be conscious of the consequences of their actions. Only people can choose to do good or bad to themselves and others. Having a conscience, whether we choose to admit it or not, strongly affects the decisions we make. And the fact that we can train our conscience to do what we think is right makes us distinct from every kind of animal. I could never accept the fact that humans have a conscience and animals don't as a minor difference in genetics. The fact that nematodes, which are parasitic roundworms that can live in our guts, share 75 percent of their genes in common with us doesn't make them 75 percent human. And we aren't 75 percent nematode either.

I decided that the reason many scientists wanted humans to be animals, and claimed they evolved from animals, was because they wanted to blur the truth about having a conscience. They didn't want to acknowledge that with freedom of choice comes responsibility for taking care of the planet, including people and animals. They didn't want to be accountable. Instead, they made weapons for killing their brothers and praised their new technology. The source of their conscience remained unexplored and unknown because they didn't care about others. They were too selfish.

The second ruin of my life was the realization that I couldn't trust most of human society, and especially the mainstream, to teach me what it meant to have a conscience. To me, the world bred lies and lovelessness because its rulers were mostly liars and loveless. The history of the world showed predictable patterns of violence. Civilization after civilization conquered each other for the same basic reasons.

The word "world" comes from the ancient Greek word *kosmos*, which means "order" or "arrangement." The idea to the Greeks was that the *kosmos* was everything that humans created as a framework for their lives on earth. It included not only civil codes of conduct and law, but everything pertaining to human inclination and temperament as mankind grew in number and in years of existence.

But by the year 50 C.E., *kosmos* took on a new connotation. The "world" was equated with corruption. In the Greek writings in the Bible, for example, the *kosmos* is characterized as the place where people practice superstition, strife, jealousy, fits of anger, divisions, lies, stealing, drunken bouts, and things like these.[2] In this context, the apostle James wrote twelve years later, "Whoever...wants to be a friend of the world [*kosmos*] is constituting himself an enemy of God."[3]

Though I hadn't read the Bible by the time I was eighteen years old and only felt turned off by what I saw of Christian ways, I knew I couldn't find fulfillment in the usual things that people seek to make them happy. So I rebelled against the world, but not because I was angry. I was searching for a greater love, not a greater hatred. I didn't dye my hair purple, smoke cigarettes, or get a tattoo to defy authority. I didn't party or drink. I didn't want to wear make-up, have a consuming job, or read newspapers.

My rebellion against the world was not made by the world. It came from the realization that nothing the world provides is designed to draw us close to the truth about life and our spiritual origins. I knew I couldn't trust the world's ways because no one who loved the world could help me understand what it was that I was looking for. I began to separate myself from the world more and more until I spent as much time as I could in nature.

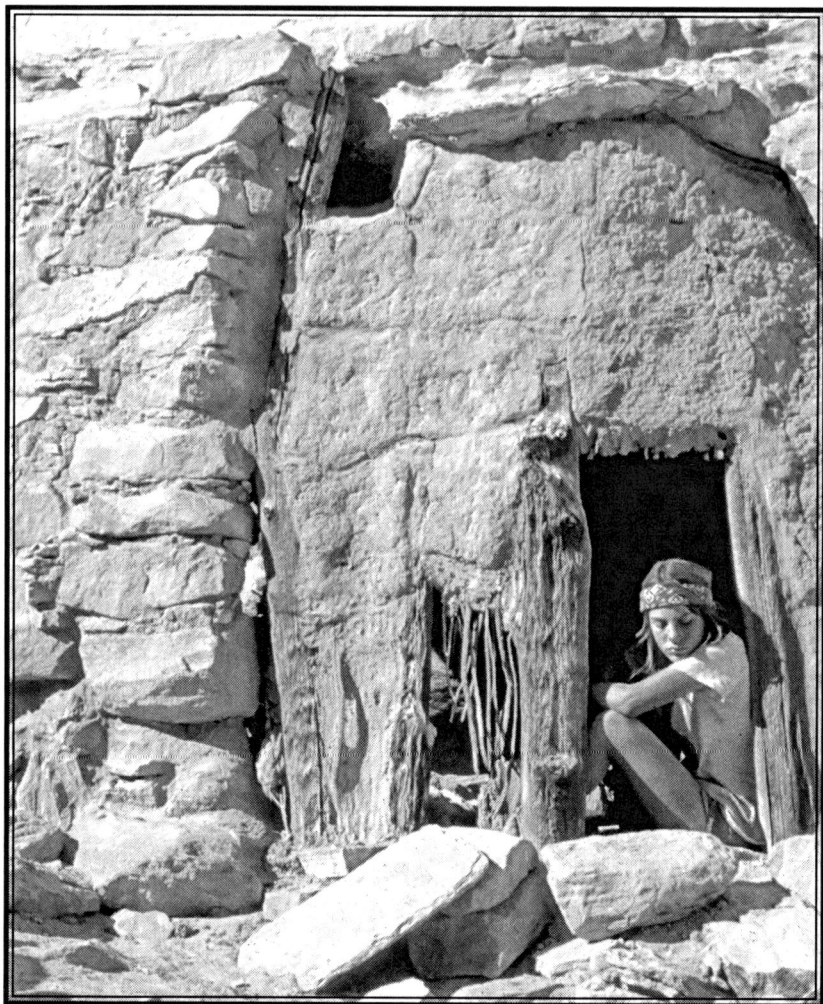

I never involved myself with school socializing, like cheer-leading, football games, or student councils. I was searching for a greater intelligence than what school appeared to offer me, but then I had been spoiled by my travels across Africa, Australia, and New Zealand. But even though I was rebellious against the knowledge that the world and its teachers wanted to instill in me as the truth about life, I was still a polite and responsible student. I always got good grades.

When I was in eleventh grade, a boy named Billy invited me to the prom. But I wouldn't go with him. The reason, as I explained to him, was that he didn't like nature enough. Probably no boy had ever been rejected at my school for the reason I gave him. And, as it was a rather unusual subject of gossip, the story spread around the school halls. A few boys asked me with puzzled looks on their faces, "What do you mean by 'nature'?"

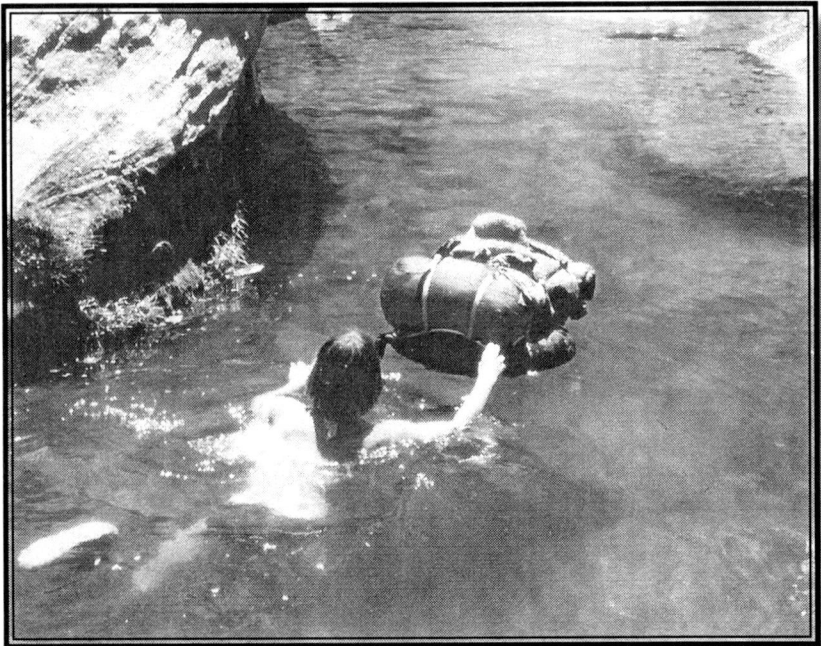

In spite of my inner discontent against the ways of the world, I was obedient to my parents most of the time and I tried to be helpful and generous. I always cared about people and wanted to please them. In fact, because this desire was so strong in me, my dad teased me for years that I was like one of our family dogs. She was a golden retriever named Annie and she always wanted to be good, and to be praised for being good. She wanted love and affection more than anything.

Annie was usually obedient, and she would tremble and her ears would go flat if you talked to her harshly. She couldn't bear to be spanked. And it was true, Annie was like me because I wanted to be good. But my dad's remarks made me wonder if he felt my giving quality was a weakness, perhaps because he felt it was too pronounced in me. I always thought that was the reason he compared me to the dog instead of the other way around.

We had another dog named Tana. She was also a golden retriever, but she wasn't at all like Annie. She had an independent spirit and was always trying to get out of the yard. When she managed to get out, we would have to chase her around the neighborhood until we finally cornered her and dragged her home. She also chewed off the top of our almond tree when it was just a sapling, and she got through the fence and killed our neighbor's pet duck.

Whereas my father compared me to Annie, he compared one of my other sisters to Tana, though I never thought she was as scheming. I'm sure my mother always thought that I was more scheming because she said it was harder to discipline me than either of my sisters. Years later she told me why. She explained that it was because she never knew what I was thinking when she disciplined me because I wouldn't show her my emotion. I had learned to hide my real feelings much of the time, especially my spiritual ones.

I shared my heart with people from the past, with people who left their voice in words. Lao Tzu, who lived about six hundred years before Christ, had an appealing way about him. He was a Taoist philosopher in ancient China. Where the world seemed to have existence figured out, Lao Tzu wasn't so sure we could ever know because of the limitations of human thinking and language. He said things like, "Existence is beyond the power of words to define."[4]

I knew what he meant. Scientists couldn't dissect beauty and say what it was or where it came from. They didn't have a clue about love or the real meaning behind the power of choice and consciousness and the creative urge in us. Their descriptions of life weren't intimate with life, but were only confined to its outlines and edges. I didn't think that words for color, shape, and spatial relationships could ever explain what existence really was, except in a superficial sort of way.

Though Lao Tzu wasn't a spiritual teacher because he didn't talk about God, he still gave me a valuable lesson. He taught me how to meditate and the value of having a meditative mind. It was a thrilling discovery. No one I knew at that time thought about the meditative mind and what could be learned through it. Lao Tzu made it clear that the goal of the meditative mind wasn't to accumulate facts and call that knowledge. It was, to the contrary, to discard useless thought processes that are only self-serving and which create pain and division among people.

Lao Tzu, who lived in the present-day province of Honan in China, based his teachings on the distinction between the ways of the human world and the ways of the natural one. I understood why he made this distinction. It was a precious understanding that I shared with him. So I honored him in the best way I could. In the morning I'd wrap up his book in a piece of white cloth and carry it to school in my backpack. At night I'd only read Lao Tzu by candlelight because candlelight was as close as I could get to firelight. Sometimes I tried to read his words by moonlight, but the print was too small to see.

Lao Tzu said that there were only two forces in the world of human making. There was the force for disunification, which created confusion and separation from joy and wholeness, and the force for unification, which created understanding and fulfillment. But to Lao Tzu, only the meditative mind could comprehend these forces and how they influenced us.

According to him, the force of disunification was the ego. More specifically, it was the drive of the ego to do its own will and keep itself at the center of the world. But the other force of unification was not a doing, like the ego, but a being. He didn't mean a being like a creature or a person. By being, he meant a characteristic of the mind that is not doing. Lao Tzu did not call it a spiritual force, but more like the natural being of the mind when it is not governed by the ego.

The bottom line for Lao Tzu was that only a person with a meditative mind could be wise because he could control his thoughts. He would not be dominated by the fears or pleasures of his ego. Why? Because he would have understood the nature of his own ego through self-examination. A person with a meditative mind would use knowledge for understanding, but not for personal recognition and gain in an egotistical way.

In Lao Tzu's teachings, which were more like poetic sayings and not long discourses, he contrasted the false "ways of the world" with the true "way of life." Not surprisingly, "the way of life" could be learned, but only by the meditative mind.

The test of the meditative mind was to understand what exactly Lao Tzu meant by his puzzling words, "The way to do is to be." It meant, essentially, that if we are not reactive and ego-dominated, or intellectually competitive, then we can understand "being."

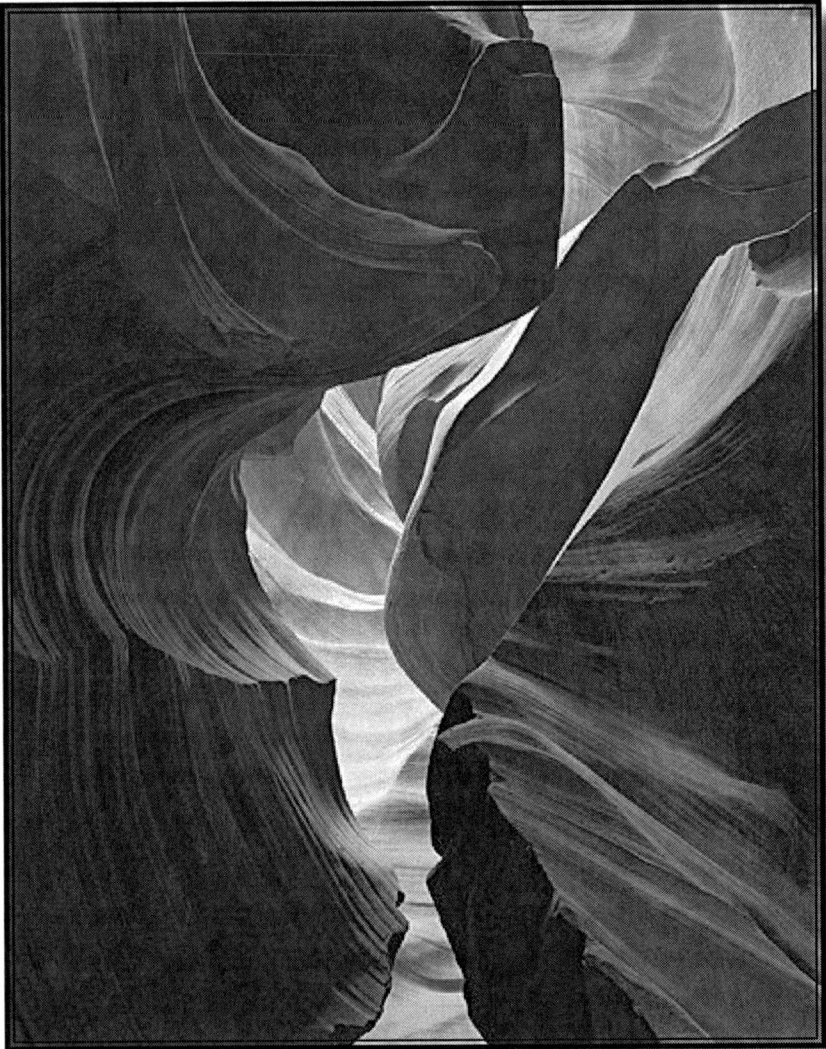

Lao Tzu also taught that "action" can be emptier than "inaction." He wanted to jolt us with these words. He wanted us to realize that action without wisdom is empty. So if action is not self-aware, then it doesn't derive from wisdom. He was pointing out, too, that inaction doesn't mean not being active, like sitting around doing nothing. By inaction, he meant not acting on the desires of our ego that constantly project themselves out on the world.

Lao Tzu challenged his listeners to study themselves, but not in the world or from the perspective of the ways of the world. He wanted us to study ourselves in nature, in alignment with natural ways: with silence, beauty, and order. Then we can understand from personal experience how our mind works, and with the help of the meditative mind we can find peace. He wrote:

> Nature does not have to insist.
> Can blow for half a morning, rain for only half a day,
> And what are these winds and these rains but natural?
> If nature does not have to insist,
> Why should man?
> It is natural too
> That whoever follows the way of life feels alive,
> That whoever uses it properly feels well used,
> Whereas he who loses the way of life feels lost,
> That whoever keeps to the way of life
> Feels at home,
> Whoever uses it properly
> Feels welcome,
> Whereas he who uses it improperly
> Feels improperly used:

"Fail to honor people,
And they fail to honor you."[5]

I agreed with Lao Tzu that the world of human doings seemed so unnatural. People could never just be, they had to always be doing, and usually things that were not helpful for understanding themselves. I understood what Lao Tzu meant when he said, "That whoever follows the way of life feels alive, and that whoever uses it properly feels well used, and whoever keeps to the way of life feels at home." But I didn't feel well used, even if I was a straight-A student. I didn't feel at home, even if I lived in a house. I felt free and accepted by my surroundings when I was in nature.

As we lived in the foothills of the Wasatch mountains of Salt Lake City when I was in high school, I often rode my bicycle up the canyons sometimes even before school started. I always hiked when I could, and often by myself. There were dozens of high mountains to climb and trails up every major drainage and connecting most of the ridge lines. It was absolutely beautiful and I always felt strong and confident in the wilderness, especially when I was alone.

One summer afternoon I was hiking up Dromedary Peak, which was more than eleven thousand feet high. My route was up a scree slope between the cliffs on its west face, as there was no trail there. "Scree" refers to small loose rocks that are piled up together and can be quite deep. Because of this, when you take a step up, you usually slide down a few feet, so it is hard going.

When I finally made it to the top of Dromedary, I was covered in dust. I sat down to enjoy the view and took off my hiking boots to shake the rocks out of them. I was wearing long green socks, cut-off jeans for shorts, a yellow bathing suit top, sunglasses, and a red bandana tied around my head. I also had my backpack with food, water, matches, and first-aid items, and my Lao Tzu book wrapped up in its special white cloth.

I heard voices behind me and stood up barefoot and turned around. There were two men dressed in wind gear, which consisted of long nylon pants and shirts, and hats that covered their necks and ears to prevent sunburn. They also carried heavy packs and wore thick round glacier goggles, though there wasn't much snow left on the east side of the peak where they had ascended. I chuckled that they were playing the role of the "good mountaineer" with all their equipment that seemed so needless to me. One even carried an ice ax. They looked so surprised, and perhaps disappointed, to see me all alone.

"Where did you come from?" one said, staring.

"Oh, the west side of Dromedary Peak," I smiled.

"That isn't a designated route, is it?" the short one asked.

"I didn't read a guide-book," I replied. "There were a few long steep shoots of scree to climb up, but no real exposure."

"Have you been up here before?" the other queried.

"No, not from this side."

"How did you find your way?"

"I always know how to find my way," I boasted.

"Don't you worry about getting hurt when you're by yourself? No one would find you easily."

"Why should I worry? The city is a much more dangerous place with so many crazy people."

"Don't you worry about falling rocks? Don't you get nervous when you're out here all alone?"

"I'm not by myself," I smiled again. I was going to give them a lesson by Lao Tzu, who was my constant companion. They must have sensed my intentions because they said they had better turn back as the day was wearing on and they wished me well and disappeared down the way they had come. That was the way most people were. They couldn't bear to talk about anything out of the ordinary, even on top of a mountain!

Since I had so much experience hiking as a kid, I had learned the ways of walking in the wilderness. I knew my capabilities and never took risks off trails. I never once hurt myself when I was alone except for a deep scratch from a dead branch on my thigh. The blood trickled down and made such a neat pattern as it blended with the dirt on my leg that I didn't clean it up for many hours.

I used to tell my friends that someday I would disappear

into the rocks, but not because I wanted to die. It was more a statement of suggesting that I would eventually learn the secrets about life that only the rocks could tell. They had been around so long. "Disappearing into the rocks" was a figurative way of saying that I would find the truth about life because I was willing to search for it in spite of the way the world wanted to distract me.

As for Lao Tzu, it was said that he disappeared one day. He was last seen on a water buffalo, riding off into the desert. No one knows where he died, but they say he was sick at heart because people refused to accept the "way of life" that he taught. I always wondered if he could have actually been disillusioned since he possessed a powerful meditative mind that wouldn't get easily trapped by the ego's ways, and especially his own ego. Probably those who were irritated by his teachings concocted the story that he ran away to die. Lao Tzu was not well-liked by scholars and businessmen because he called them a corrupting influence over those who wanted to be wise.

Like Lao Tzu, I wanted to leave the world. I tried all of my life until I finally succeeded. But I initially thought I had to be like him and physically separate myself from the world's ways and live in nature. It was so easy for me to love the wilderness. My parents had taught me and my sisters to appreciate being out of doors since we were very young. Their appreciation was mostly in the form of enjoying visual beauty, for recreational accomplishment and pleasure, and for acquiring knowledge of plants for science. But I had to find out more about the connection between self-knowledge and the wilderness experience. I decided to go out on an extended journey by myself. To me, the most beautiful place on earth was the desert canyon country of southern Utah.

I had years of experience hiking in those sandstone canyons, and had started backpacking when I was seven years old. Though I knew how to walk on slanted rock, climb boulders, cross rivers, make fires, and sleep under ledges in the rain without a tent, I hadn't experienced being alone for more than a day.

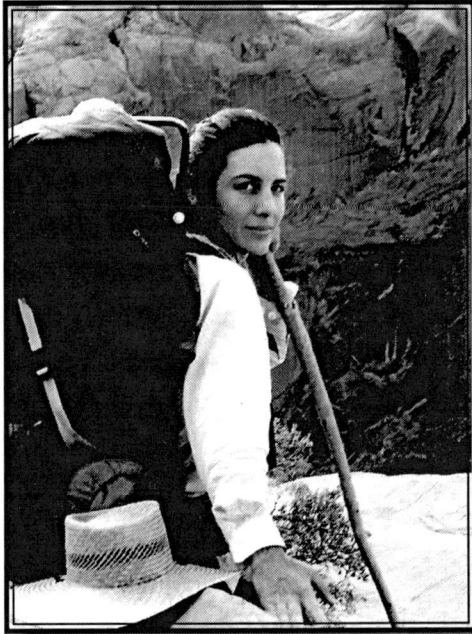

The desert is a complex place to be by yourself. You notice everything. All your senses become magnified. You observe every detail about where and how plants grow together, how they smell, and how the morning light falls down the canyon walls. You notice how the shadows of evening feel on your sunburned shoulders, how the sound of a hollow rock tells you that it will not be strong enough to hold your weight, and how the stars cross the night sky.

You hear, especially, every little whisper your mind makes. You can follow your thoughts, be aware of all that you are thinking. You can observe patterns, too, about what feelings motivate your concerns and activities. You become aware of your mental and physical habits, like the sorts of thoughts you find yourself thinking most often. You watch yourself chewing your food, tying your shoelaces, and listening to the swifts, swallows, and ravens.

You get into the rhythm of walking for hours, and your mind doesn't think to interfere with your feet. It just watches them moving over long stretches of sandstone, or up and down boulders in a wet or dry streambed, or sometimes weaving around banks of poison ivy, or chimneying through a narrow passage in a slot canyon. And sometimes the ground is slippery where you walk on algae-covered rock where clear water flows from springs lined with maiden hair ferns, monkey flowers, and orchids. But when your mind doesn't worry about slipping and falling, it hardly ever happens. You become amazed at your dexterity and balance.

After a few days, you settle into a quietness that underlies all the chatter of your usual mental activity which makes up your daily life in the interactions with the people you normally see. You realize that being alone in the wilderness makes you present to yourself in a way that nothing else can. In the wilderness, you learn to feel your real feelings instead of the ones that you hide behind when you don't want others to hurt you. You can ask yourself to be more courageous and not mask what you feel inside just because you fear others won't understand.

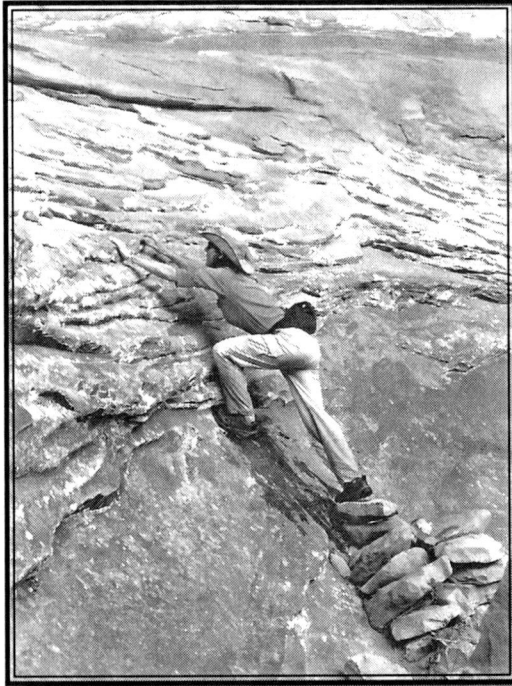

Your mind changes when it is not confined by agendas because it's not busy making plans. It doesn't whirl around a schedule. When there are no distractions to feeling yourself, nothing to do but be with yourself completely, you begin to get in touch with who you really are. Without lights, TVs, or anyone to talk as a way to distract yourself from feeling what you normally don't permit yourself to feel, you learn to face yourself. You get in touch with your fears and strengths because there is nothing to prevent your self-encounter.

In the beginning, you cry at night because you feel infinity all around you, and it's overwhelming. It's not sleeping outside under the stars that is difficult, but rattling around in the space that you normally fill with conversation. And for a while each day, your footsteps sound too loud as they echo across rock ledges and scrape up sandstone faces, sweeping for footholds. Sometimes you still worry about putting your hand on a rattlesnake as you move upward, hugging a crack in the red rock, grabbing for grass clumps or desert shrubs that have managed to grow in a vertical groove.

Slowly, after a few days, the ways of the world start to fall away and your memory of them seem to have no relevance. Neither do your achievements, reputation, or bank account. In silence you learn how to pray. You talk to the immensity outside of you. You seek the source of life, of intelligence, of beauty. You ask to be worthy of knowing what is absolute, beyond what is relative to your own desires and judgments, and those of others whom you know and love.

On my first trip alone, I went to a canyon eighty miles long with numerous side canyons to explore. Fifty miles from the nearest town and a few days hike away from any road, I was searching for Anasazi Indian ruins tucked up under overhangs and on sandstone ledges high above the streambed. To me the ruins symbolized the hidden part of our lives that is always there, but difficult to find unless you search for it in a careful way. In a spiritual sense, the ruins stood for what has to be rediscovered and renewed by each one of us if we want to know the truth about who we are and what we are really capable of knowing. The ruins were my connection to what was forgotten but still existed, like spiritual truths that were not made by man, but given by God.

The name Anasazi means different things to different people. According to some archeologists, it means "ancient ones" which refers to the people who lived in the desert canyons of the Four Corners country (where the borders of Utah, Colorado, New Mexico, and Arizona come together) for two thousand years, from 700 B.C.E. to around 1300 C.E. According to others, though, the Anasazi arrived later, around the first or second century. But the modern Pueblo people, who are considered descendants of the "ancient ones," don't like to refer to the Anasazi. They consider the reference to be an ethnic slur for some reason. And then there are the Navajo who define the Anasazi as the "ancient enemy or ancient outsider."

But to me, in those days, the word "Anasazi" meant all that was mysteriously beautiful. It defined silence and sun-baked sandstone canyons. It also expressed what was sacred and separate from the ugly plundering ways of modern society. I didn't know at that time, nor did I want to know, that the Anasazi were not a peaceful people who lived in harmony with each other outside of the civilized spaces of the cruel races. In the collapsing ruins of their adobe city in Chaco Canyon of northern New Mexico, which is thought to have been the center of their culture, was found evidence of their practice of human sacrifice and cannibalism.

The ruins that I searched for were not large structures made of adobe and I didn't associate them with any large society or any horrendous social practice. The ones I found were only small dwellings and granaries where corn was stored and protected from rodents. Their walls were often made of clay that covered a lattice of sticks and were usually anchored to a row of foundation stones. And if you looked carefully at the construction of them from the inside with a flashlight, you could see finger marks dried in the clay where someone had worked it into the lattice of sticks.

But there were also some ruins almost wholly made of stone that were carefully shaped, or sometimes not, but always held together with clay and mud mortar. Stone ruins seemed more sturdy and well-protected, and I often wondered what it would be like to spend the winter living inside one.

Once I stuck my head into a small stone ruin and something huge lunged up and hit me in the face. I was so startled that I almost lost my footing and fell backwards, down the broken cliff

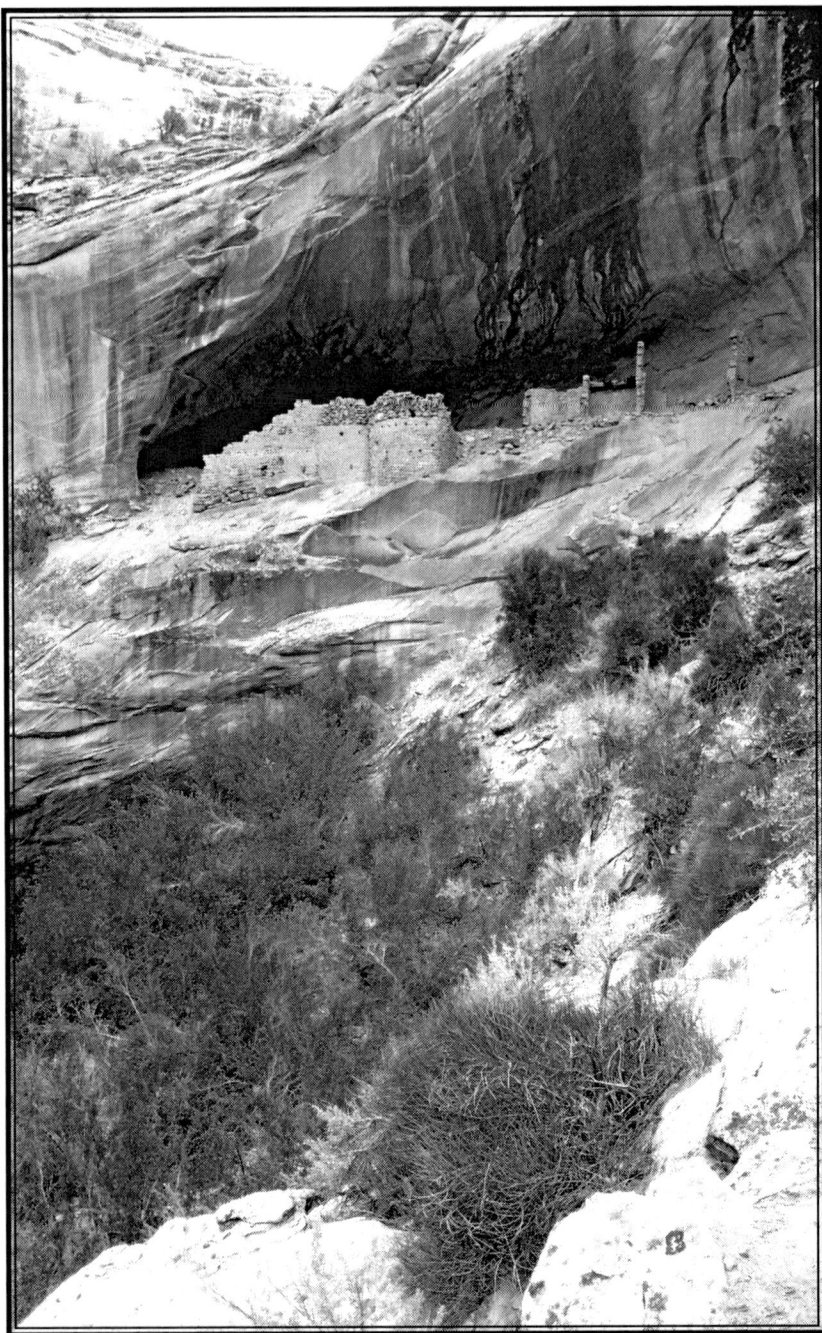

I had climbed up. But instead of being a raving spirit creature or a mountain lion, it turned out to be a great horned owl that was trying to protect its nest inside. The great horned owl is enormous; it is at least three feet tall with a wingspan of up to five feet.

On my first solo trip, I wanted to enhance my feeling of separation from the high tech world and its chaos. So I buried my clothes in a plastic bag, though I carefully marked on my map where I put them, at the base of a tall juniper tree near a rock pillar that was easy to spot when I returned to dig them up. I pulled out of my backpack a tan springbok hide that had come back with us from Africa. It was soft and hairless and I wore it in such a way that it worked both as a shirt and a skirt for the most part, though there were large openings in my outfit where I got sunburned. I tied the front arms of the hide under my armpits from the back, and the hind legs around my waist, so that they hung down my thighs. I knew that I probably wouldn't encounter anyone out where I was, so I didn't worry about being seen.

I also wore a twine necklace with a burnished brown clay pendant. I made the twine from silky threads of the dead red stems of a plant called *Apocynum cannabinnum*, which is commonly called Indian hemp. It grows near streams or springs and has tiny greenish white flowers and milky white sap. Whenever I found the broadest and straightest clumps of dead stems, which can grow over six feet tall, I always tied a bundle onto my backpack for twisting into string.

Twisting the Indian hemp into string is a long process. First you have to separate the inner bark, where the fiber is found, from the outer bark. Then you roll the fibers between the palms of your hand and weave them together. To make a long thick cord takes a lot of hemp and a lot of finger strength. After completing one, my hands would be sore for days.

The clay for the pendant I found in a moist clay deposit on the banks of a stream. It was pure clay and not mixed with sand so it could hold together well, even if it wasn't fired to give it strength. I burnished the pendant, which was the shape of a teardrop and about two inches wide, with a small smooth stone. I etched on the pendant the twisting pattern of the canyon walls that seemed a thousand feet high. They were streaked with beautiful black watermarks, called desert varnish, which is made of clay particles, iron, and manganese oxides.

I also wore earrings that I made the same way as the pendant, which were attached to thin strings made of Indian hemp. In my hair I wore the dry open pods of a giant milkweed. The pods had split open long before I found them, releasing their silk-tufted seed to the wind. Milkweeds have a sap called "latex" which is poisonous and contains compounds that can affect the heart. The descendants of the Anasazi Indians evidently used it to make arrow poison, but they also used it medicinally to treat boils, infected wounds, and other skin problems.

Around my ear I kept a little snake. Its black-forked tongue flicked at my face, wondering what on earth I was. But it was a nice warm place for it to hang in the morning. He had round pupils and markings that were obviously not those of a pit viper, which are venomous. There are only seven venomous species of snakes in Utah, and all of them are pit vipers (rattlesnakes). Pit vipers get their name from the pits on their faces between their nostrils and eyes. They also have elliptical, or slit-shaped, pupils and rattles at the end of their tails.

As for my little friend the snake, his flicking tongue wasn't a friendly gesture like a dog's lick, but an ingenious way to determine if I was friend, foe, or food by the way I smelled. The forked tongue collects data for a special chemical receptor called the Jacobson's organ in the roof of the snake's mouth.

I wasn't afraid of rattlesnakes, even if they were venomous. The reason was that since their venom is mostly hemotoxic, I likely wouldn't die if one managed to sink a fang in me.

Compared to the African snake venoms which are mostly neurotoxic, and absolutely deadly, rattlesnake venom seemed harmless though I knew it could kill an adult on occasion. Hemotoxic venom primarily attacks blood cells, breaks down blood vessels, and prevents coagulation, but neurotoxic venoms attack nerve cells and cause respiratory collapse and heart failure. Also, another reason I didn't fear rattlers was that up to 25 percent of their bites are dry, which means they don't inject any venom. Warning bites, too, are considered to be less dangerous than food-related bites because they don't inject so much venom.

Most rattlesnakes are not aggressive and they usually slip away when they hear you coming. But if you happen to get too close, they almost always warn you before they strike. The explosive sizzling buzz of their rattles is unmistakable and gets so imprinted on your hearing that sometimes when you step on dead leaves you think it is a rattlesnake nearby.

I tried to avoid an encounter with a rattlesnake by letting it know I was approaching. I used a beaver-chewed branch from a cottonwood tree as a walking stick. It was sturdy and straight and besides acting as support for balancing maneuvers that I made when I was climbing down boulders or areas of broken rock, I used it to part tall brush and places where I couldn't see the ground. In dense willow areas that surrounded springs in dry canyons, and even on the lush sand benches above the stream in spring-fed canyons, I always probed and tapped the ground in front of me. Most of the time rattlesnakes hang out in rocks, though I have seen them on sand bars lying in the morning sun. I often saw snakes in the water, but they weren't poisonous so I'd pick up the small ones and carry them with me for a while.

Besides not hiking without my stick, I made an agreement with myself that when I was alone I wouldn't go anywhere without my shoes except around camp, and I didn't allow myself to run. It was a way to minimize the chances of hurting my feet, something I never thought about when I was with others. Having an injured foot would be impossible to move on unless I was able to crawl.

When I was alone, I also liked to sleep with my back against a big boulder or a canyon wall so I wouldn't have to worry about being stalked by a cougar. I never carried a tent. But being up against rock meant I had to watch out for black widows and scorpions. Only once did I sit on a scorpion in my campsite and it stung me on the behind. Though my lymph nodes swelled up for a few days, the sting wasn't much more potent than a wasp's sting.

Southwest Utah is home to dozens of species of scorpions but only the small bark scorpion, which is barely one and half inches long, can inflict a dangerous sting that can cause considerable dizziness and extreme pain. But black widows are more of a problem than scorpions because they will wander into your shoes and clothes at night. Their bites are severely painful and so as a rule, when in widow country, you always shake out your shoes in the morning.

One dawn, when the canyon wrens were singing the most beautiful song on earth, I prepared to set off to search for Indian ruins. The sunlight had not yet reached my camp as I packed my day pack with my map, first aid items, lunch, and taxonomic key (a heavy book) and hand-lens for identifying plants. I also took a paper bag for gathering the white blossoms of Robinia, a tree in the pea family. The edible flowers taste like fresh sweet snow peas, and I liked to eat them with my bagel and cream cheese and also in my soup.

My camp was situated under a small overhang, where the sandstone wall is undercut and provides protection from the rain. Before I left for the day, I secured things so if the wind came up they wouldn't blow away. I hung the food from my big backpack in a juniper tree so that ravens and pack rats couldn't get into it. Pack rats are small, have bushy tails, and are cute like squirrels. They make nests of sticks and cactus in a big messy mound called a "midden." Most of the time, you find packrat middens in rock crevices or under overhangs.

My shoes were still wet from crossing the stream the day

before, though my socks were dry and stiff where I left them hanging on the branch of a cottonwood tree. I put on my socks and shook out my shoes before I put them on at the water's edge. I headed off down canyon, swinging my walking stick. My destination was the west fork of Rock Creek, about three miles as the crow flies but more like five or six miles by the bends and twists of the canyon.

When I reached the west fork, it was dry. There was no sign of water running in the wash. But there was a magnificent sandstone monolith that marked the west fork, which was a side canyon off the main canyon. The monolith stood five hundred feet tall and looked like an elephant's head. Geologically speaking, it wasn't technically a monolith because they are made of metamorphic rock which is formed by high temperature and pressure. Sandstone, though, is a sedimentary rock which is made of sand grains glued together by calcium carbonate and silica. I had studied the geology of southern Utah and knew that originally the entire canyon system around me had been part of an ancient sea of sand, but had turned into sandstone over time.

I named the pillar "Elephant Head" and wrote it on my map. Around Elephant Head, the canyon walls were broken and didn't form sheer faces, and I thought there must be many ruins in the area. I saw cougar prints in the sand heading up the wash so I followed them. I hummed a Navajo song that I had heard years before. I always hummed this song in the desert, but only when no else could hear me. It was a secret sound of my own, like a voice of my inner being, and intensely private. When I hummed it for a while, especially when I walked with my eyes closed, I felt intoxicated with a fierce independence and capability to explore myself like I explored the desert canyons.

This feeling of strength fueled my longing to understand what I didn't know about God, and to discover what was still hidden from my mind and heart. In this way, the Navajo song was connected to my search for ruins. I willed the song to be like a soft wind blowing out of me that would sweep away everything that stood between me and them. It was like I used the song to try and call the ruins to me, to somehow will my awareness to them. And even though the song had no power but what I imparted to it, it so focused my intention to find ruins that I nearly always found them. Discovering ruins was so important to me because it was like discovering a hidden part of myself that I knew existed, but which I didn't know how to reveal in relation to other people.

Near the ruins, I often found paintings called "pictographs" that the Indians drew on the sandstone or "petroglyphs," which were figures carved into it. I also looked for artifacts lying in the sand. They included pieces of broken pottery, called "pot shards,"

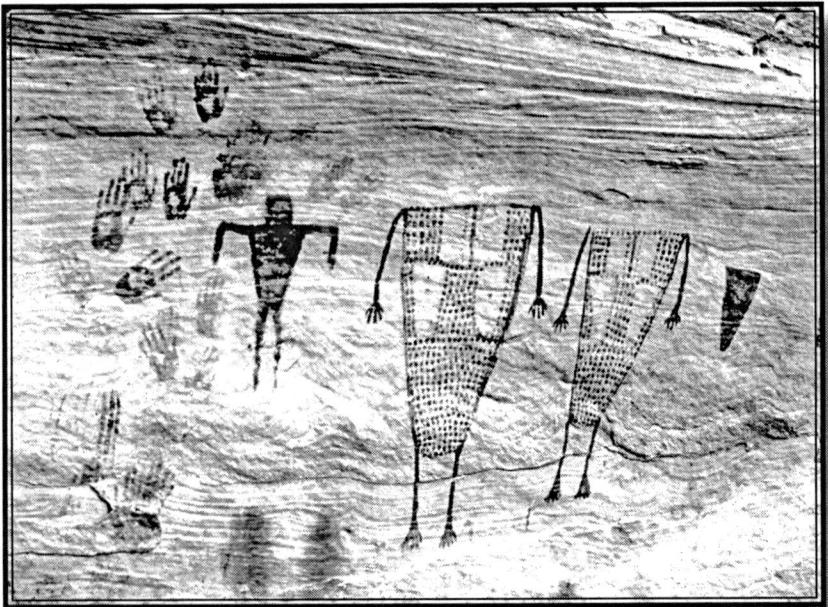

and broken or whole arrowheads. Over the years, I found many arrowheads of different colors, shapes, and sizes. But I decided to return them all back to the desert except for one, which was especially meaningful to me. It was uniformly white, about an inch and a half long, with a symmetrically perfect point. I had found it when I was around twelve years old up on the Kaiparowits Plateau, on the night of a total lunar eclipse. It became a symbol to me of all that our modern culture had lost because people lived inside buildings, couldn't walk on uneven surfaces, and refused to sleep on the ground under the stars.

There was also the thrilling discovery of the human skull years before. It had looked like an old cracked gourd on the top until it was lifted out of the sand. Dry mummified skin was hanging over the side of the face, and teeth still lined the jawbones. Where the ear had been was a piece of abalone shell shaped as an earring with a hole where it had attached to the ear.

Knowing the treasures hidden in the sand, I carefully searched the area around Elephant Head for artifacts, especially where flood water couldn't reach. I deliberately planned each of my ascents up to ledges where I thought that ruins might be found. I had to be cautious so as not to get stranded. If I went up a cliff or a crack in the rock that I couldn't get down, then I would be in trouble. I could die on the ledge and probably no one would ever find my bones.

After climbing around on the rocks and scanning for overhangs, where ruins are often situated because they are well protected from the weather, I finally spotted a small stone granary. But it would be hard to reach. The ascent included climbing up about thirty feet of Indian-carved footholds called "moki footsteps." Moki footsteps are more like simple climbing aids that gave the Indians a place to hold onto the sandstone with their fingers and toes. They aren't at all like the full flat steps of a conventional staircase that prevent you from falling down.

Though I tried to make it all the way up the steps in the sandstone wall, there was too much exposure in case I slipped and fell. So after climbing up about twenty feet, I climbed back down and looked for another route up to the ruin. As I was trying to find another access way up to the ledge and was chimneying around a bunch of boulders, something caught my eye. There was an almost square opening between them, but square is not a common desert shape. I peered into the opening. There was something inside, I felt sure of it. I took out my flashlight and shined it inside while shielding my eyes from the sun.

It was so silent that I felt faint and my ears began to ring. What I had discovered wasn't a typical ruin, but something like an underground chamber. It wasn't constructed like a kiva because it wasn't made of bricks, though there were stones around the opening stuck together by mortar made of mud and clay. I shuddered, daring myself to go inside, and prodded the darkness with my walking stick. I realized there was a sort of irregularly shaped open space where the undersides of the boulders came together and formed the walls of a room. I had often been underneath big boulders like these and found spaces of a similar kind, but here I saw something that I had never seen before.

There were pictographs, five of them, on one long, slanting flat surface of sandstone. With my flashlight, I saw that they all had the same bizarre triangular-shaped bodies with odd heads and thin, short legs and arms. The paint was red and thick in places, and the biggest figure was about four feet tall. Coming out of the outline of each triangular body were short perpendicular lines that looked like they were supposed to be hairs, but the lines were not close together.

It felt so hard to breathe inside the room that I had to come out a few times and sit in the sunlight before I could finish sketching the figures in my notebook. For many years I had gauged Indian ruins by how hard it was to breathe in them. I had decided that the harder it was to breathe, the less likely it had been that anyone else had been there since the Indians. I don't know how I came up with that idea, but I always felt there was some truth to it.

The pictographs up the west fork were remote and well-hidden, and one of my special discoveries. I only told one person that I found them and exactly where they were located. I felt so exhilarated by finding the pictographs, I decided to continue climbing up to the rim of the canyon to see if I could find a way back to the main canyon (and my camp) down one of its side canyons further north. I never made it to the ruin above me on the ledge, but instead went searching for a bighorn sheep trail. The bighorn always know the shortcuts through canyon country, and have well-established routes up on the canyon rims if you can find a safe way up to them and don't get scared of being on the edge of incredible drop-offs.

The wind began to blow as I climbed up higher and higher out of the west fork until I reached the top of the mesa, above the canyon walls. The late afternoon sun lit up towers of

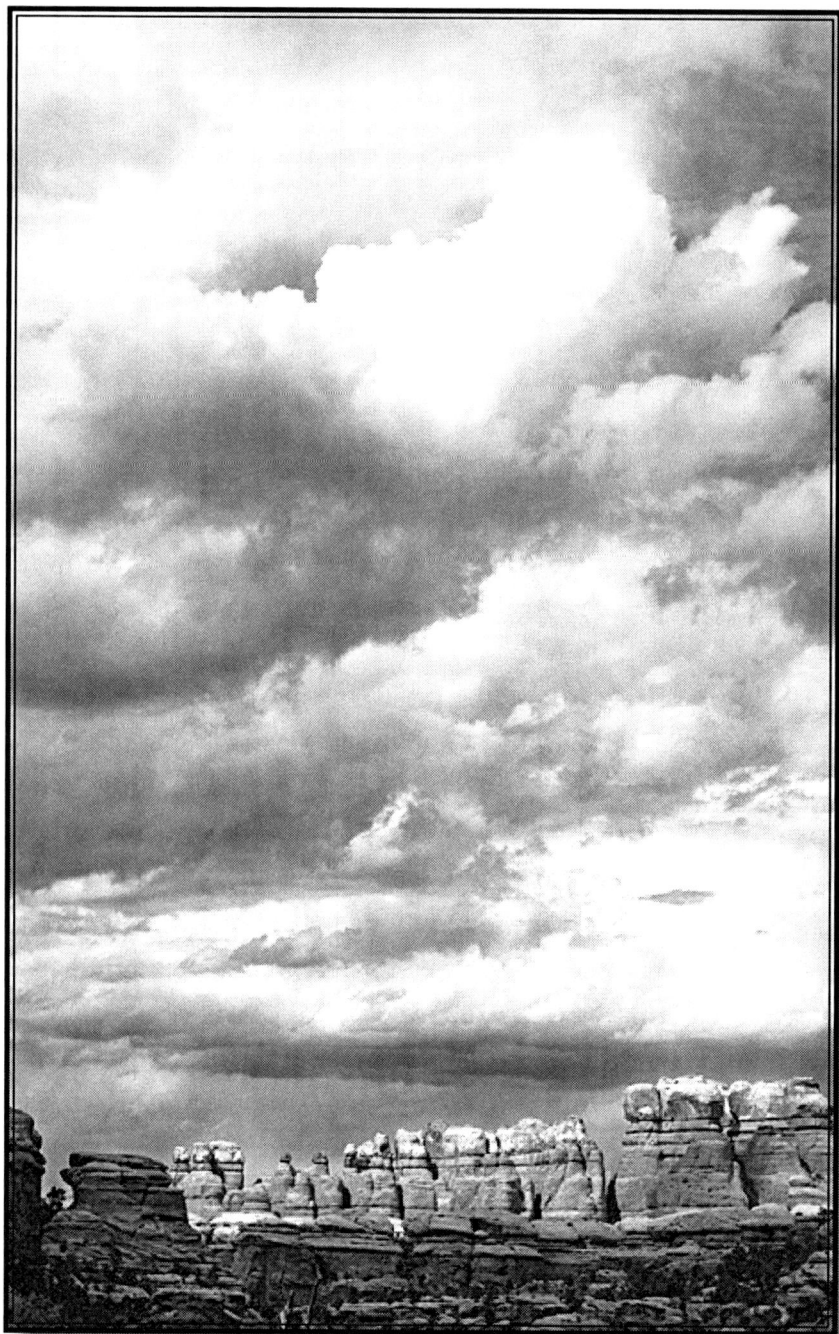

Navajo sandstone carved by wind. It was a rolling sea of stone and clouds. Walking on the edge of the rim, I finally found a sheep trail which was marked by their droppings. "Way to go!" I congratulated myself out loud and continued my conversation with myself. "Looking up as an ant what do you see? Just the immense sky? And looking way down into the twisting canyon below? Just a stream that winds like a snake?"

It is easy to get philosophical and ask yourself questions, especially questions about how you decide to believe what you can and cannot know. Up in all that silent space with cliffs falling everywhere around you, and nothing to obstruct the sky, you feel there are few limits to your inner and outer perception. You can practically see in all directions at once. In that environment it is natural to think you can get closer to the answers to questions that perennially haunt the human mind.

At that time in my life, I always wondered what it meant to have a mind that could be aware of itself asking about meaning and purpose. No animal, by contrast, could be either fascinated or frustrated with this insight because no animal could be self-reflective in this way. To me, implied in the question of what is the meaning and purpose of having a mind is the essential nature of the mind, which can learn from the past, make choices in the present, and look to the future. This quality of consciousness, I reasoned, couldn't be just an advanced physiological specialty of human life. It didn't show up as an arbitrary consequence because we walk upright. I couldn't believe that self-awareness could have a physiological origin even if thinking about it depended on physiological functions.

I considered self-awareness to be as apparent a dividing line between voluntary choice and involuntary instinct as air was between the boulders. To me, the constituents of intelligence, and the ability to be self-reflective, couldn't be understood as well in physical terms as it was in spiritual ones. For unlike the internal physiological mechanisms that respond to environmental triggers and define instinctual behavior in animals, humans will and often do make choices that go against their own survival. Though we can choose to starve ourselves, animals don't have that option. Animals can't defy what is hardwired into them.

People have to choose to live, and how they want to live, and so they are not like animals. And a meaningful human life involves infinitely more than the proper functioning of all the physical parts of our body and how many children we contribute to the gene pool. Choosing life means recognizing our responsibility to find out the purpose of having a mind and a heart.

When it comes to defining the purpose of life, there seem to be three kinds of people: scientists, philosophers, and seekers. Perhaps most scientists can't venture a definition because they aren't supposed to deal with such subjects. As empiricists who believe that all knowledge comes from the senses, most scientists can't think in terms of what isn't defined by mechanism, by form and function. To them, it is easier to ignore certain questions about life as if the answers don't exist or matter.

Most philosophers, though, are a lot like Protagoras who lived nearly five hundred years before Christ. Regarding the question of the purpose of life, Protagoras said that the answer is wholly subjective, that "man is the measure of the world," which means that things are whatever we want to say they are. To him, like most people, truth is relative to what we want to believe. But is this accurate? Does it mean that what is true is only relative to our own egos, its likes and dislikes?

Of course when you're in the desert, where you walk is relative to the time of day, the canyon you want to access, and how much water you are carrying. So, by extension, it is easy to reason that everyone's knowledge is relative to his own experience and cultural ideals, including religious beliefs or lack of them. For example, a person's physical attributes are relative to genetics, climate, and how he eats and exercises. His accomplishments are relative to others, and so, then, is his sense of self.

But there are people who are not satisfied by making up their own hodgepodge of truths and calling it a day. These are the seekers. They look for a deeper understanding, for underlying realities that explain why truth is not relative to the mind, even though it may appear that way to those entrenched in the physical aspects of life. The seekers aren't afraid to combine their heart, mind, and strength to search in a concerted way for meaning that is not made by any person. They search for spiritual truths that are not made by the world, by those who create religion for their own purpose as a way to exploit others.

There are stories of these seekers. They wore animal skins, lived in caves and on mountains, and wandered about in deserts. They understood that to be nobody, by the world's standards, was to be someone. To them, true values did not shift with society because truth was not made by men. The seekers were not ordinary people because they wanted to learn what was greater than they were. They weren't seduced by the desire to be famous or by anyone who had money or power.

I wanted to be like them, and recognized by them, even if nobody else knew I was a seeker. I hopped down from boulder to boulder in my springbok skin with the wind howling through my hair. It was getting late in the day, just a few hours before dark. I didn't carry a watch in the wilderness because I liked to rely on my own senses to tell me how much light was left in the sky.

As it turned out, I couldn't find an easy way back to the main canyon because my little side canyon seemed to be a dead end. There was a wall of sandstone in front of me, but I noticed a horizontal crack at its base. As I bent down to look into it, I could see light on the other side and realized it was a passage to the main canyon where I wanted to be. But it would require twenty-five feet of wriggling on my belly to get there. I decided I could probably squeeze through, but it took me a while to get up my nerve.

The crack was so narrow I had only a few inches above my head as I extended my walking stick in front of me, with my palms and elbows down. Pushing with the balls of my feet, I somehow slid forward little by little. I managed to pull my pack beside me, and it scraped against the rock like the heels of my shoes. I kept my eyes on the end of the darkness in front of me, and hoped I wouldn't bump into a snake den or a nest of daddy longlegs.

It wasn't really a dangerous way to get from one canyon to another unless there were strange creatures burrowed in the passage that would come to claim me between the worlds on either side. And I wasn't too worried about getting stuck, though it was scary to think that it could happen. "Getting stuck" was mostly a metaphor for living in an uninspired way where you never strayed from your comfort zone.

When I finally made it back to camp just as the last light faded, I named the crack "the abyss that you have to enter." To enter the abyss means that you renounce what your ego values in a meaningful open way. For the seeker wants to be enlightened, not stuck in a mind-set. So crossing the abyss is a metaphor for not being afraid to change, to show the courage needed to grow beyond the limits of your present self-awareness. And, of course, the literal act of crossing from one canyon to another, like crossing from a lower state of awareness to a higher one, has to be enacted somehow. In my case, my zeal for advancement compelled me to slide along on my belly as if that degree of difficulty would make me more worthy of finding what I so wanted: the meaning of life in relation to the truth about God.

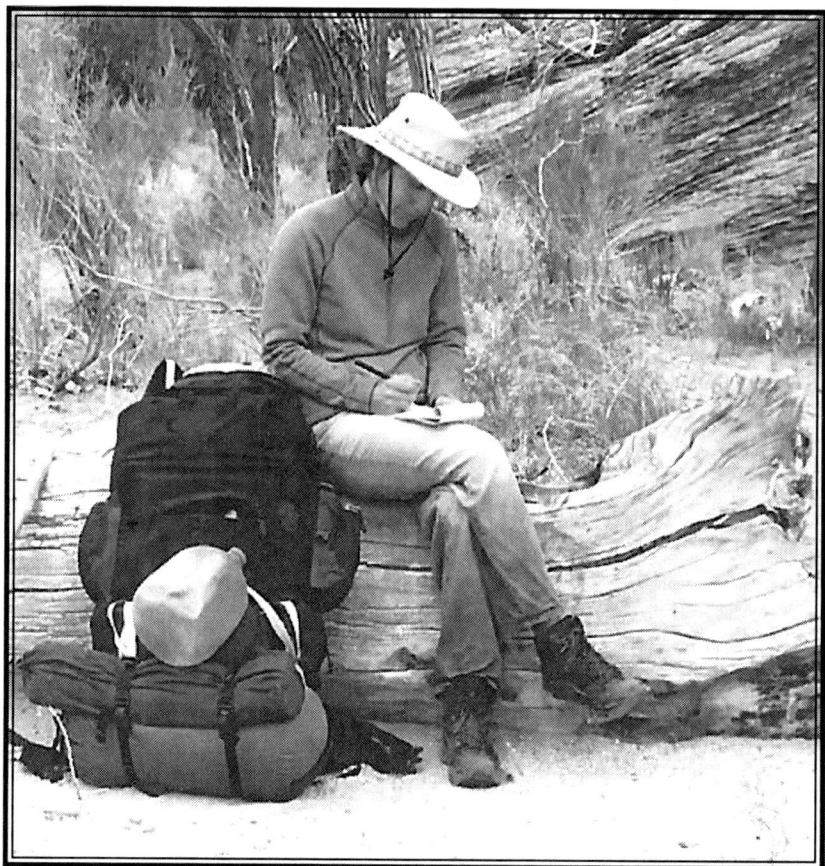

It is one thing to show a man that he is in error, and another to put him in possession of truth.

John Locke (1632-1704), English Philosopher

CHAPTER FOUR

Rumors of a Well

Har Swaroopji told me a story one day down on the banks of the Ganges River, where the water is clear and swift as it pours out of the foothills of the Himalayas. I used to pass him often on the river trail to Laxmanjhoola, the town with a white-washed post office, a few miles from where I lived in a forest the Indians called "the jungle."

To get to Laxmanjhoola I had to cross a bridge about two hundred feet long made of metal wires and wood planks, and it wasn't ever easy. The red-faced macaque monkeys were a terror to anyone who wasn't prepared to defend himself. They dropped like a mob if they saw me carrying fruit and they robbed me many times. As careful as I tried to be, they always knew when I had bananas hidden among the carrots, potatoes, squash, and greens that I carried in two red cloth bags slung over each shoulder.

The monkeys were so clever. They knew I was a foreigner because I didn't scream the usual abuses at them. I didn't know any swear words in the Hindi language, though I had been studying it for over a year. So though I tried to fake a strong confidence in the tone of my voice when I yelled at them to go away, they could still sense my nervousness. They chattered their teeth at me even if I didn't look up at them. Raju, as Har Swaroopji called a large male with scars on his face and a stumpy tail that had been bitten off at the end, was always on the lookout for me. When he saw me, Raju (which means "king" in Hindi) screeched a piercing call to gather the other monkeys to rally with him. Even though I always carried a strong stick to try to protect myself from his taunts, he always harassed me. I realized it was his way to distract me and slow me down so that he could observe the shapes and smells of my bags.

I would become so afraid sometimes that I wouldn't know what to do but get off the bridge and stand very still. I didn't dare sit down, though my bags were usually heavy. I'd just wait for someone to come along who would cross with me and knew how to deal with the monkeys. On one of these terrifying occasions, Har Swaroopji came to my rescue and beat off the king and his

cohorts. With only a few scolding words, and by hurling his fists in the air, he got them to retreat down the cables of the bridge.

But Har Swaroopji appeared anything but tough. He walked with a limp and must have been at least eighty years old. Tall and thin, he was like the willows that swayed when the wind blew down canyon and pushed hard against them. Though he wasn't physically strong, he had a dignified presence. And even though he had only one dirty white *kurta* (a type of shirt that hung down to his knees) but no front teeth or shoes, he had a genuine love for people.

"Namaste, Sitaji," he said one early afternoon, politely bowing his head as he approached me at the bridge where I was waiting for someone to cross with me.

"Kya hal hai?" [How are things?] He smiled seeing my frustration with the screaming monkeys.

"Meharbani hai, sab thik hai. Ap kaise hai?" [Thank you, everything's fine. How are you?] But I shook my head at my predicament.

"Mai bhi thik hu, sukriya," [I am fine, thanks] he nodded.

Then he teased me, "Yah jagahah shant hai hi!" [This place is truly peaceful!] and he laughed at the monkeys making taunts on the bridge and smacked his lips in amusement.

"Aie, baithie! " [Come and sit down!] he urged me to rest. "Vahan na jaie." [Don't go over the bridge now.]

"Accha," [Okay] I agreed, knowing he wanted the monkeys to calm down first.

"Idhar nahin baithie!" [Don't sit over here!] he gestured with a long finger as I prepared to sit close to the bridge with him to protect me.

"Udhar baithie!" [Sit over there!] he pointed to a black

boulder with a flat top down on the riverbank.

So I walked down to the boulder and sat down with my fruits and vegetables safely beside me and he told me this story:

Once upon a time, there was a frog who lived in the ocean and he swam as far as he could in all directions. But one afternoon he decided to visit a well some distance from the seashore. When he arrived at the well, he jumped in and started to swim.

Then he met the frog who lived in the well and asked him: "Have you ever been to the ocean where I live?"

"What's the ocean?"

"A huge amount of water." The ocean frog's eyes rolled wide open to emphasize the bigness.

"Is the ocean as big as the space between by arms?" asked the well frog.

"No, it's much, much bigger."

"Is it as big as the space between my feet?" The well frog stretched his legs as far apart as he could.

The ocean frog shook his head. "It's unbelievably bigger."

"Can it be as big as the distance across my well?"

"No, no…it's millions of times bigger!"

But the well frog couldn't compute such a size. "You're a liar!" he accused him.

Har Swaroopji didn't tell me where he had heard this story and if he really understood what it meant. I was amused that he thought frogs could live in the ocean, but maybe he was just trying to make me laugh. But even if he didn't know the truth about frogs, which was more likely, it didn't discredit what they represented in the story.

I always remembered the point of his story, which was simple to understand. It is that we can be either open-minded or narrow-minded when it comes to learning new things about life and the truth of our circumstances. For though both the well frog and the ocean frog may live inside us all at different times in our lives, it is likely that each one of us will resemble one frog more than the other. Either we can constantly seek to defend our point of view and bolster our beliefs so that we don't ever let anything challenge them, or we can be open like the ocean frog and swim across our own mind as if it is as expansive as the ocean.

The story also illustrates the thought that when we have a chance to learn something new from someone whose perspective appears to be broader than our own, we better pay attention. It is our special opportunity. The ocean frog can teach us something important about our lives, but it is up to us to listen. If we refuse, then we are just like the well frog who represents a stubborn resistance to stepping outside of his comfort zone. If we are like the well frog, then we are saying that our ego is all we know and all we want to know.

But it is such a pitiable way to live when we get trapped by our own ego. Like the well frog, we can only paddle in small circles around the confines of our limited knowledge of ourselves and our relationships with others. Our well will be like a prison because we have no vision of anything grand and no opportunities to be inspired. We will be like the well frog who can't make any discoveries on his own because he needs outside information and influence to learn something new. Yet if he is fortunate enough to have the ocean frog visit his well, then he can ask him questions. He can ask where the ocean is, and how he can learn to swim without his habitual confinement.

So the moral of the story of the two frogs is that we have to find out which frog we best represent. If we can admit we are like the well frog, then we can learn how to be more open-minded. But if we call the ocean frog a liar, then we close ourselves off from learning who he is and what he knows. We will also refuse to accept a more accurate understanding of ourselves because we have too much self-importance.

It might seem tricky to be in a position like the well frog. On the one hand, if you're not open to learning new things about yourself then you stay trapped by your ego in your little well of habit. But on the other hand, you can't believe every frog that jumps into your acquaintance and says he's seen the ocean. What if he isn't telling the truth? And how can you tell if he's genuine? There are answers to these questions, but we have to find them out for ourselves.

When I was thirteen years old, I met Maria Mathlangoo. She was a Zulu woman with big bones and a big bottom who lived in a shack behind our house in Pretoria, South Africa. She knew the rules of the South African apartheid and believed her worth depended on how well she served the whites and obeyed them. But to my family, she was a maid who worked for her income. We happened to bump into Maria's life, like ocean frogs jumping into her well, when we rented the house where Maria worked. We stayed at the house for some months while my father worked at the University of Pretoria and conducted various field trips to collect plants.

Maria called me "Winjee." She raked the carpet with a lawn rake so that the grooves made a tidy parallel pattern across the living room floor. She had a sponge bath every night from a sink attached to the red brick wall outside my bedroom window. She sat cross-legged on the kitchen floor and refused when the new madam, my mother, suggested she sit at the table with us. Her previous master and madam had gone to France and she was bewildered by our ways.

We had no intentions of upholding the bigoted beliefs of white supremacy, and yet poor Maria had no ability to trust why we seemed so different. Though she did not dare to use the silverware we offered her, as she was conditioned to believe her lowliness, she gratefully ate the good quality meat we shared with her. Most blacks had to eat "servant's meat," a grizzly punishment for their pigment. It was purchased for next to nothing in every butcher shop and were probably just scraps swept up from the floor.

Maria knew I cared about her because I always tried to make her laugh. One afternoon after trying to catch lizards running around the whitewashed walls of her shack, I decided to play a trick on her. I went to my dad's closet and put on one of his hats, a heavy coat, and a pair of his gloves. Then I went to Maria's door and knocked so hard that her tin roof rattled. I disguised my voice in the deep low tone of a man, but she couldn't understand anything I said because my words weren't real. I spoke a made-up gibberish in the cadence of Zulu, which I had often heard her speak to others who had come to see the strange new family, especially the mysterious madam.

Perplexed by the babble coming through her door, she volleyed questions back to me. We went back and forth for a few minutes until she opened it up a crack to see who on earth I could be. Quick as I could, I thrust out my man-sized glove stuffed with toilet paper around my wrists and fingers. Scared, she started yelling until I exposed who I was. Then she chased me around the yard, trying to whack me with her sandal. "Winjee, you bad girl. Bad girl!" she laughed. Then she hugged me.

One day I took it upon myself to teach Maria something new. After trying to explain that I was born in North America and why I couldn't take a bus from there to Pretoria as she had inquired of me, I took down an encyclopedia from high up on the living room shelf. Contained in the sections under "United States" were many pictures attempting to frame the virtues of America. In one picture, black and white men were working together dumping trash into garbage trucks. They were smiling and wearing the same white shirts, dark pants, and shoes.

Maria stared and stared at the picture, but she couldn't believe what she saw. "Huh?" she exclaimed, pointing at the white men working with the black men. "Winjee, you lie! You lie!" she accused me, and grabbed the book out of my hands. She threw it down hard on the floor and stomped outside to her little hut of hopelessness.

"Maria!" I called her. "Maria, come back here. I'm not lying!" But she wouldn't answer. She was too hard-hearted.

I wondered then, and I wonder more now, if someone else had been in her position, if that person would have learned something new and important. For one thing, he or she could have reflected on why the hearts of white people are not all the same. Just like the aspirations of all people are not the same either, regardless of our color, education, or position in society. For when it comes down to searching for the truth of our existence, what we eventually find depends on what we have in our hearts.

If you think about it, there are only two ways to be fooled from learning what is true, but you have to be a well frog in both cases. One way is to refuse to believe what is true, like Maria, who wouldn't accept the picture I showed her. Though she knew there was no way I could have concocted such a picture to mislead her, she still refused to talk about it with me. She wouldn't ask a single question.

The only other way to be fooled from learning what is true is by believing what is false. This can be confusing, especially when many people are involved. Imagine the pressure to believe what is false when what is false is proclaimed as the truth.

This happens all the time in the circles of science and reli-gion when some prestigious or powerful person assigns a value of truth to what is false, simply to serve some selfish purpose. But, we have to remember, just because false ideas are made to masquerade as truthful ones, it doesn't mean that truth doesn't exist in principle. We have to be careful about what we claim is truth, regardless if our outlook is primarily scientific or religious. In our desire to establish "the truth" we have to be cautious not to be like well frogs and defend a false position.

For example, many scientists may say up front that they can't engage in questions about the origins of life, especially hu-man origins, since they profess that they have to stay within the guidelines of scientific empiricism in stating what is true. In other words, they can only talk about physical forms and functions when it comes to defining laws of life according to their own criteria. If they stray beyond these boundaries, if they leave the touchstone of scientific testability as the basis of their claims, then they smuggle science into metaphysics where it isn't supposed to be.

But this actually happens when evolutionists call matter the "Maker" of life. They step outside an empirical mind frame and break their own rules. How? When they state their belief that humans (and all life) evolved by accident, they usurp "the truth" of established religious absolutes and announce their own. When they dub religious absolutes as simply relative to the cultures with which they are historically associated, they are making a metaphysical statement. Why can this be said? Because they redefine religious absolutes under their own faith claim that life evolved by chance. But evolutionary theory is not a proven fact and cannot stand squarely as one. The reason is that belief in the spontaneous generation of life is not scientific.

The causal mechanism for the development and evolution of life cannot be identified. Of course, this is not to say that natural selection is not a real process. It does work fine for explaining certain limited kinds of variation, for small-scale change. But there is an astronomical difference between selection processes acting to make minor changes in an existing structure of an organism and the origin of that structure itself. Variations in color, size, and shape can be the outcome of selective pressures, manifesting as functional advantages, which are passed from one generation to the next.

Charles Darwin was familiar with domestic breeding because he had experimented with pigeons. He knew, too, that people had been breeding them for centuries. Pigeon breeders had been able to make dramatic changes in pigeon populations by selecting only certain pigeons to breed in order to pass on specific traits. For this reason, he must have suggested that the same processes could operate in nature. But pigeon breeding assumes an intelligent source, a pigeon breeder who methodically selects for traits by the controlled breeding of the pigeons. Without a pigeon breeder, pigeons wouldn't show dramatic changes in their minor structures. Without breeders to select for traits, pigeon variation couldn't be engineered. It couldn't come about by accident.

Darwin's mistake was to think that small-scale changes, such as those applied to pigeon breeding for different varieties, could explain the real complexity of life.[1] For selected small changes in the structures of feathers and beaks is an entirely different scale of phenomena than the changes required to create one organism from another. And yet Darwin wanted to make the impossible possible. He wanted to explain the appearance of order and transformation without intelligence. He wanted to acknowledge the appearance of design, but not by the hands of a designer.

Chance, however, cannot be defined as a causal agent, as a mechanism for change in the same way that an intelligent designer, like a pigeon breeder, is. A mechanism has to be repeatable and rational in order to have a basis for observation by the scientific method. With regards to chance, there is no mechanism that can explain the action of how single cells became multiple ones in the supposed evolutionary sequence of fish growing legs, reptiles growing wings, and mammals losing legs to become human. Saying such an immense journey of life happened by accident means that there is no understanding of what caused the accident to occur in the first place and allows it to continue occurring. Attempting to explain the accident with the catch-all phrase of "random genetic mutations" alone is not logical because science clearly shows that mutations (lethal alleles) in existing organisms overwhelmingly result in birth defects and death.

It was once believed that the earth was flat, and that if you sailed off of it then that was the end of you. But now it has been established as a certainty that the earth is spherical in shape. And though Aristotle and Ptolemy established the idea that the earth was the center of the universe and that everything revolved around it, they were wrong. But the idea held true for almost two thousand years in the Western world until the sixteenth century when the Polish astronomer, Nicolaus Copernicus, proposed a heliocentric model of the solar system. Eventually, it was proved that the earth rotated around the sun.

In order for Darwin's theory of evolution to be accepted as a fact, it has to be established as a fact by the scientific method. This method has a given number of components, no more, no less: First, observe. Next, based on your observations, form a theory as to what you think is true. Then, test your theory by further observations and experiments. And finally, ascertain if your predictions, based on your theory, can be maintained.

It has not been possible to use the scientific method for establishing evolutionary theory as fact. The reason is that nothing can be verified as to a starting point. Experiments cannot reproduce a beginning. Predictions based on the theory cannot be fulfilled. If it is not possible to use the scientific method to establish the origins of life in a scientific way, then it doesn't make sense to elevate the theory to the level of a fact. It isn't honest either.

The evolutionist Loren Eiseley admitted this back in 1957 when he wrote, "After having chided the theologian for his reliance on myth and miracle, science found itself in the unenviable position of having to create a mythology of its own: namely, the assumption that what, after long effort, could not be proved to take place today had, in truth, taken place in the primeval past."[2]

But even though evolutionists don't play by the rules in proclaiming how we came to be, this isn't to say that religion does. Every religion should agree with the findings of science, at least with the basic physics of life, such as the shape of the earth as we know it today and how it hangs in space. A true God wouldn't pronounce the sphere of the earth flat or oblong or as being supported by an elephant standing on four turtles when gravitational forces explain its position.

Establishing a truthful relationship between science and religion is actually not as hard as establishing a true relationship between the religions of the world. For there is a big problem that exists when different religions all give God a different name. Different names signify different qualities, just like every human name identifies a different person. If God is supposed to define an absolute, which means God is not a creation relative to people but instead the Creator of them all, then it is not logical for God to be defined in different ways and mean different things to different people.

Both religious and non-religious people throughout the centuries have tried to solve this contradiction. Karl Marx was one of them. In 1844, he spouted out that "religion is the opium of the people."[3] Though his remark seemed to take a cheap shot at religion, it accurately pointed out that there is some mischief going on somewhere when different religions make the same claim that they alone know the truth about God.

As a political philosopher who had no ties to any religious inclination, Marx wanted to show that there is in the nature of religious organization some kind of powerful indoctrinating force that can dull our minds just like opium has a sedating effect on our consciousness. He was right about that. Unless we think for ourselves, and don't fall victim to addictive sedating influences, we won't be able to find out for ourselves what is true about God. We won't, so to speak, be able to ask the ocean frog questions.

But in spite of his zeal to be free of false influences, Karl Marx turned out to be another well frog. For even though he was

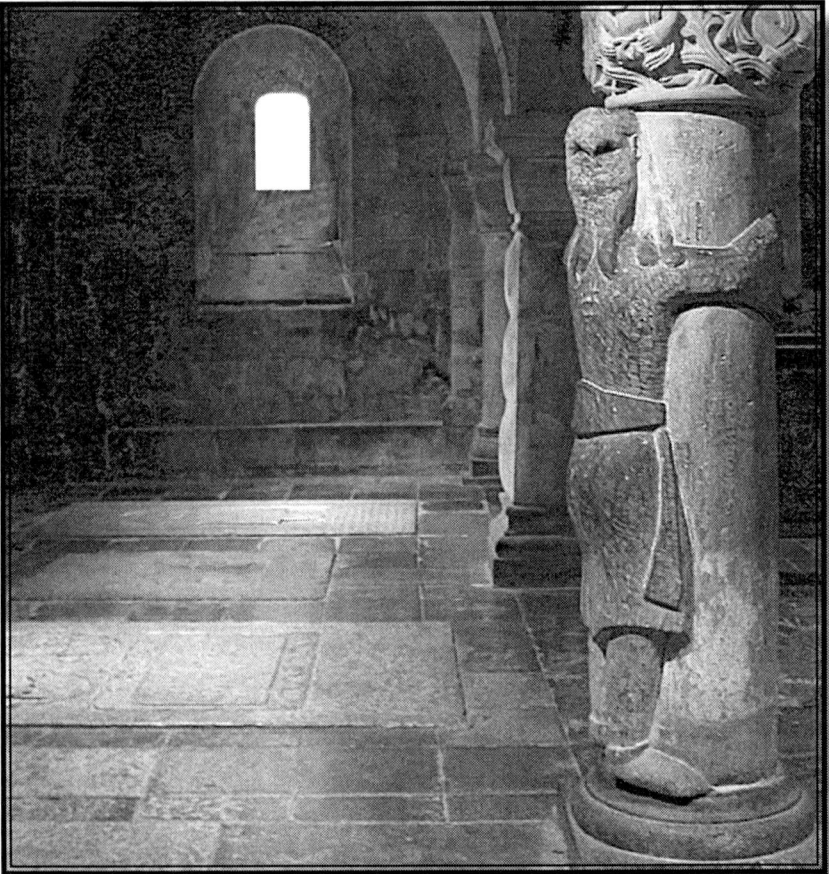

not fooled into believing what was false, he still refused to believe what is true. Why? Because he believed that spiritual concerns are not primary to human nature but are just secondary consequences of how people struggle with economic injustice over time.

As he said, "Religion is the sigh of the oppressed creature, the heart of a heartless world, and the soul of soulless conditions... the abolition of religion as the illusory happiness of the people is the demand for their real happiness. To call on them to give up their illusions about their condition is to call on them to give up a condition that requires illusions."[4] To Marx, then, religion was just a relieving sigh, an illusory consolation to ease the hearts of people burdened by struggle.

To him, the history of the world was always a history of class struggles. And though this may be obvious to everyone, what isn't so obvious is why there has always been such strife. But Marx didn't address the cause of greed and from where the desire for selfish prominence really originates. For even when people have enough to eat and enough means to live a good life, they still aren't satisfied.

Most people don't want or appreciate economic equality, as we have seen when people are forced into such a circumstance. Communist societies don't guarantee a happy end to struggle, and Marx didn't live long enough to see that his ideas were not a solution to the problem of human suffering. When people in communist societies are freed from forced equality, they fall back to their own inner inclinations. Some will want to dominate, which means that others will be dominated.

The fundamental shaping of human society, then, is not based on economics. Economics is simply an outward expression of a deeper choice. What determines economic status depends on what people choose to do. And choice stems from a desire to help or hinder when it comes to sharing food and the necessities of life. It comes down to what motivates people to be generous or greedy. It comes down to what we cultivate in our hearts.

It is an interesting fact of history that when it comes to being forced to be violent and fight for food, some people have refused. They make a decision not to be violent like those who oppress them. Though some may want to argue that willfully starving to death is as violent to the body as fighting for food, they miss the point about why some don't choose to fight. They don't fight because they choose to be non-violent.

Marx couldn't understand the basis of human suffering because he didn't want to understand why there is a fundamental difference in the hearts of people. He couldn't see that class struggle is a spiritual problem before an economic one. But he was a materialist who believed only in matter, including the mind and intelligence, as the basis of life. For this reason, he had to deny the truth that people choose to worship a Creator not just because they are oppressed, but because it is fundamental to their nature. Humans have always sought to worship qualities that they consider transcendent to themselves.

Instead of trying to understand the nature of religious experience and why some people have a spiritual need and others appear not to, Marx envisioned that the solution to all suffering would be a new classless society. But this would mean that good-hearted people would be forced to kill bad-hearted people in the struggle of the working class to completely overthrow the ruling class. Though his ideas were meant to liberate society from oppression, ironically they couldn't be implemented without perpetuating pain.

Like all of us, Marx projected his own inner inclinations onto the world. In his case, his political philosophy was a reflection of his own unhappy life. Wherever he went, he stirred up trouble. Though he tried to create a united German republic and joined several revolutionary movements, he was thrown out of Germany. He also lived in Paris until the French government kicked him out. The same thing happened in Belgium. His comings and goings were hardly in the interest of anyone, as Marx sought to capitalize struggle and dethrone God.

But Marx was quick to recognize Darwin as an ally because his theory of evolution through the survival of the fittest justified struggle. On January 16th, 1861, Marx wrote to Ferdinand Lassalle, a German jurist and political activist: "Darwin's book is very important and serves me as a natural scientific basis

157

for the class struggle in history."[5] H. G. Wells, an English writer, confirmed how people like Marx took up the idea of struggle and used it to support oppression. In his book *The Outline of History*, Well's wrote that "prevalent peoples at the close of the nineteenth century believed that they prevailed by virtue of the struggle for existence, in which the strong and cunning get the better of the weak and confiding. And they believed further that they had to be strong, energetic, ruthless, 'practical,' egotistical."[6] Notably, Darwin's ideas about the survival of the fittest were essential to Hitler's doctrine of racial superiority.

Like many others, Marx didn't want to acknowledge that only loving qualities, and not violent ones, would enable a ruler to use power in the right way for the benefit of everyone. Only loving qualities are unselfish, considerate, and responsible. Only loving qualities end oppressive situations. Though Marx wanted all men to be economically equal, he didn't realize that the desire to be equal could not be in the hearts of everyone because the disposition to share equally is a spiritual quality more than a physical one.

Marx's political philosophy was an ideal not matched in his personal life. Though he wanted to appear like the true champion of the working man, he refused to work to support his wife and children. Three of his seven children (one was the result of an affair and lived with another family) died in childhood because they lacked proper food and medical attention. In a letter to Friedrich Engels, his wealthy political friend, he wrote: "My wife is ill. Little Jenny is ill. Lenchen has some sort of nervous fever. I could not call the doctor because I have no money to buy medicine. For the past eight to ten days I have been feeding the family solely on bread and potatoes, but whether I shall be able to get hold of any today is doubtful…How am I to get out of this infernal mess?"[7] In another letter he wrote: "At present I have to pay out twenty-five per cent to the pawnshop alone, and in general am never able to get things in order because of arrears…The total absence of money is the more horrible, quite apart from the fact that family wants do not cease for an instant, as Soho is a choice district for cholera, the mob is croaking right and left (e.g. an average of three per house in Broad Street) and "victuals" [food supplies] are the best defense against the beastly thing."[8]

Though Marx did receive financial help from Engels (whose father was a textile manufacturer and one of the bourgeoisie capitalists that they both hated but ironically still depended on) he squandered the money on liquor, tobacco, and travel. Two of his three surviving children later committed suicide. A Prussian government spy, describing Marx to a judge, related about his habits: "In private life he is an extremely disorderly cynical human being, and a bad host. He leads a real gypsy existence. Washing, grooming and changing his linen are things he does rarely, and he is often drunk."[9]

In contrast to Karl Marx was Ralph Waldo Emerson, an American poet and writer who was born in Boston in 1803, fifteen years before Marx. He was known to make a good impression on people because he was a kind person with a positive outlook. Once he met Henry Crabb Robinson, the British diarist, who didn't like Americans because they kept slaves. But he was won over by Emerson. He wrote about him, "In an instant all my dislike vanished. He has one of the most interesting countenances I ever beheld, a combination of intelligence and sweetness that quite disarmed me…He conquers minds as well as hearts wherever he goes."[10]

The poet Walt Whitman said about Emerson, as he stood

by his grave in 1882, that he was "a just man, poised on himself, all-loving, all-inclosing, and sane and clear as the sun."[11] Louisa May Alcott wrote to her friend, "Emerson did much to help me to see that one can shape life best by trying to build up a strong and noble character through good books, wise people's society, an interest in all reforms that help the world, and a cheerful acceptance of whatever is inevitable."[12]

I was also attracted to Emerson because I liked the intelligent love I felt in his writing. I also appreciated that he wrote on many subjects including nature, love, spirituality, friendship, history, and beauty. He was an integrated person. Since he was a friend of life and opened himself to discover its secrets and truths, he didn't have to be dogmatic. He wasn't arrogant either. He had a relaxed and playful humor and the knack for telling anecdotes. And though there is a lyrical quality to his writing, he was still matter-of-fact and said things like they were.

For example, he wrote: "A little consideration of what takes place around us every day would show us that a higher law than that of our will regulates events; that our painful labors are unnecessary, and fruitless; that only in our easy, simple, spontaneous action are we strong, and by contenting ourselves with obedience we become divine. Belief and love, a believing love will relieve us of a vast load of care. O my brothers, God exists."[13]

I just loved the casual way Emerson said that "a little consideration of what takes place around us every day would show us that a higher law than that of our will regulates events." It was as obvious to me as it was to him. But I didn't know exactly what he meant by "contenting ourselves with obedience." I knew it had to do with knowing what spiritual laws we are under, but at that time I didn't know where to find an accurate knowledge of them.

I also didn't know exactly what Emerson meant when he said that "a believing love will relieve us of a vast load of care." But I thought it meant that if we have the right attitude, then we can discover that love is the basis of higher laws. By higher laws he meant spiritual laws, and these laws can bring us an end to our painful labors if we live in harmony with them. When he said that pain is related to what is unnecessary and fruitless, as an expression of what is not believing and not loving, he also implied the opposite. Joy is the fruit of believing and loving.

In another place in the same essay, he repeated that "we only need obey." And he went on: "There is guidance for each of us, and by lowly listening we shall hear the right word...For you there is a reality, a fit place and congenial duties. Place yourself in the middle of the stream of power and wisdom which animates all whom it floats, and you are without effort impelled to truth, to right, and a perfect contentment."[14]

I was intrigued by his words that it is "by lowly listening we shall hear the right word." I understood that by "lowly listening" we will be open to what is true. Emerson gave me the hope that I desperately wanted because, as he said, if we are open to learning about spiritual laws, we will find out what they are, but not as a matter of dogma or indoctrination. Dogma prevents true knowledge because it prevents openness and self-understanding.

As for having a relationship with God as the Originator of spiritual laws, Emerson had one. He even expressed that there is one true relationship and many false ones when he said, "The multitude of false churches accredits the true religion. Literature, poetry, science, are the homage of man to this unfathomed secret, concerning which no sane man can affect an indifference or incuriosity."[15]

I was amazed when he stated that no sane person can be indifferent about the "unfathomed secret," as Emerson called the essence of true religion. I had a sense of reverence for what he alluded to as the true religion, but for me it was always found in the wilderness and, ironically, not around people. In the beauty of nature I felt in my heart the "unfathomed secret," even if I couldn't explain what it was in words. But I still constantly searched to find a person who knew about it too.

I respected Emerson because he urged people to learn to think for themselves. He believed in the importance of self-reliance as an essential quality of the truth seeker. He wanted us to be courageous and question the validity of ideas that pervade our society and shape our minds. He urged that we learn to trust our intuition because it takes the lead in helping us unveil the truth about our life and purpose before we gain accurate knowledge.

He wrote, "To believe your own thought, to believe that what is true for you in your private heart is true for all men, that is genius. Speak your latent conviction, and it shall be the universal sense; for the inmost in due time becomes the outmost...A man should learn to detect and watch that gleam of light which flashes across his mind from within, more than the lustre of the firmament of bards and sages."[16]

Emerson supported my concerns, and I loved him for that. He didn't want me to fall victim to the pressures of the well frogs of society. Though he didn't specifically use the metaphors of the well frog and the ocean frog, he would have certainly believed in them as principles. He pointed out that the self-reliant person follows his intuition as the safest guide until he can meet an ocean frog to teach him what he needs to know. Emerson didn't care what other people thought of him, and he didn't let others condemn his thoughts as offenses against the mainstream or as a deviation from the norm.

He let the self-reliant one stand up for himself as he too had done. He refused to tow the line of society and mimic any established voice. To him, truth was not allowed to be a consensus of the masses, but the insight of a few. He said, "Society everywhere is in conspiracy against the manhood of every one of its members...The virtue in most request is conformity. Self-reliance is its aversion. It loves not realities and creators, but names and customs...Whoso would be a man, must be a nonconformist."[17] He confirmed what I knew. Truth seekers are courageous. They are willing to stand alone.

He also wrote, "Trust thyself: every heart vibrates to that iron string. Accept the place the divine providence has found for you, the society of your contemporaries, the connection of events.

Great men have...confided themselves childlike to the genius of
their age, betraying their perception that the absolutely trustwor-
thy was seated at their heart, working through their hands, pre-
dominating in all their being. And we are now men, and must
accept in the highest mind the same transcendent destiny; and
not minors and invalids in a protected corner, not cowards fleeing
before a revolution, but guides, redeemers, and benefactors, obey-
ing the Almighty effort, and advancing on chaos and the dark."[18]

Finally for Emerson, the truth couldn't come from pas-
sively receiving instructions from others. Instead, it had to originate from a desire to receive the truth in ourselves by seeing

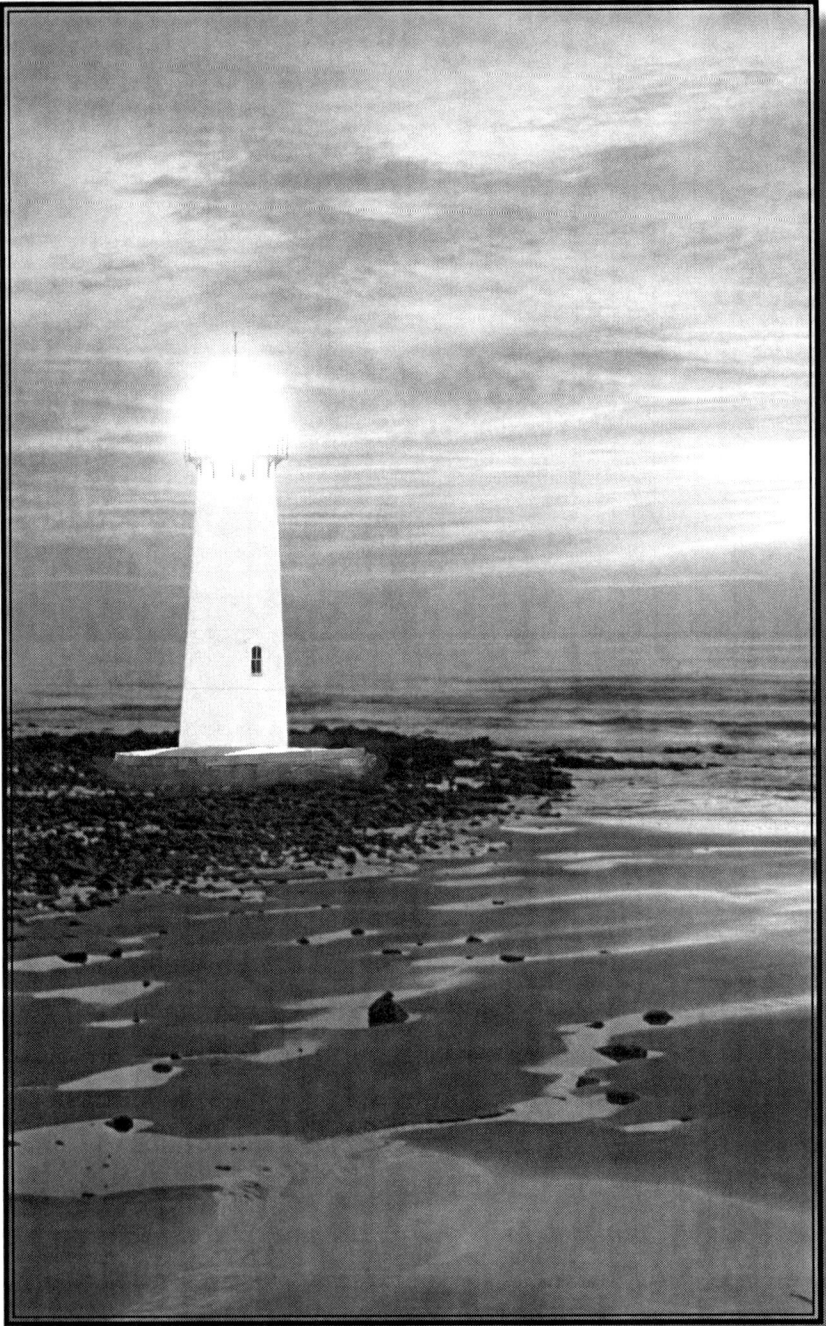

what is real, without being hypnotized by the fear of standing alone and being punished for it by others. He wrote, "What I must do is all that concerns me, not what the people think. This rule, equally arduous in actual and in intellectual life, may serve for the whole distinction between greatness and meanness. It is the harder, because you will always find those who think they know what is your duty better than you know it. It is easy in the world to live after the world's opinion; it is easy in solitude to live after our own; but the great man is he who in the midst of the crowd keeps with perfect sweetness the independence of solitude."[19]

I knew what he meant. I went to study at the University of California at Santa Cruz in the autumn of my eighteenth year. Though I didn't know how to stand up for my independence in terms of bringing my love of nature to my academic life, I knew my independence meant that I wouldn't stop searching for the truth until I found what I was looking for. I decided not to go the usual route and take an established major. I created my own, which I called "Science and Society," with the help of a few professors to direct me. I wrote my senior thesis on "Scientific Methodology as a Belief System," which was a series of essays about the philosophy of science and the effects of science on the modern mind and heart. I was given honors on my diploma.

My committee of professors who oversaw my coursework were a cultural anthropologist, a geologist, and a historian. My coursework was mostly science, including inorganic and organic chemistry, molecular biology, cell biology, zoology, physical anthropology, plant morphology and taxonomy, plus many other subjects. I also studied the theories and practice of science, besides the facts established by it, so I could understand the repercussions of a scientifically-based belief system on society and how it affected the moral and spiritual decisions of people. But since some of my interests didn't fit the usual undergraduate curriculum, I arranged to do many independent courses with various professors in the departments of history and philosophy.

The historian on my committee was named Noel Q. King. He would never tell me his middle name though I always tried to guess. I supposed it was "Queen" from something he said and it became a joke between us. He always lectured barefoot and left his sandals by the classroom door. He opened the windows wide and the wind often blew our papers. But he never got cold in the winter, even if we students did, because he wore a thick cotton kurta. I never saw him in a tie though he was a tenured professor and well respected as the head of the Department of History.

His hair was wispy white and always wild, and he constantly pulled on his long white beard. His body was shaped like a pear, soft and plump in the middle. On the inside he was usually gentle, but on the outside he was sometimes hard.

When I'd stop at his open office door, we'd have a little ritual, sort of like a British cup of tea in a quick conversation, complete with proper manners, before he'd invite me in. "Professor King, how are you today?" I'd always start out speaking from the hallway.

"I'm busy as usual," he'd say with his unusual accent.

"Are you available now during office hours?" I'd ask as politely as I could.

"Only if you're searching for more meaning."

"Yes, it's true," and I'd try not to laugh.

"Do you want to ask me a question or share a thought with me?"

"Yes, if I could please."

"Well, then, come in, but don't close the door completely."

There were books stacked on books, on shelves, on the chairs, and even on the floor. There were also papers floating everywhere on his reverential love for literature. In all that clutter there was no apparent formality to his learning, but he was still intensely focused and committed to the mind and heart's search for meaning. He would listen to whatever I had to say and then ask me questions. He appreciated me in a way that none of my science professors ever did. But then again, I never found a single science professor at UC Santa Cruz who would talk to me about the conceptual foundations of science from even a philosophical point of view.

"Conceptual foundations of science" were my own special buzzwords for the description of what I studied when people asked me about my independent major. I usually found that those four words were enough to shut down anyone. But not Professor King. He was interested in what I meant by the "conceptual foundations of science" and why I had a bone to pick with scientists. He understood my reasoning on why I considered scientific methodology to be a belief system, with the same dogmatic features as religion.

"Look at this, Professor King," I complained one day. "Can you believe it?" I had arrived at his office with the latest issue of the *National Geographic* magazine.

"What's the problem with that?" he asked me playfully.

"Look," I said, pointing to the cover. "This little piece of fossil jaw is supposed to be the latest missing link."

"So?"

"Do you think a little chunk of fossil jaw is enough evidence to redraw the tree of man's supposed evolution? Do you think that is adequate information? What are these scientists thinking?"

"What does the article say?" He was flipping through papers and not acting real attentive.

"I don't have to read the article because the drawing says everything I need to know."

"So what is your objection, dear?"

I scowled. "Just look at the newest version of the tree of human evolution. For one thing, it is presented as a factual representation. And we are supposed to believe that this new link is the true link when the old links, which were once on centerline a short time ago, are now cast-offs leading to extinction?"

Professor King refused to show disdain. Instead, he said rather nonchalantly, "It's obvious evolutionary science is all about conjecture. Let them think they've found a needle in a haystack. Why should that bother you anyway when you don't believe that humans evolved in the first place?"

"Because it invalidates the scientific method," I replied.

"Why?"

"Because their scientific point of view doesn't arise from a method that can guarantee high-quality conclusions. Do you consider this high quality?"

"Let them think they can fool you." He pulled thoughtfully on his beard. "But you and I both can see that the method they use tells more about themselves than their subject of study."

"That is precisely my point," I agreed. "But doesn't it make you mad at science?"

"Why should it?"

"Because it is a lie. They want me to believe their lies. Do you know how many human fossils these scientists claim they have found?"

"No, I don't know." He chuckled at my consternation.

"Really just a handful. They are so few that they can fit on the top of a single desk. Don't you think that's a pitifully small number of fossils from which to draw an evolutionary tree that is supposed to span a few million years? Don't you think these kinds of scientific claims make scientists look more like mythmakers than liberators of the mind?"

On another occasion I told Professor King how my organic chemistry lab was a torment to my soul. It was absolute torture to titrate some unknown chemical that had no relevance to the questions that occupied me. I always impatiently turned up the heat source and my unknown chemical, the identity of which the experiment was supposed to reveal, boiled up out of the glass and inevitably fell on the floor. I'd quickly stoop down and scrape it up when I thought no one was looking.

Professor King chided me for being impatient, but he also was amused.

"You have your own fire to deal with inside of you," he clapped his hands. "But don't you worry so much. We know scientific and chemical processes are surely not the whole explanation of life, but they are a good base from which to view the rest." He always scolded me that I shouldn't blame science just because it couldn't teach me what I desperately wanted to learn.

One afternoon I related to him that Ernst Mayr, a prominent evolutionary biologist of the twentieth century, actually believed that Charles Darwin had brought about a revolution in man's mind and his place in the universe.

"Why?" I asked rhetorically to make my point. "Because Ernst Mayr believes that Darwin destroyed the anthropocentric universe, as Copernicus before him had destroyed the geocentric cosmology." But in my mind, Darwin's ideas didn't liberate us. They wouldn't let us see the divine. They would turn us into dull heartless stones without a sense of our spiritual vitality. Darwin wanted us to be made in his image: afraid, lonely, and burdened.

By contrast, Professor King was an eclectic scholar who didn't mind drifting into many areas of inquiry, especially spiritual ones. He wasn't afraid of any subject. He was so different than my scientist professors who would only hang out in the safety of conversation on cell membranes or whatever warty toads they hid behind. And even though I would listen to all their lectures, they wouldn't listen to my questions during their office hours.

One late afternoon towards the end of my senior year, Professor King took a book down from his shelf that changed my life. He said, "You have never met Rabindranath Tagore, have you?"

"Who is he?" I was excited by such a mysterious name.

"Tagore was from India, but he was well educated in the ways of the Western world and he lived and studied in England."

"What did he write about?"

"He wrote, my young friend, about the magnificence in the human will that desires to know transcendent truths and to live by them, too." His eyes danced as he watched my reaction.

"Will you read me what he said?"

"Yes," he nodded and opened the book, called the *Gitanjali*, to a marked page. Before reading, he related that Tagore had translated the original contents of the book from Bengali to English to share with the West in 1912. "Now close your eyes," he said.

That I want thee, only thee--let my
heart repeat without end. All desires
that distract me, day and night, are false
and empty to the core.
    As the night keeps hidden in its gloom
the petition for light, even thus in the
depth of my unconsciousness rings the
cry, I want thee, only thee.
    As the storm still seeks its end in peace
when it strikes against peace with all its
might, even thus my rebellion strikes
against thy love and still its cry is, "I
want thee, only thee."[20]

I was amazed at the sweetness of Tagore's writing and didn't want to open my eyes.

But Professor King wouldn't let me swoon. "Who is the 'thee' that Tagore is seeking? Do you know?"

"Of course I know. It's God," I replied.

Professor King put the book in my hand before I could ask him any questions, and said I could take it on the condition that I would take good care of it and meditate on the poem he read.

When I returned a week later, I announced that I was in love with Tagore because he wrote so openly about his longing for truth in a spiritual way.

"So you don't mind the old English style of writing with 'thees' and 'thous'?" he teased me.

"Why should I care about that?"

"Would you like to know more about Tagore's life in England?" he asked me.

"No, I don't care about his outer life, it's his inner one I want to know." Even though Tagore died in 1941, he was still a kindred spirit.

Professor King then attempted to teach me a lesson that I already knew. He said that I should study a person's outer life, especially someone like Tagore's, because it would reflect what was on his inside. For, as he explained, it is out of the heart that the mouth speaks.

"Simply stated," he said, "we think and talk and write about the things that matter most to us, whether it's to further our ego's hold on our life or to diminish it."

"Yes, I understand," I agreed. "Now let me read you two more that are full of depth." I began to read with so much pleasure and gratitude:

By all means they try to hold me
secure who love me in this world. But
it is otherwise with thy love which is
greater than theirs, and thou keepest me
free.

Lest I forget them they never venture
to leave me alone. But day passes by
after day and thou art not seen.

If I call thee not in my prayers, if I
keep not thee in my heart, thy love for
me still waits for my love.[21]

"Very beautiful," he smiled softly. "What's the other one?"

"The other one tastes like a fragrance. Do you know what I mean by fragrance?"

"Yes," he surprised me by saying.

"I'm amazed you understand what I mean." I felt so thankful for his loving kindness.

"Okay, now read it please," he urged me.

When the heart is hard and parched
up, come upon me with a shower of
mercy.

When grace is lost from life,
come with a burst of song.

When tumultuous work raises its din
on all sides shutting me out from beyond,
come to me, my lord of silence, with thy

peace and rest.

When my beggarly heart sits crouched,
shut up in a corner, break open the door,
my king, and come with the ceremony
of a king.

When desire blinds the mind with
delusion and dust, O thou holy one, thou
wakeful, come with thy light and thy
thunder.[22]

I found a secret place at the university to meditate on Tagore's writings, but it wasn't in the library. It was up in a tall Douglas fir tree that I found I could climb in the back campus. It was so high I could see the Monterey Bay from the top. I carried Tagore's book with me and tucked us together up in the branches. When the wind blew, I tied us in with a piece of rope. We often stayed up there until the sun set. It was my haven away from the insistent reaches of the academic world that somehow, strangely, didn't want to perceive or couldn't reveal the truth I wanted.

At my graduation ceremony, Professor King told my father something about my spiritual search and my restless heart. I didn't know exactly what Professor King had said to him because my father related the incident some time later. My father did tell me, with some disbelief, that Professor King said that I was a religious person and would have a hard time settling down because of it. My father had no idea that I possessed an intense spiritual side because he never asked me about such things. It was always so strange and confusing to me that he didn't search for spiritual meaning. After all, he loved adventure and seemed willing to explore any country of the world, regardless of the challenge.

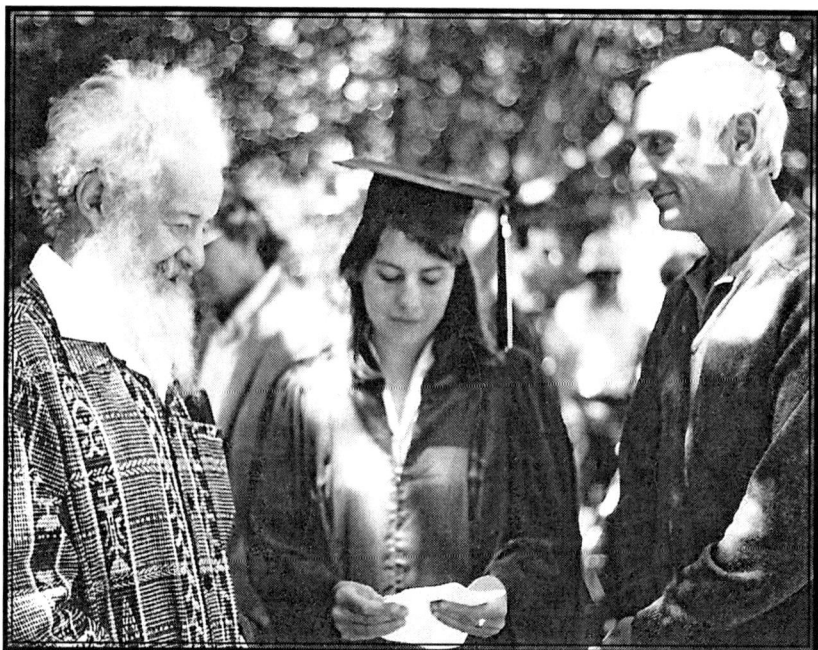

The last words Professor King ever said to me took many years to understand. He held my hands and whispered to me, "You need to be pummeled and broken to become what you want to be." I knew he wasn't being unkind, but I must have looked surprised and hurt. It was meant as a resolve, as a sort of encouragement and promise from him that if I endured that pummeling, whatever that involved, I would find what it was that I wanted. His eyes were soft and somehow sad.

Science without religion is lame and religion without science is blind.

Albert Einstein (1879-1955), Physicist

CHAPTER FIVE

In Parched Places

A chilling fog was pouring down from the mountains and across the meadows of wild flowers and tall summer grass. Though the birds and bees were silenced in the eerie darkness of the early afternoon, the rumbling calls of bison were getting louder.

"We've got to get out of here!" I yelled out to my horse, Oly. I ran to where he was tied to a tree and unbuckled his harness. "Let's go find the others," I urged him nervously, putting on his bridle. I pulled my raincoat out of a saddlebag. The temperature was dropping fast and water was beginning to drip from my hair, but I didn't feel cold. I was too worried. The fog was getting thicker by the minute and I couldn't see the bison. If there was a herd of them, then we could be dangerously surrounded and caught on the inside.

It was mating season in the month of August when the bulls paw the ground and aggressively gouge out chunks of grass and soil and challenge anything big that moves. I was relieved that Oly didn't seem concerned as I swung up onto his saddle and we headed down the valley, hugging the trees wherever we could. There was no established trail, but the ground was easy to ride on except for the marshy ponds, called "kettles," and fallen trees we had to go around.

Each of my companions, all with horses, were out checking the five-by-five foot bison enclosures, made of welded re-bar, that we dropped by helicopter a month before. We were a group of five botanists employed by Yellowstone National Park to study bison and elk grazing patterns. The enclosures were scattered throughout our study site in the Lamar Valley in the northeastern range of Yellowstone. Our goal was to provide statistics on grazing, which would be implemented in the bison and elk management programs. Our field work involved determining how much vegetation, according to species, had appeared to be grazed significantly outside the enclosures in contrast to the inside where animals couldn't reach.

We all rode horses as a precaution against running into

grizzlies and their cubs. The Lamar Valley is only roughly seven miles long and two miles wide, but is known to have more grizzlies per square mile than anywhere else in Yellowstone. As there had never been a documented grizzly attack involving horses, even though a grizzly can sprint faster than they can, we decided it was a good idea to ride them to our study sites. I had to wonder, though, as I was alone with Oly in the fog, how often a grizzly lunged at a single rider who came too close to her cubs. I didn't know the answer, but I consoled myself by thinking that bears had to be less of a concern than the bison in the breeding season.

When the smaller groups of males join the larger groups of females and their young, the combined herd size numbers in the hundreds. Besides the bulls being erratic in their rush to display their strength, the females are also unpredictable. Those that had calves in the spring will charge anything that appears to threaten them. And though bison have a good sense of smell, they have bad eyesight and so Oly and I had to be extremely cautious.

In Yellowstone, bison actually injure or kill about four times more people than bears do. But the bison victims are usually the unwary tourist types who step out of their cars to photograph them. At six feet tall or more at the shoulders and weighing around two thousand pounds, male bison are massive animals. In comparison, male grizzlies seem like lightweights at around eight hundred pounds.

Many of the park scientists called the Lamar Valley "the Little Serengeti of North America" because of the number and the variety of animals living there. And though the Lamar Valley seemed tiny in comparison with the Serengeti plains of Africa, which span 5,700 square miles and are filled with tens or hundreds of thousands of animals, the Lamar is still home to thousands of elk, hundreds of bison, and smaller groups of pronghorn antelope, mule deer, and bighorn sheep.

To me, the Lamar Valley was more beautiful than the Serengeti plains, even though I had seen its stunning double rainbows after rain. The Lamar was more personal and had a soft intimate beauty with its curving river, rolling hills and meadows, and clumps of pine and aspen trees. Its intense colors affected me in a way I didn't dare mention to the others. Scientists don't usually swoon with emotion, especially the inspirational kind. But I didn't consider myself as much a scientist as a lover of the wilderness.

But I tried to act like I was as involved as the others in gathering data. Still, whenever my mind would let my heart be free, I'd fly. I winged around the trees like I was a hawk, dipped in the river like a water ouzel, and sang like a yellow-throated vireo when the sun rose. I wasn't interested in scientific endeavors as much as spiritual ones, though I didn't think they were mutually exclusive.

Science showed a complexity of life that pointed out an intelligence that humans couldn't recreate, but could only try to mimic in their own inventions. Bird wings were the idea behind the design concept of a highly maneuverable aircraft. The boxfish, which has surprisingly low drag for its shape, was the inspiration behind a vehicle concept. And Velcro is the synthetic equivalent of a burr's tiny hooks that cling to animal fur and clothes.

I was amused when I was introduced as a scientist to park visitors or other visiting scientists. It was supposed to be an honor, I knew, but I was a lover of life, a seeker for what was beyond parameters, especially the ones that our botany crew established. But, then, I didn't believe our scientific methods could determine with any accuracy what was going on with bison and elk grazing patterns in the Yellowstone rangeland. There were too many variables. Besides, I was aware that it was really big game hunters who decided on elk and bison herd size much more than the findings of our studies. We were just a cover up for park politics, but nobody liked to admit it was true.

I played along and acted useful. I knew the flora of the Lamar and the surrounding areas in Yellowstone. I had a broad knowledge of taxonomy because I had studied plants for years on my own. I could rattle off their Latin names, including family, genus, and species, and whatever plant I didn't know, I could easily "key out" (in botanical lingo), though the grasses were hard and often required a microscope.

I was hired at Yellowstone because I had worked in a similar capacity at Olympic National Park. I had worked there for two seasons with a group of botanists that studied the effects of mountain goat grazing and impact in the alpine plant communities. Our studies in Olympic, like our studies in Yellowstone, were meant to help establish herd management policies.

The problem in the Olympic mountains was that the mountain goats did not naturally occur there. Hunters had introduced them in the 1920s, but when the park was established in 1938, hunting was prohibited on the park lands. As a result, the mountain goats multiplied quickly in the absence of predators. They were considered a threat to the continued existence of the alpine flora in general and especially to species of plants, called "endemics," that occur only in isolated areas of the Olympic Mountains and nowhere else on earth.

Our botany crew was dropped by helicopter on top of re-mote mountains in the Bailey Range where there were no trails. Our job was to draw maps of the alpine plant communities. We called these trips "reconnaissance expeditions" as we surveyed the high regions where the mountain goats lived. We were also part of an operation that captured the goats by darting them with a sedative and then dragging them into crates. They would then be transported to the Rocky Mountains. The crates of goats would swing in the air as they were lifted by helicopter, and I always wondered how many would survive the trauma of being sent to a new home.

Sometimes it would take many days to return to head-quarters after a reconnaissance expedition, and the hiking wasn't ever easy. Though there weren't any grizzlies in Olympic National Park, only black bears (which we heard and saw on occasion), there were shoots of snow to make our way down and we always had to carry heavy packs full of equipment for our research. There were also huge fallen trees that we had to climb over and under, besides crossing rivers and finding our way to established trails once we came down from the mountains.

I felt a strange combination of physical freedom and mental slavery. Though I loved being in the mountains, I hated treating plants as numbers. I also doubted we could determine with any accuracy the impact of goat activity on the alpine plants because our methods were too crude. We each used a one-by-one meter square made of PVC plastic pipe for taking "percent cover" (as we called it) of alpine plants that lived in our study sites.

To take percent cover, we'd assemble our PVC pipes that we carried in our backpacks, and which were sectioned into a hundred little grids by strings. The idea was to determine roughly how many grids appeared to be filled by each species in our one-by-one meter study plots. But our assessment of how many grids were filled by a specific plant depended on "eyeball work," and not on objective measurement. This meant that a large degree of subjectivity would be the basis of our data. Back in the lab, we'd run the data through statistical computer programs, which were designed to tell us which plant species appeared to be increasing and decreasing in the alpine plant community as a reflection of mountain goat grazing and impact over time.

The basic hang-up I had was that many of our study sites were located on steep scree slopes in alpine plant communities. When we walked around the sites for a couple of hours, we dislodged tons of rubble and loose rock. I always believed our impact in these areas was much more than the mountain goats. They were much more sure-footed than we were, and hopped easily through the scree instead of carving heavy troughs and tracks like the five of us did. It bothered me that my fellow workers weren't concerned like I was. I felt that our disturbance to the slopes rendered useless the data we spent hours collecting, and I often grumbled about it openly.

Usually, we each had to complete about 8 one-by-one meter plots every day. I noticed that we all finished our plots more quickly when it was raining or when the wind was blowing hard. I wondered how the data could amount to anything meaningful when it was so much influenced by the weather and also, for that matter, by our appetites. When it approached lunch time, regardless if it was raining or not, I looked around to see people's pencils moving faster than normal and making the tallies too quickly. I realized that what was "normal" seemed to have its own strange mood swings in the mountains, but I didn't think it was right. Scientists always boast (and usually flaunt) objectivity as the sound basis for us to believe what they find and say to be true. But it was obvious to me that the findings of our studies would be mostly relative to our physical and emotional needs. They wouldn't reflect an empirical accuracy regardless of how official our data looked in the reports we printed.

I was twenty four-years old when I was hired at Yellowstone National Park. In spite of not liking to treat plants as data, I was happy to use my knowledge of plants to earn a living. My goal in those days was to be in the wilderness as much as I possibly could. I was desperate to avoid the ways of the world, like the customary eight-hour workday in a stuffy room, like the chatter of people who are uncomfortable with silence, like thinking that making money for ourselves can stifle the pain we feel for starving people who have no money.

I also refused to conform to a standard of life made by ideologies that didn't encourage openness and exploration of both the physical and spiritual aspects of life. I hated advertising and social pressures like make-up and high heel shoes that made your feet weak for vanity, like the illusions of "the good life," "the evolved life," and "the religious life." Regardless of what society taught me and the education that was jammed down my throat, I didn't believe I could create meaning and purpose as a matter of personal preference. To me, meaning and purpose couldn't be determined as a simple choice, like the way we choose to have mashed potatoes for dinner instead of rice simply because we like them better.

I longed to be in the wilderness because it didn't shift with the facts, fads, or politics. It wouldn't tell me what I was supposed to know. There I had to figure it out for myself. The wilderness was a primary reality, the primary beauty, far away from the self-serving civilized mind. It was the only place untouched, with integrity. Its defining characteristic was simple: a place where there weren't humans except for the occasional wanderer.

In the wilderness we can wake up to what is true about ourselves. If we are there alone long enough, we can admit what we have become dependent on and distracted by. We will eventually come to realize that there is something arbitrary, and often deceptive, in the way we have allowed our cultural affiliations to define who we are, such as what we are supposed to know, accept, and nurture as ideals.

Once there was a scoundrel of a man who wasn't afraid to point this out. His name was Diogenes and he wanted to show people how easily we tend to get lost in our own lies. But it wasn't through the written word, or any pedantic or academic mentality, that he expressed his wisdom. He used his way of life as his most effective teaching tool.

He lived in ancient Greece in the fifth century B.C.E., and according to the *Phaedo*, Plato's fifth and final dialogue, he was there when Socrates was put to death on the charge of corrupting Athen's youth. But Diogenes was more clever than Socrates because Socrates claimed that he "knew nothing" when, in fact, he had to know something.

Though Socrates' claim to knowing nothing was probably meant as a clever device to show that he didn't want to live by the clamor of his ego, but by a more benevolent humility which could admit what he didn't know, his claim still proved ineffective. He had to die for not knowing what he should have known, at least by the standards of the politicians and civil authorities.

But Diogenes used a mischievous disguise for his intelligence, and it served him better than Socrates' professed ignorance. He played tricks on people's egos and still avoided being punished. At least he didn't have to drink the hemlock, the poison they used to kill Socrates. And Diogenes had no qualms showing what he knew for sure, which was that people who are determined to be rich, powerful, or famous fall into a trap.

Diogenes made it easy to understand that people who care more about themselves than others, and who seek to bolster their egos at the expense of others, betray their only means to be happy. Why? Because being happy means we are connected to others by love, and we will want to love others as much as (or more than) ourselves. We give to them and consider their needs as much as our own. For this reason Diogenes planned to be poor. And though he was dubbed a beggar, it didn't mean he was a mooch.

He just didn't want to be a slave to the social system as a reflection of the selfish ruling ideology. Instead, he preferred to play pranks. Since he didn't have anything to lose in terms of reputation, rank, or material possessions, he was shrewd and free.

My favorite story about him was when he lit a lantern on a blazing sunny afternoon. Then he walked through the outdoor market swinging it to the left and right with a puzzled look on his face, and scratching his head on occasion. He showed, as he raised his lantern and searched with squinting eyes, that he was seriously looking for something that only its light could reveal. People must have shook their heads and turned away when they saw him coming.

"Hey, Diogenes," some good-natured fellow probably called out to him, while the others pretended not to hear, "what are you trying to prove with your lantern? Why is your lantern lit when we have the afternoon sunlight to see by?" The man had to state the obvious because that was all he could do. But at least he wasn't mean.

"I'm looking for something," Diogenes egged him on with wide exaggerated eyes," but you won't believe what it is!"

"Well? Tell me!" The man was curious. He liked Diogenes because Diogenes was playful and different.

"Something you don't know how to find," Diogenes pointed at his lantern, trying not to smile. He knew the crowd was listening too.

"What is it?" The man pursued an answer.

"You really want to know?" Diogenes sounded serious.

"Yes," the man emphasized. "Tell me." He was hooked.

"Ok, then," said Diogenes. "I am looking for an honest person. Do you know where I can find one?"

"What? What do you mean!" The man raised his voice in confusion and protest.

But this is the way wisdom speaks sometimes. It may seem strange at first until you look more deeply at what is being said. Diogenes' reply can be well taken. It is hard to find an honest person. But this isn't the kind of honest person who just doesn't cheat on his taxes. There is more to Diogenes' conception of honesty, but he didn't say what it was. It is up to us to figure it out, as well as the symbolic meaning of his lantern light and why he used a lantern in the first place. Of course, the lantern light was a clever device to get peoples' attention, but it had a deeper purpose.

Diogenes meant, by an honest person, one who questions the validity of his perceptions and doesn't just blindly serve his own ego. He meant that an honest person doesn't get stuck in someone else's truth, whether scientific or religious, and adopt it as his own just because it is popular or especially because of peer pressure or family pressure. He meant, too, that an honest person doesn't get angry if someone presses him about what he believes and why he believes what he does. An honest person can pleasantly share the logic of his thinking and doesn't have to be defensive. He knows that kindness is more honest than anger.

If we think about Diogenes and his scams on those who took themselves too seriously, he can make us laugh. He must have won the hearts of some, but only those who valued being open-hearted, only those who were willing to poke fun at their own imperfections instead of always trying to hide them from themselves and others.

Diogenes wasn't afraid to speak out for what he thought was true, though sometimes his displays of defiance may have seemed too crude. For this reason, many philosophers throughout the centuries have labeled him a cynic, though cynics are usually angry. But he struck me, though, as more a clever man than an angry man because he mocked the haughty and exposed the self-serving, but wasn't put to death by them.

To me, Diogenes' daytime lantern light symbolized awareness. I believed, when I was in Yellowstone, that my awareness came from the wilderness. Being in the wilderness gave me freedom to think without the confinement of small mental spaces that conform to four square walls. Whereas the wilderness made my senses sharp and my self-understanding grow, the work space of most people seemed to do the opposite. They never learned how to walk on uneven surfaces or be comfortable alone in silence. They never learned the spirit of exploration where money wasn't involved.

One of my favorite places near park headquarters (at Mammoth Hotsprings) was Blacktail Valley, which was about twelve miles from where the botany crew lived in mobile homes. If it wasn't too late in the day, I'd ride my bicycle out on the main paved road through Yellowstone and arrive at Blacktail Creek, where there was a locked gate across a little dirt road. I'd carry my bike around the gate and hide it in the willows until I returned a few hours later.

Though high summer was over, the days were still long. I could hike up valley along Blacktail Creek and usually get back to my bike before dark. I loved Blacktail for many reasons. The first was its beauty. The valley was much like the Lamar with rolling hills, meadows of grass, and clumps of trees, but it also had boulders covered with orange lichen. There were many coyotes always yapping in the valley and I hoped that one day I would open my eyes after a meditation on the top of the ridge and see them sitting quietly nearby, though I'm sure I would have heard them coming. I was always alert for the sound of footsteps, especially the four-legged kind. But the coyotes were afraid of me and always ran away, though I assume they became familiar with my smell. I never worried about being attacked by them because they seemed more like large rabbits in comparison with the wolves and bears that roamed the area.

The dirt road up Blacktail Creek ended after half a mile at a small log cabin where one of the park biologists lived. Her name was Mary, though I thought she looked more like a Maggie or Margo. She was a flaming redhead in her late fifties with short cropped hair, freckled strawberry skin, and a nervous fleeting smile. She was a loner in the true sense and had never married and seldom spoke, though I noticed she still had a sense of humor.

She didn't like groups of people, and appeared emotionally detached from everyone on the rare days the botany crew and the park scientists met to talk about our study sites. She sat in the corner of the room, as still as the elk head mounted on the wall. But she didn't want to be as visible, and so tried to pass the questions that were asked of her on to someone else to answer. When she did talk, she spoke in an articulate, measured way and tried to avoid looking into peoples' eyes.

But there was something about her that struck me. Though I assumed she would have to agree with park scientists on matters of biology, I wasn't sure she was an atheist. There was something open-minded and even, perhaps, spiritual about her despite her aloof ways and shifting eyes. I wondered if she had learned truths deeper than bison and elk biology as a result of her choice to live alone.

I was curious to find out who she really was, but I knew I'd have to track her like a mule deer. I decided that during my visit to Blacktail Valley, I'd go near her horse's corral and slowly let her feel my presence. I found a rock in Blacktail Creek that was flat enough to sit on to play my small wooden recorder that sounded like a flute. I was sure her horse, Pete, could hear my music, though I didn't think Mary could hear it over the sound of the water.

After a couple of weeks, Pete allowed me to pet his nose. He was a real timid type because, as Mary told me later, the bears walking down the road to lower Blacktail Valley made him nervous. But I wondered if he was so nervous because he took on Mary's traits. He had lived with her for a long time.

One evening when the sun was about to set and I had said goodbye to Pete, Mary finally called out to me. I knew she was aware when I was around. Pete was her closest companion, and he always told her what was going on by the direction he pointed his ears. She also knew that I was aware that one day she would talk to me. But I had to pass her test of patience first.

I turned and waved, but she wasn't friendly. She was standing near the corral, holding Pete's harness in her hand, her body language stiff and bristled.

"Why do you always come here?"

"Because, for one thing, there are so many red-tailed hawks up creek and the coyotes are always singing here. And I also love the orange lichen on the boulders up high on the ridge."

"Did you know," she asked dryly, fleeing from me into the safety of factual knowledge, "that lichens are among the oldest plants on earth?"

"No, I didn't know."

"Yes, in harsh climates they can shut down their metabolism and go dormant for years."

"That's surprising," I tried to sound interested. I wondered if she was punishing me with a lichen sermon because she sensed I wanted to talk about more personal matters.

"Lichens also produce over five hundred chemical compounds in order to control their micro environment."

"Why is that?" I asked with a sinking feeling, and wondered if it was a mistake to think I could talk to her about spiritual things, which no scientist had ever allowed me to do.

"The chemical compounds repel herbivores and somehow serve to control the light exposure to the plant. They can also kill microbes."

"It doesn't surprise me at all," I replied, standing as still as I could. I had learned at the university that my science professors felt more comfortable with me if I didn't move when they gave me the facts. I had to be careful not to let my eyes smile or be playful in any way so that their encounter with me wouldn't awaken their emotions or make them feel self-conscious. I made my face fall flat and silent.

The scientists I knew could only entertain thoughts about physical things, at least outwardly. Mention anything metaphysical, even a question, and that was the end of the conversation. They had to remain safe in the zone of facts and figures, as it seemed they couldn't trust themselves to speculate about truths not empirically measurable, or even admit that they were interested in them.

Mary started up again. "So, you like Blacktail?"

"Yes," I turned to look up valley so I wouldn't make her nervous if she got the feeling I was too focused on her. "It's one of the most beautiful places on earth, and you get to live here all summer!"

She gave a tiny nod of approval and I knew that I had won her acceptance, at least for the moment.

We walked past her cabin, but she didn't invite me in. And even though the moon was getting full and would have provided enough light for me to see by if I stayed after dark, she gestured that I should head down to the main road. She informed me in her matter-of-fact way that she'd seen a grizzly passing in the twilight almost every evening for a week.

How strange, I thought, as the light was fading fast, that she'd send me out to bump into the bear. But she must have known what I was thinking because she offered to walk me half-way down to the gate. She added that the grizzly must be a male, as she hadn't seen any cubs.

"You don't need to worry," she said without emotion. "The sows are the dangerous ones." But I didn't feel comforted.

I was back the next day, though I arrived earlier with hopes that she'd invite me into the cabin for conversation, but neither she nor Pete was there. His harness was hanging on the fence post, so I knew they were out riding somewhere. I decided to hike up valley, and I willed myself to find them, though I didn't come across them or see them from the ridge. I was careful to get back down to the gate before sunset, as I didn't want to meet the grizzly before I got on my bike.

I couldn't find Mary at the cabin for days, and I wondered if I frightened her or if she was just playing hard to get. But I kept trying. One early evening I found her out in the corral with Pete. I approached them from the creek and stood near the fence and said, "Hi Pete."

She managed a polite "How are you doing?" but she sounded suspicious.

"Fine, thanks. It's nice to find you home." I replied in a similar tone.

"You're like a wild animal," she almost accused me. "You aren't afraid to be alone."

I was floored. She knew I was seeking her out, but didn't know why.

"What is it you want from me when you can have the whole valley to yourself?"

I tried to answer, but she bashed me with more words.

"You aren't like other people," she blurted out sarcastically, though I didn't think she was trying to be mean.

"Neither are you," I said with a little smile to show I wasn't afraid of her bluntness. She left Pete's side and moved a little closer to me. I leaned against the fence in a comfortable sort of nonchalant way. I wanted my body language to be relaxed and help her to let down her guard.

"I really like people," I tried to engage her, "but so much of the time they don't want to talk about what really matters because they are too afraid. They want to convince you to believe what isn't true." I caught myself talking and stopped. I didn't want to overwhelm her.

After a silence, I tried to lead her into a spiritual conversation by asking a question. "Why do you live out here by yourself?" But she didn't take time to reflect.

"Because it is obvious how ugly society is becoming," she said without pause and scraped her cowboy boot against the fence.

"But why, Mary?" I couldn't conceal my passion.

"Because people value money more than beauty," she replied flatly.

"But why do people do that? Why do they make that choice? I'd really like to know. Wouldn't you?"

"Don't push me!" she erupted, the words thrown out violently from deep down inside her.

The sun had set and I knew I had to get going down the road before twilight faded into darkness. I was used to facing darkness alone, especially the closed hearts of people who were afraid to feel. But I wasn't as courageous as I must have seemed, and it wasn't because I was afraid of the bear. I was so tired of encountering people who were so locked up in their hearts and tense in their bodies.

"Well, I better head back to Mammoth as it's getting late. Bye, Mary. See ya, Pete."

She let me go without saying a word, and I knew that's what she wanted. She probably always had to have her way because she was so inflexible. It was a cover for her fear, even though she wanted to look so tough.

As I walked down the road, scanning the twilight for the grizzly, I realized that our unenlightened lives are organized around only two tendencies: that of seeking pleasure and avoiding pain. All our pursuits serve one or the other as the flip sides of our ego that won't budge from its place as the self-appointed dictator of our life, governing our actions until we want to be free and put up a fight. A spiritual awakening means we break away from our ego's hold on our heart and mind. Then we can seek a greater understanding of our purpose in life, and redefine what is important to accomplish.

When I reached my bike, I switched on the light attached to my handlebars. The light dispelled the dark road just like the stars dispelled the dark sky. But physical darkness isn't like spiritual darkness. Spiritual darkness can't be dispelled like a light you switch on. It can only be dispelled by a conscious effort that involves humility in the heart which enlightens the mind to use knowledge for understanding, and not for the ego's personal gain.

As for Mary, she could face a grizzly in the dark as though it was a squirrel, but she couldn't face the un-lived life inside her. She probably wasn't even aware of why she wanted to avoid me. All she knew was that the alarm went off inside her. She had to give me the silent treatment, just like she gave herself.

I wondered what she meant when she said that I wasn't like others. It could be just her simple observation that I was content to come to Blacktail by myself. Or she could have meant that I was unlike others because I sought her out. Nobody else, as it seemed, tried to be her friend because that would mean having to break through her armor, and that was too much work.

But maybe Mary thought I wasn't like others because I was open about what I wanted to understand, and she knew I wasn't afraid to search for answers. I decided that she sensed my intent to question the rules that scientists agreed to live by, and it scared her. She didn't dare to be personal. I had found that most scientists fit the stereotype of not wanting to look too deeply at themselves. For this reason, they only studied the outer world, but not their inner one. They were terrified of the tangled web of their own psyches. They were afraid of the darkness inside themselves.

What a coward she is, I couldn't help but think as I pedaled fast and watched my light pouring over the pavement. She wants to appear intelligent and scientific about life, but she doesn't know how to connect with people. It was such a hoax! Scientists boasted about being great explorers in uncovering the secrets of life, but they failed to explore themselves and their fears and failures around love.

I always felt so disappointed, even crushed, when I came to see again and again that so many scientists ran into their little pens of protection when they saw me coming. Their pens of protection amounted to their acknowledging only a fraction of what existence involved. "The empirical" and "the testable" were the whip-like leashes that tethered their hearts to the ground so they couldn't feel the immensity. They couldn't touch the spirit of being alive. They couldn't come to know it in themselves. I always had the sense that people like Mary could live in open silent spaces where it was so quiet that they could hear their own blood ringing in their ears, but they couldn't bear to hear from another what was missing from their heart.

A couple of days later, I was surprised to find a message from Mary tacked to the herbarium door where we kept our dried plant collections and microscopes. Only four words were written on the note, in the same measured way that she spoke: "Come see me again." So I rode off to meet her later that day, wondering what was going on in her mind.

So as not to seem like an intruder, I usually approached her cabin from the creek. But since I had an invitation, I now walked openly up the road. When Mary saw me, she acknowledged my presence and waved her hand. When I reached her at the cabin door, she asked me to join her for dinner.

It was like a dream in mountain time. The front door of her cabin opened into a small kitchen heated by a roaring woodstove.

Along one wall was a small wood table set with two yellow place mats and green cloth napkins. Attached to the other wall was a warped pine plank about four feet long that served as a cutting board and a place to prepare food. There was a blue ceramic wash basin at one end that was half full of water with carrots floating on top. Above and below the plank were cupboards made of pine, and on the floor was a pail of cold water from the creek.

On the window ledge near the door was a vase arranged with sagebrush and dried grass. It showed a feminine touch, and was the only sign that a woman lived in the cabin. The hardwood floor made the perfect clunking sound as Mary walked like a cowboy in her boots over to the hook where she hung her hat.

In the middle of her main room was a queen size bed with heavy wooden bedposts. Her bed was covered with a red and black woven-wool Indian blanket tucked in carefully at the corners. Her pillows were meticulously placed a few inches from each other, displaying the perfectionistic traits of her personality. Across from her bed was a large window that looked out at Pete's corral and upper Blacktail Valley. Eagle feathers were stuck in the cracked logs of the walls around it, along with a bird nest and elk antlers arranged on nails. She also had a mirror and two shelves of books on a wall above a short desk that held two carefully-placed oil lanterns. There was also a standing cabinet for her clothes.

We ate black bean soup, rye bread with butter, and raw carrots for dinner. When the sky turned shades of grey and black, she lit both lanterns and put one on the kitchen table.

I was careful not to startle her, and made slow deliberate moves and used my best manners during dinner. I talked about things equivalent to the weather and our studies in the Lamar Valley. Her face slowly relaxed and showed a greater range of expression than I'd seen before.

After we finished eating, she cleared the plates off the table, and then asked me as she sat down: "Now tell me, again, what brings you so often up to Blacktail?" The corners of her mouth lifted almost imperceptibly, and I knew she was trying to be funny and somehow also obliging.

"Let's see," I said, wanting to hug her for her humor. But I was careful not to get carried away. I knew I had to appear seriously grounded and have a determined, flinty forehead. It was her language, the masculine outer front to conceal the vulnerable softness inside her.

"It's because I wanted to talk to you about why you have chosen this way of life and what you've learned living by yourself." I expressed myself without moving my hands and kept them folded quietly on the table in front of me. I played the persona of a judge. Mental, aloof, in control.

"I knew early in my life," she offered without restraint, "that I wasn't one to be married or live with other people." It was a fact not open to discussion.

"I understand the desire to be alone," I proceeded cautiously, looking anywhere but in her eyes so as not to scare her, "because I have that too, but I also love to be with people."

"Yes, but you have a magnanimous quality." I knew she meant it as a compliment, though she didn't really seem to trust the word and spit it out of her mouth like it tasted bad.

"I think that being interested in wanting to get to know people is a good thing because it is by being with others that we learn about ourselves." I tried to speak slowly and keep my words from leaping with excitement.

"But you don't need people to know who you are!" She raised her voice in an emotional way. I noticed that though she always tried to steer clear of feelings, she blurted them out nonetheless.

"Yes, I know we have to learn to depend on ourselves," I replied quietly, ignoring her reaction, "and it is good to be able to be alone, especially in the wilderness. But others can be like a mirror to us. I mean, sometimes it is only by being with others that we can see certain aspects of ourselves that we might not otherwise see or want to see."

"Well, my horse is my mirror," she balked. She seemed to be slipping down her fear tunnel like a gopher retreating into the ground.

She didn't want to admit or realize that it is initially others who teach us most about ourselves, but not because they know who we really are. They teach us only if we are willing to observe ourselves carefully and see how they react to us, especially if they challenge our image.

In our efforts to seek what is pleasing and avoid what is painful, our ego projects its own perspective as if it is the sun shining over all. But slowing down to observe ourselves, especially when we are being rebuked unfairly by others, is an essential part of cultivating self-awareness and the first step to becoming a spiritual person.

I tried a different tactic, as I couldn't climb the slippery wall of Mary's defenses. "You know, Mary, I get the feeling when I'm alone in the wilderness that there is so much more to life than most people want to accept or admit. Do you ever feel that way?"

"I don't know" was her answer, but I noticed she was listening. She was fascinated by my persistence in trying to speak with her, but she'd never admit she liked the attention I gave her.

"It's like there are clues to the essence of life. You can see them here in Blacktail Valley, in the way it lives and moves. It is so beautiful. Beauty is so powerful." I paused for emphasis. "Beauty can teach us so much if we see it for what it is in itself, and not translate it only in mental terms of natural laws in a detached, impersonal way." I looked up for permission to keep talking.

"Go on." She picked at her nails.

"Well, how can beauty be something made from what is not beautiful? How can intelligence be made from what is not intelligent? How can order be created from disorder?"

"Oh," she spouted and looked up easily. "I see where you're going."

"You do?" I was so surprised.

"You mean to say that life is not an accident."

"Yes," I said, "because if you notice it, anything beautiful in the human world is always made by someone in a careful, deliberate way. Haphazard actions can never create order."

"So what's your point?" She played the devil's advocate, like I had played the judge.

"Well, a person, for example, who throws things around in her house can't ever make the house clean, can she? She can demonstrate that even if she throws things around forever and ever, her stuff will never be organized. Order has to be planned as the outcome of an intelligent force like conscious intention. What is random can't be specific, can't be determined."

"So?" Mary clicked her tongue as a way to bolster her presence.

"The force of order, or the power of conscious intention, is apparent at every level of life," I answered, "not only in the natural world, but especially in the human one."

"Are you talking about order as being what people call the design of God?" She didn't hesitate to pronounce the word "God." I had a hunch she was raised as some sort of Christian because her name was Mary, but I didn't want to put her on the spot and ask about it. At least she wasn't allergic to the subject as were so many scientists that I knew.

"You could call the force of order 'God,' if you wanted, or you could call it 'determinism' like Einstein did," I said. Do you know what Einstein meant?" It was more a rhetorical question and an indication that I wanted to build the conversation slowly. I was eager to talk about God, and love, once a framework was set for an intelligent discussion that couldn't be tipped over by her fearful emotions.

"Yes, it's basic stuff," Mary sniffed. "It means that things just don't happen without a cause, like the old idea of spontaneous generation tried to account for processes that were not scientifically explainable. Events can't occur without a causal agent, regardless of how you define that agent. Every branch of science, whether physical or biological, shares this assumption." She sounded pleased with herself.

"Exactly," I praised her. "That is what Einstein meant when he said that God doesn't play dice with the universe. He was pointing out that whatever happens is not a simple matter of chaos in action, but an exact expression of order, of causality. In other words, nothing happens by chance."

"So did Einstein believe in God as 'The Determinator'?" Mary laughed at her own joke, and she looked so sweet in the lantern light. She was melting like a candle.

"No, as far as I know, Einstein didn't believe in a Determinator, in the sense of it being a personal God. He believed in an intelligent but impersonal force, though he still called himself a religious man."

"How's that?" Mary yawned, and her gentle sweetness disappeared. She was getting tired, as I knew she was up well before dawn and she was usually in bed by this hour.

"Let me tell you what I mean," I replied quickly, giving her the cue that I would go home soon. "Einstein called himself religious in the sense that he was a seeker of truth. But he equated being religious with an absolute confidence in the rational explanation of the nature of reality."

"That doesn't make sense to me," Mary accused me in her old suspicious way. "Einstein couldn't mean that religion can be rational!"

"Yes, that is what he meant, even if most religion appears irrational because people use it as a pious cloak to serve their egos."

"Well, that is too much to think about at this hour," Mary yawned again, making it clear that her hospitality was winding down. "I hope your visit to Blacktail gave you what you want," she concluded, indicating that she had done her part.

I thanked her for dinner and realized how much more there was still left to be said. I wondered why she had invited me to dinner as it seemed we had reached no conclusions in our conversation, but had only scratched the surface. I was putting on my sweater when she asked if I wanted to stay the night. I was so surprised, I couldn't help but wonder if she was gay. For why else would she want me to stay in her cabin all night long when she was unwilling to share any intimate detail about her beliefs around religion and God?

I told her that I couldn't possibly stay because I'd be sorely missed at headquarters. If I didn't check in like I always did when I came back from Blacktail, they would probably send out a search party to look for me. But I told her I'd like to take a carrot out to Pete before I went on my way. It was an indirect way to show her affection.

When I came back from the corral, Mary was waiting at the cabin door with a flashlight in her hand. We walked down to the gate without a word. When I gestured to give her a hug, I was happy that she let me. I told her that her willingness to talk with me was a gift from Blacktail, and I'd always remember the evening.

"Such gifts are mutual," she said formally, her voice staccato and scared.

As I rode off on my bike, my mind was spinning. There was so much left unsaid in our conversation. I felt so deeply grieved that no matter how hard I tried to find a person who might be capable of discussing the relationship between the physical and the spiritual aspects of life with me, I could never seem to find anyone who could sustain a conversation.

I was disappointed that I hadn't found out if Mary was an atheist. We didn't even have a chance to talk about how she thought life began on earth and if she would rely on Darwin for an answer. Of course, Darwin didn't claim that life originated from non-living matter. But he did write about the magnificence of life that he believed was originally breathed by the Creator into a few forms or just one, as he said, which then miraculously mutated into millions of different forms over time.[1]

Strangely, though, most scientists opted not to know this

about Darwin, or tended to easily forget that he wasn't an athe-ist himself. Regardless of whether atheists have used his evo-lutionary theory as their engine for atheism, Darwin's theories didn't make any contribution to the question of the biological origins of life. Why? Because he didn't know what was the basic unit of heredity. Under his microscope with low magnification, a cell looked like a gelatinous blob.

Naturally, Darwin couldn't think about the origin of the essential building blocks of the cell because he couldn't identify what they were. But with modern technology, cell components can be magnified thousands of times. Cell biologists have discov-ered that a simple cell has a complexity that Darwin could never have imagined. In fact, the workings of a single cell have been compared to the complexity of New York City.

Even single cells are made of thousands of types of proteins, which are large complex molecules. Proteins, in turn, are made of smaller chemical units, called "amino acids" that are linked together in long chains. In nature, twenty types of amino acids are used to construct over thirty thousand distinct kinds of proteins, but only a specific order of the amino acids will make functional proteins. There is nothing random or hodgepodge about the arrangement.

A comparison of the twenty amino acids with the twenty-six letters of the English alphabet shows the high degree of specificity that is required to make proteins, just like letters make meaningful words. For example, if we don't combine our letters in exactly the right way, then we won't have a functional word. So, too, for amino acid chains. But in the case of amino acids, if they are not in the proper sequence, then the protein will not form. Also, though a recognizable word is constructed of a few letters, a functional protein is constructed of hundreds, and sometimes over a thousand, amino acids.

Interestingly, the longest word currently listed in the Oxford English dictionary is forty-five letters long. It is a scientific word for a lung disease called "pneumonoultramicroscopicsilicovolcanokoniosis." The length of this word, which would take some time to learn how to spell and pronounce, highlights the complexity of the information required to create a functional amino acid chain. For, even if this word was misspelled by a few letters, a medical person probably could still figure out what word was meant in spite of the mistakes. But it isn't the same with amino acids.

Though it is obvious that human intelligence creates the high degree of specificity that makes up words and language, it isn't so easy to say what creates the high degree of specificity in the linking of amino acids. Where do such directions come from?

In the 1950s and 60s, cell biologists figured out the basic answer. There is a large molecule in the nucleus of every cell called DNA (the commonly known acronym for deoxyribonucleic acid), that stores instructions for sequencing the amino acids for every single type of protein that constitutes a functioning cell (regardless of the kind of cell). For this reason, DNA is called the chemical code or language of life because its information is incredibly detailed and highly elaborate. In contrast, human language would seem exceedingly rudimentary.

So what is the source of the information in DNA? There is a narrow set of options. It couldn't originate by chance alone because the probability is too remote. The genetic instructions required to build the proteins in even the simplest one-celled organism would fill hundreds of pages of printed text. So how could the complexity of DNA be adequately explained by chance? Even the most elementary experiment with chance shows its limitations to create meaning. For example, if you dropped Scrabble letters for hours and hours on a flat surface with enough space that they wouldn't pile up on each other, the probability is almost nonexistent that you would find a simple recognizable sentence.[2]

For the same reason, Darwin's theory of natural selection can't account for the concise and detailed information in DNA either. Though atheists use his theory to explain that natural selection had acted upon existing molecular systems in primordial seas, the logic doesn't work. By definition, natural selection can only operate on a cell that is fully functional. In other words, a self-replicating system has to be already in place before natural selection can act upon it. So the question still remains: how could the source of information in the DNA come to be without the proteins that construct it? Logically, you can't use natural selection to explain the origin of DNA.

I had wanted to ask Mary how she would propose to solve the difficult problems of logic that arise with life, structure, and specificity by accident. But I never had the opportunity because I never sought her out again. I decided it was pointless.

When I left Yellowstone National Park, I went to study the history and philosophy of science at Indiana University. I had almost a full scholarship to do a doctorate program that would take about four years. But I only stayed for one semester.

My professors could teach me the facts about the Enlightenment period of European history, the fascinating time that began in the seventeenth century when there emerged a conflict between science and religion. My professors could teach that, up to that time, European culture was dominated by dogmatic religious beliefs, which were mostly the result of the work of Thomas Aquinas who wed Aristotle's "scientific" philosophy with church politics. My professors could also explain how the scientific discoveries of the seventeenth and eighteenth centuries questioned the wisdom of such futile orthodoxy. But they wouldn't question that maybe, though the orthodoxy was an expression of ego, there was some religious truth that was wrongly represented by the church. Just like science feeds politics and big business most of the time, so, too, the Church Fathers did the same. They weren't interested in true spiritual knowledge. My professors were like them. They couldn't see the divine beauty behind nature and natural law.

I began to wonder if the resistance to the idea of intelligent design (never mind the personal name or nature of the Designer) was created by some dark force in the universe that blinded people to knowing what was true. I decided I had to start from the beginning, to figure out what was the basis of true knowledge so that I wouldn't be deceived like so many seemed to be. So I went to study the history of consciousness, the history of human thought, in a graduate program in Newfoundland, Canada.

I specifically focused on the philosophy of religion. None of my professors had a scientific background so they weren't reluctant to talk about God. They spoke easily in terms of ontology and epistemology. As philosophers, they seemed so much more relaxed in a mental way.

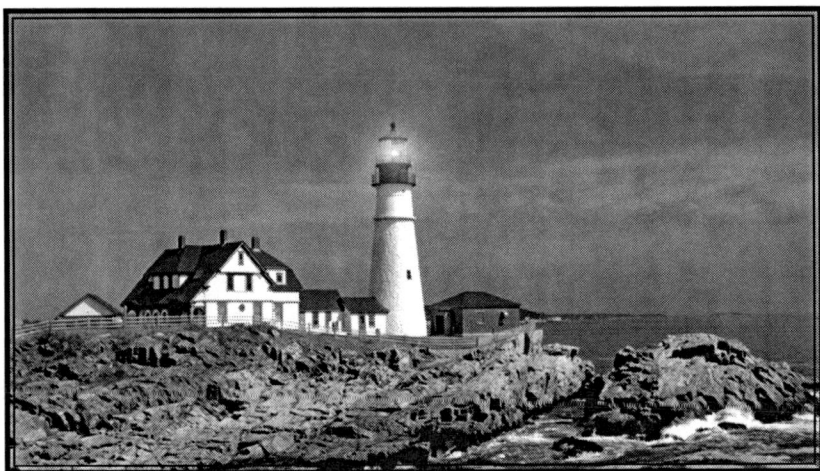

It was a happy time for me in the sense that I could speak a language that other people appreciated. They weren't afraid of the concepts around the existence of God and how people throughout history had contemplated them.

I spent three years in Newfoundland, a frigid empty northern land where light drizzle and fog was the weather for nine months at a time. There were old English-style pubs with fireplaces and icebergs floating in the harbor.

But my studies still couldn't satisfy me. I was longing for practical wisdom and spiritual knowledge that I couldn't find in the books that I read. Though I studied Eastern and Western philosophy in much detail during my course work, I still didn't know how to describe why I had a spiritual need. Just like I couldn't find satisfying scientific answers to my primary questions about how humans came to be, what was the purpose of our life, and what did the future hold for those who found out, I couldn't find the answers in my study of philosophy.

"The Newfies," slang for Newfoundlanders, always called me a "come from away," the local jargon used to refer to a foreigner. I wondered when and where I would ever find my own people. I loved what Rumi, the Sufi poet, wrote sometime in the thirteenth century: "Take your attention off of forms and focus on what's inside...If you're on this way, choose companions who are also pilgrims. No matter their shape, color or national origin, if they are your people, go with them."[3]

I used to wander the narrow, steep streets of the old part of the city of St. Johns looking for my people, especially in the evenings. In that section of the city, the houses were one line of connected buildings that ran along through almost every block, all the way down to the harbor.

On many nights when it was bitter cold, I'd walk the streets by myself in a long black coat that almost reached down to my ankles. I'd look in people's windows and watch them eating dinner. Once I saw a family praying. I always believed that if I wandered long and hard enough, I'd find my people. I even fantasized over and over again that I would come to a door where someone would open it and say to me, "Come in, we've been waiting for you." But it never happened.

Then I moved to Vancouver, British Columbia, to write my thesis, the last requirement to complete my master's degree. My thesis was a book-long discussion, through Plato and his successors, about how the soul chooses to move from ignorance to wholeness. It was a spiritual subject, but I didn't have, at that time, the right understanding of the soul because Plato didn't have it either.

Near where I lived on Fourth Street was a famous bookstore called Banyan Books that featured books on religious philosophy, poetry, and art. I decided to spend a couple of hours each day reading in the bookstore. I read books mostly about religion. I wasn't looking to belong to any organization though I was open to Buddhists, Sikhs, Hindus, and Sufis, but not to Christians or Muslims. The history of the Catholic Church convinced me that the Catholic clergy was evil, and that there was such a thing as Satan.

I also read some Gnosticism (which was really weird stuff), more on Lao Tzu, Chung Tzu, Confucius, and the Neo-Confucists. I studied the Sufis in some depth and also read much about Buddhism, particularly Madiamika philosophy, Mahamudra, the Heart and Diamond Sutras, and Zen. I also read Hindu books including the Bhagavad-Gita, the Vedas, Upanishads, Puranas, and part of the Muslim Qur'an. I also read books by the bizarre Guru traditions of Chogyam Trungpa and Osho. I also read the traditional Gurus from India like Ramana Maharishi, Yogananda, Ramakrishna, and Vivekananda. There was also Alan Watts and the writings of Ouspensky and Gurdieff, besides many others.

One day a Buddhist monk came into the bookstore. His orange robes dusted the edge of the shelves as he passed along the aisles. He appeared to be the real thing, at least a true Asian, maybe even from Tibet. He was around sixty years old with a shaved head and was drawn to the books on Tibetan Buddhism.

I thought I had a way of testing people back then, though it really amounted to nothing. I'd just watch them meticulously and see how "together" they acted. So I watched the monk and how he touched the books he was reading. He appeared to treat them well. But then he made a horrible sound and wiped his nose on his robe in a sickening way though he didn't see me watching. I decided he was too crude to know the delicate things of the spirit.

Some months later I noticed a sign on the door of the bookstore. It was announcing a monk from the Himalayas who was visiting Vancouver. He had a Hindu name, Swami Divyananda Saraswati. He was going to give a talk at the vegetarian restaurant across the street, and so I attended one week later.

He wasn't like anyone.

He was clean and elegant, willowy but strong. His black hair was tied neatly with a piece of orange string, and it hung in a long ponytail down his back. His long beard was grey and carefully brushed. He wore an orange dress-like robe.

The Swami's posture was straight and polite as he sat poised in his chair. He seemed to notice no one in particular. I watched him carefully, but he showed no sign of agitation. His mind seemed perfectly relaxed and he didn't fiddle with his nose or nails like academics often do.

His long fingers were gracefully folded on his lap and his bare feet were still, though they must have been cold because it was rainy outside.

A woman named Ruth introduced him to his audience, about twenty of us. Only his eyes occasionally moved, as if to highlight one of her words. Otherwise, he sat completely still.

We learned that he was born in India in 1912. So he was eighty-two years old, but he looked more like sixty. He was raised in a wealthy family, as his father worked for the British and the railroad. But the Swami renounced his wealth and took to the spiritual life. Before Gandhi was assassinated in 1948, the Swami had lived with him in his ashrams and had learned the ways of non-violence.

The Hindu word for non-violence is *ahimsa*, and the concept includes not only a non-violent way of treating others who have different religious beliefs, but a non-violent way of thinking in one's own mind. When Gandhi died, the Swami made a school for poor children and then took to living in remote mountains by

himself. He had lived the past forty years in the Himalayas, in Badrinath, the seat of the Ganges River and one of the most northern pilgrimage sites in India.

Ruth said that some trekkers had found him in his little *kuti*, a meditation hut at the base of three mountains in a valley called Charan Paduka at nearly twelve thousand feet in elevation. They invited him to Canada to share what he had learned.

The back of my spine prickled. So here was a man that knew silence, and even more silence than I had known. I felt thrilled. Maybe he knew the truth about life, the truth not created by the human mind, but the other way around. He would know truth because the truth had made him.

Then Ruth asked each one of us to stand up and announce our name, age, horoscope sign, and occupation. I knew it wasn't meant as a way to welcome the Swami, but more as a way to drum up business for Ruth. She seemed to be some sort of Sufi who needed spiritual seekers to support her financially.

When it came to be my turn, I said, "My name, my birth sign, and my occupation are not important to state when I am in the presence of a person who knows the value of silence. Why don't we all listen and learn, for once, instead of talking about ourselves." I was furious.

Ruth replied, pointing out the color of my blouse, "Dear young woman in the purple, Swamiji can enjoy all the facets of our existence." But I wouldn't budge and banter about stupid things, such as my birth sign and how I paid for my rent. The Swami didn't show that he sided with either Ruth or me. He just sat there without any expression on his face, though I thought I saw him smile slightly. Then finally everyone grew tired of talking about themselves, and it was time for the Swami to speak.

His words flowed like a mountain stream. He knew the King's English because he said he had been schooled in a Christian boarding school. He never stumbled on a word, or paused with an "ah" or an "um." His speech was fluid and highly educated, witty but pleasant. He was youthful though certain, and laughed freely at his own jokes. But he was strict and strong about what he said was the value of living a meditative life. He talked about the importance of knowing how to read and write, but that higher education, as his own graduate degree in physics, gave him no privilege when it came to attaining spiritual knowledge.

His hands were flying and kept up with his words, illustrating them in wide gestures and sudden dives. He told stories about the disciplines needed to overcome the ego life, about how Canadians were punctual and considerate, about the power and beauty of the Himalayas.

The message he gave was simple but profound: "Understand and cultivate the meditative mind and overcome your ego. Then you can know God." His accent didn't confuse me.

After the talk I went to shake his hand and thank him for what he had shared. He smelled like perfume, but I later learned it was coconut oil that he used in his hair because it is good for the scalp. He took my hand kindly, as if he already knew who I was. He said, looking calmly into my eyes, "You have the same eyes as I do." I wondered what he meant, but when I asked him, he didn't give me a satisfactory answer. He just smiled. So I just stood by and listened as the others met him, but he didn't say that to anyone else.

Two women who were astonished by his age started to obsess over the smoothness of his dark brown skin. With mischievous eyes he told them, "There are no wrinkles on my face because there are no wrinkles on my heart." They laughed like girls and he playfully slapped their cheeks. They moaned that they were thirty years younger than he was, but had many more wrinkles.

When I left him that afternoon, I wanted his special words to me about my eyes being like his to mean that he recognized my spiritual aspirations. More than anything, I wanted that recognition to be a cryptic promise that he would help me to understand what I was searching to know.

Over the course of a few weeks, I listened to him speak about the way of *sadhana*, which means a meditative life, and the path of love and the work of self-knowledge. I liked that he didn't flatter people, though he appeared good-hearted and respectfully tried to answer our questions. He didn't seduce us with the tales of mystical gifts or astral travels that flooded New Age books on spirituality, books which made God out to be whatever it was one wanted. In fact, the most prominent New Age teaching was that we are perfect as we are, and don't have to do anything to train our consciousness.

But the Swami's message wasn't at all like that. He didn't want to tickle our egos. He made it clear that if we chose to walk the spiritual path, then we had to expose our ego and conquer the bad habits that it hid. He said we would learn to become more conscious, and more loving, the more we dismantled our ego's hold on us.

He talked about his life in India and the importance of humility, discipline, and living in a healthy way. Through Gandhi he had studied naturopathic medicine, and was called "Dr. Swami" by the villagers whom he helped in exchange for a meal and not for money.

I wanted to find out more about who the Swami was because he was not afraid of being alone, and he wasn't afraid of being around the commercial insanity of the world like I was. I wondered if at last he was the one who could teach me the truth about God. Maybe he was part of "my people" in the way that Rumi had written.

I always loved Rumi's idea that "the pilgrims of the way" could distinguish the highest truth that universally applied to everyone from those that arose out of specific cultures and traditions. For, as Rumi emphasized, those who really wanted the truth about God would recognize each other regardless of their race or national origin. I had always searched for my people.

They would have the understanding that the heart and mind are united in a common goal to find out the purpose of being alive and the truth of our existence. They would also know that the physical and spiritual aspects of life are not opposed, and that physical matter did not create spirit as a whim, like the scientists who believed that the evolving human mind made God up as a way to cope with the finality of death.

Since the Swami had studied science, and even had a master's degree in physics, it showed that he was not afraid to be rational. He understood math as an expression of physical laws, and did not reject science just because he had a spiritual need. Many people of Christian, Muslim, and Hindu origin rejected the truths of science because they were unable to fit scientific truths into their version of religion. But the Swami knew that having a spiritual need was not irrational, but instead the most natural and dignified expression of being human. He didn't use science to mock or reject the inner life and spiritual awakening, like so many scientists did who were unwilling to consider that humans could have a spiritual origin.

Above all, the Swami wanted to teach people how to love in a principled way and not just with emotion because, as he said, emotion can serve hatred as much as it can serve good. But a principled love is not selfish or sentimental. Love endures all things and never fails.

Life is too intricate
to have random origins.

Dr. Harold Morowitz (currently the principle investigator
on a National Science Foundation grant to study the
molecular processes of how life emerged on earth)

CHAPTER SIX

More Mirages

I was shaking with excitement when he opened the door." Good afternoon, Mr. Swamiji," I stumbled through his name, not knowing exactly what to call him. "Sorry I'm late. I got lost in the rain."

He made a joke about what monkeys looked like in India when they were as wet as I was, but I couldn't come up with a clever reply. I was too nervous.

I looked down at my soaking shoes and socks and wondered where to leave them. He was aware that I knew I had to take them off, and he pointed to the place where I should put them.

When I stepped inside, I noticed he was barefoot. He seemed to easily ignore the cold tile floor, but my feet were freezing. I followed behind him watching his long arms hanging loosely at his sides. From the back he looked like a woman with his long dark hair and slender Indian build. He wore the traditional Indian kurta, dyed orange, and a *dhoti*, a rectangular piece of cotton cloth that was also orange and tied at his waist, hanging like a skirt to his ankles.

He led me without a word to the room where he was staying in the house of a fish salesman named David.

"In India," he explained, "my bed serves as my couch, and my table, and a warm place to sit in the daytime. But oh my Lord, it isn't big like this one."

His queen size bed was neatly made with a soft blue blanket that was piled with books and papers on one side. I strained to see the titles of the books as I was curious to know what he had left to learn about life from other people's words. Perhaps he enjoyed history, quotations, or reading about herbs.

I waited for him to instruct me where to sit. He pointed to a chair by the window and gestured that I should pull it up near where we stood. While I wondered where to position the chair, he climbed onto the bed and sat cross-legged, leaning against the wall. He was so limber that all his movements flowed effortlessly like he was twenty years old instead of eighty-two. He waited silently for me to get situated, and I noticed he sat completely still. From where I sat, I couldn't face him and he would have to turn his head if he wanted to see me directly. I wondered if it was his way to keep his distance from people, especially young Western women who came to ask him questions.

I was impressed with his profile. He had only a small white pillow between his straight back and the cold winter wall. I pictured him sitting just like that in the Himalayas, only on a bed made of planks and wool blankets. He had mentioned in one of his public talks that his kuti, which means "little hut" in Hindi, was "cold as a fridge." He had no heat source except for the wood he used for cooking, and he had to use that sparingly. But he had also remarked that he knew how to regulate his breathing, which helped to keep his body warm.

I knew he was referring to a practice called *pranayama*. I had read accounts of Tibetan monks who sat in the snow wrapped in wet sheets and could apparently dry them with their body heat. This feat was not considered a magic trick that was accomplished with the help of gods or demons, but was supposedly just a physiological result of breath control. I was curious about whether it was true, but I didn't give it much attention. Even if it was possible to do such a thing, it wouldn't be an indication of spiritual attainment. To me, the real mark of attainment was the extent to which a person showed unselfish attention to others as a reflection of his loving kindness and peace of heart and mind.

The Swami seemed to personify the peace of nature. Though I had only seen him speak a few times in public places, I never saw him make any agitated, repetitive movements. He never picked at his nails or cleared his throat nervously. And his eyes never darted around betraying a lack of focus. He wasn't like the average modern man whose driven, exhausted mind couldn't be in the present moment, but was always projecting into the future.

Still, the Swami wasn't slow in speech, or weak in expression or reason. His mind was sharp and refined and he was eighty-two.

I was thrilled to meet him because he knew the wilderness like I did, and he obviously wasn't afraid to meditate on spiritual truths in silence by himself, as I had also done. I was eager to ask him if he had learned what no one else seemed to know: the truth about God, the reason for our existence, and what was really important to accomplish in our lives.

He continued to sit silently. I thought he was probably so aloof because it was the first time we were alone together, and his meditative posture was a guard against me. But I had decided not to bring anyone when I came to see him for the first time because I knew it would have resulted in a more superficial kind of conversation. I trusted him, though, like I wouldn't have trusted others. He seemed childlike and unusually small, though he was about five feet eight and that wasn't unusually short for a man. His smallness was more like an innocence or an inability to be domineering like men could often be.

"How would you like me to address you?" I finally broke the silence. But I could have kicked myself for sounding so formal. I never trusted people who sounded like I did, but I was glad he didn't seem to notice.

"In India they call me Swamiji." He turned his head toward me, and I realized he had been waiting for me to speak to him.

"Do you know what a swami is?" His expression showed he was curious to find out what I knew besides the superficial stuff.

"Yes, a swami is someone who wants to know the truth about God. He foregoes seeking an image of success in the world because he doesn't believe in its lies. For him, success is a matter of spiritual attainment, and not whether he owns a house or has a lot of money."

He was amused at my reply and laughed at me, but there wasn't enough light in the room for me to see the full expression of his eyes. Heavy white curtains covered the wide windows.

"May I turn the light on?"

He nodded.

"That's better," I said, and he remarked how he didn't have electricity in India and wasn't used to overhead light. I wondered how long he'd been in Canada, as I guessed it was only a few months, but I wanted to save my questions for more important subjects.

He continued with how to define a swami. "'Swami' is a Sanskrit word, and Sanskrit is an ancient Aryan language. Have you ever heard of it?"

"Yes, I know about Sanskrit," I assured him.

He turned toward me and said, "'Swami' means master, in a spiritual sense because a spiritual master knows the difference between a spiritual man and a physical man."

"That's an interesting contrast." I was impressed he could make the distinction so easily.

"Yes," he noted my enthusiasm. "The physical man, of course, lives like an animal because he only wants to cultivate animal qualities, and live by the laws that govern them."

"You're right, Swamiji!" I exploded with appreciation. "I know exactly what you mean. And the physical man isn't only the scientist who believes he's an animal because he evolved from one. The physical man is also the so-called spiritual man who creates false doctrines, like false gods, as a way to dominate others. His godliness is just an expression of his selfishness."

"It is so," he agreed. It seemed old hat to him. But I was floored that he understood me without question.

"And what is essential," he added, "is that the spiritual man, which includes the spiritual woman, knows why he is not an animal. Do you know why he knows this?"

"Please tell me," I replied, though I had some idea of how he'd answer.

"It's because the spiritual man has submitted himself to higher laws of love and intelligence beyond the ego's selfish narrow-minded ways. He cultivates spiritual qualities, and this eventually breaks down his ego, though it may take a long time."

"Excuse me, though, Swamiji," I had to say abruptly, "but I don't think it's safe to label ourselves as a "master" just because we understand the difference between the spiritual man and the physical one, and make the effort to cultivate spiritual qualities."

"Why not?" He seemed surprised and shifted his posture for the first time.

"Because it's too ambitious a title." I was adamant. I was disgusted with the self-appointed spiritual masters, regardless of their religions, who were more like spiritual caricatures that littered the land in almost every country of the world.

"Why ambitious?" he asked me to clarify.

"Because labeling ourselves a spiritual master simply because we have some spiritual insight doesn't mean we have arrived anywhere in a spiritual way."

"So you don't think spiritual perfection is possible?"

"Not in this world, anyway. But my point is that our egos are masterful hiders. They are like a virus that infect our mind and heart in spite of everything we try to do."

"Ah," he smiled, "so you know the difficulty of trying to overcome the ego's ways?"

"Yes, I do. I hear it's only possible with divine help! But I don't know who or what the divine really is, do you?"

Swamiji didn't reply to me and I wondered why. Perhaps

he thought I was rude for speaking out so strongly, or maybe he was contemplating what I said. I didn't want to push him to continue the conversation so I tried to match his stillness, but my feet were so cold I wanted to rub them on the rug. I decided to suffer silently and let him know I was a patient person.

Neither of us were the New Age spiritual types who considered it vogue to become "masters" of some spiritual art in one weekend. They were a dime a dozen. I could always spot them pushing around their spiritual shopping carts, picking and choosing whatever their egos liked to identify as the "perfect" spiritual lifestyle regardless of how much liquor, marijuana, or sex it involved. These people were especially attracted to ideas and practices in the Hindu, Buddhist, and Christian traditions, and they were in attendance at some of Swamiji's talks. But they didn't seem to care, or were not smart enough to notice, that the ideas in different religions conflicted with each other when it came to the means to enlightenment, or salvation, and the goal of spiritual life. Their beliefs were riddled with contradictions and such individuals seemed so easily influenced by things that didn't make any sense.

In contrast to the modern New Age grabbers of enlightenment were stories of the seekers of the old ways. In these accounts, especially in India and Tibet, there were many tests and trials put to them. If they aspired to learn from a Himalayan sage who had supposedly renounced the mundane life in the world for a more celestial one in solitude, then their training would be anything but blissful. The main thing these stories had in common was that only those who wanted to endure the sufferings of their egos would succeed. For the true method of acquiring knowledge did not cater to a worldly person (regardless if they masqueraded as religious) who, above all, seeks glory in the eyes of others.

There was one story that I always remembered, though I can't remember the names of the student and teacher in the story. They were famous in Tibet, and were apparently not just legend. The story was about many belabored and exhausting tests that the student had to undergo to show that he was actually in the process of renouncing his ego and willing to forego the false pleasures that it brings. In Buddhism, and Hinduism too, the idea is that the ego creates a false life and so whatever it achieves is only ephemeral and illusory.

Most of these stories are about a series of difficulties that the student undergoes and overcomes in order to pass various tests designed by the teacher, who is presumably enlightened. Of course, this gets tricky to assess because if the teacher is not enlightened, then the student will probably live a life of futility and exhaustion. But enlightenment still means different things to different people, according to what they seek and what they want to believe.

In the case of the story I remembered so well, the student had been busting his heart and mind for years in order to show his commitment to his spiritual training. And one day after climbing down a steep and dangerous cliff to get water, he climbed back up and reached the top, huffing and puffing. But before he could

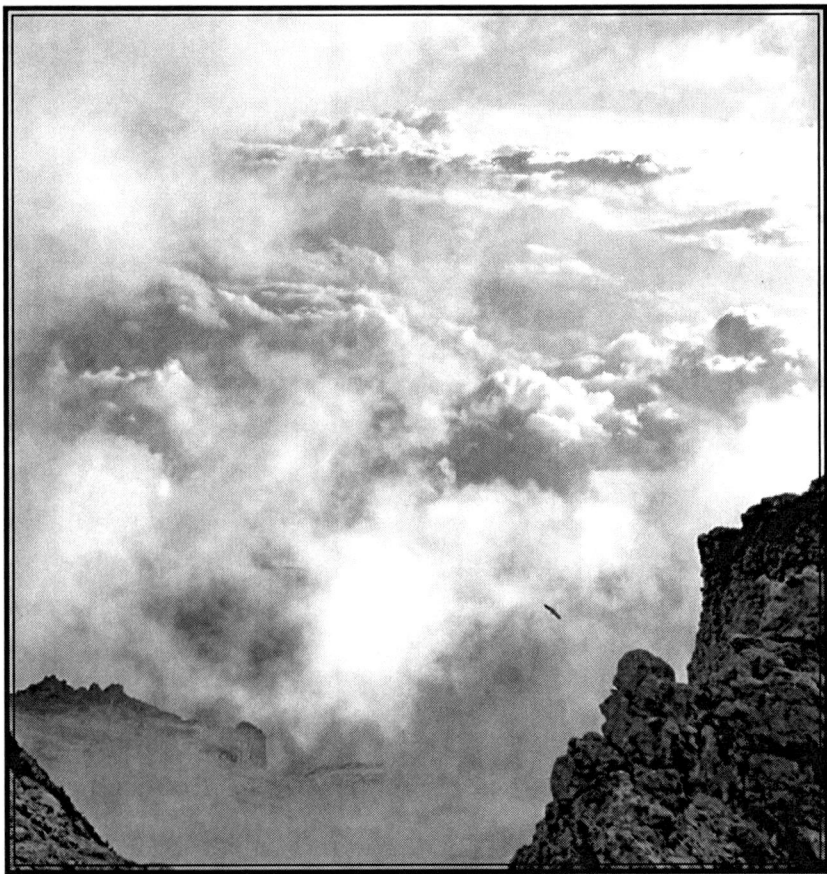

catch his breath, his master came out from behind a rock and whacked his student in the forehead with his sandal. At that moment the student became enlightened, or so the story celebrates.

I was wondering how whacking someone in the forehead could be the means for passing enlightenment from one person to another when Swamiji finally spoke again.

"Do you know that choice dignifies our life and raises us above animals?"

"Yes," I answered more carefully than before. I wondered if he was enlightened or not and how he would define enlightenment. He did not appear to be a narrow-minded person and he showed loving kindness in an open-hearted and sometimes playful way.

But he continued the lesson in a serious mood and spoke without turning his head to me, as he had previously done. "What you choose to believe is important because what you believe will make or break you as a spiritual person." It seemed to be warning me, and I was glad he was so grave.

"I agree," I said, and then added, "I have always thought like you do."

"Then don't be afraid to think more deeply," he almost scolded me. "To be a master of yourself means that you know why you believe what you do and that you understand the consequences of your choices. Your choices will be integrated, tempered by your mind and heart together."

I understood what he meant by an integrated choice, but I still wondered how a person could honestly call himself a "spiritual master," even if he did much spiritual work to cultivate spiritual qualities.

I had to ask him again, as politely as I could, "How,

Swamiji, can we be sure if we know when we have become a master? Our ego is such a slippery devil and wants to be master of everything, when all it knows is itself. It deceives our ability to think and love in a selfless way, and mixes up our choices and the reasons for them."

"You are right," he said squarely. "It can't ever be you who tells you when you have surrendered your ego and are living by higher principles. Only your teacher can tell you."

"But what if your teacher is a fake and wants to use you like a slave?"

"What if?" he repeated. "Don't worry about that. You will know if your teacher is more enlightened than you are. A serious student will attract a serious teacher. It is the way things always work."

I was longing for a teacher to teach me the truth about God, but I didn't dare reveal that to him because I didn't want him to accept me or reject me. I didn't know him well enough.

"So who was your teacher?" I changed the subject.

He told me his teacher's name, but it was complicated and composed of many foreign words.

"Can you say it again?" I must have had a muddled look on my face. He seemed to want to tease me a little because he said the name faster the second time. When he smiled at my consternation, I noticed he only had a few front teeth.

"Would you mind writing it down for me?"

"I can," he replied pleasantly and reached for a piece of paper on his pile of books. He gently held his pen and wrote with a delicate and adoring concentration. I could see how much he loved his teacher by how slowly he wrote his name. When he finished writing, he handed me the paper without a word. I could tell by his elegant handwriting that he was well educated. But I didn't know how his education applied to spiritual truths or the validity of what he could teach me.

I liked the idea of learning directly from one person who assumed the role of a sort of spiritual parent. It made more sense to me than trying to learn from a book written by someone who only conceptualized spiritual truths but didn't live them. Writers of spiritual books both East and West, like most academics and armchair scientists, were expert gymnasts of the mind. But they didn't know how to feel life and be vulnerable and admit that they didn't know themselves very well. Their intellects were an obstacle to their discovering important spiritual truths that are only known by the heart, by feeling, and not by thinking.

Even philosophers, who are supposed to be more well-rounded than scientists because they involve more than just mechanical ideas in their search for truth, still haven't integrated knowledge and emotion in their own personal lives. They often teach one set of ideals but live by another.

My own professors, for example, could be the wise sage to some of their students while trying to literally or figuratively seduce others. And they usually liked only some of their colleagues, but fought with the rest. I had observed their splintered lives in many forms and disguises. Famous philosophers esteemed for their minds were just the same, though their dysfunctions were forgiven, or maybe just forgotten, simply because they were dead.

I was intrigued by Swamiji because his understanding of a wise person, as an expression of self-mastery, involved the integration of all the aspects of the self. Unlike academics, he didn't give a primary position to the intellect. He pointed out that a spiritual person is an integrated person who knows how to combine thinking and feeling so that he can act with understanding and not just with knowledge, as intellects tend to do. But he also emphasized that it takes a lot of self-observation and self-study before we can obey spiritual principles instead of our egos. For, in their essence, such principles train the mind and heart to rise above the ego's self-serving ways and narrow-minded outlook about what is most important to achieve.

I knew what he meant by the ego's self-serving ways. When I was studying philosophy at Memorial University in Newfoundland, I usually wore earplugs when visiting professors came to lecture to us. They were puffed up with pride and felt they knew the truth about life, according to their limited knowledge of some philosopher who assumed the role of God to them. They, in turn, proselytized for him and tried to convince us to think like they did. But I never believed their propaganda.

I never said anything rude to them, but just sat as still as I could during their talks and drilled my eyes into them. It was my special way of taking notes. I asked them silently what they really knew for sure about their own hearts, and how much they contributed to the welfare of other people. I begged them to be honest. Though they always noticed me, they avoided looking in my eyes. And not one of them ever had the interest to come and ask me who I was or question why I stared at them. They were too uneasy.

But Swamiji wasn't afraid of me. He expected a deep encounter. He wasn't uncomfortable with silence either, and didn't have to fill the void with words like academics usually do. He used much more than his mind to make sense of life and to convey it to others.

After we talked about his own teacher, I decided it was time for me to go. I had heard enough to think about. I also wanted to leave before my ego said something stupid, which egos invariably do. Though it was raining harder when I left the house than when I arrived, I didn't care about getting wet. I walked through the puddles and didn't bother to go around them. I felt vindicated, like nobody or nothing could stop me now.

Like me, Swamiji didn't accept the promises of politicians or the discoveries of scientists or philosophers to give him hope for the future. And though he was born in India and raised in completely different cultural circumstances than I was, he still knew what I wanted. He was not suspicious of my spiritual need, and didn't balk at my desire to uncover the mysteries of life.

Though I hadn't received any specific spiritual instructions from him in terms of how to arrive at the truth about God and our relationship with him, he still encouraged me like nobody else ever had. He valued and appreciated my inner aspirations. He knew they were the most important part of my life because he felt the same way about his.

And, like me, Swamiji didn't care much about money though he knew the value of what it could buy. He didn't fall for the lie that money could buy happiness, even if it did buy power and prestige. He didn't scorn the seeker as an unproductive member of society. But best of all, he didn't give me one strange or confused look when I talked about wanting to find out the truth about life from a spiritual perspective. He seemed to know me better than anyone, and I hardly knew who he was. Though this was perplexing, it was even more intriguing.

On my way home, I sat in traffic watching people driving mindlessly. I realized it wasn't fair for me to judge them as mindless, but most people do take their beliefs secondhand and without examination. If people did examine what they believed, it would show. In that case, greedy money mongers and power seekers wouldn't be ruling governments because they wouldn't be able to convince others to vote for them. No one would believe their lies.

But to be a master of ourselves, like Swamiji said was possible, means that we understand why we believe what we do. We will be aware that our beliefs act like anchors to hold us upright in the shifting seas of our life. We will know what constitutes them, including the history of their influence upon people and how they came to us. For what we call our personalized beliefs are not usually our own.

The religious, scientific, and even political beliefs that we hold can be hundreds or thousands of years older than we are. So, actually, much of what we accept and choose to identify as our beliefs are not what we think they are. We can find out that we, too, have been deceived like the others whom we call "the poor fools" because we think they have accepted blindly what we consider to be false.

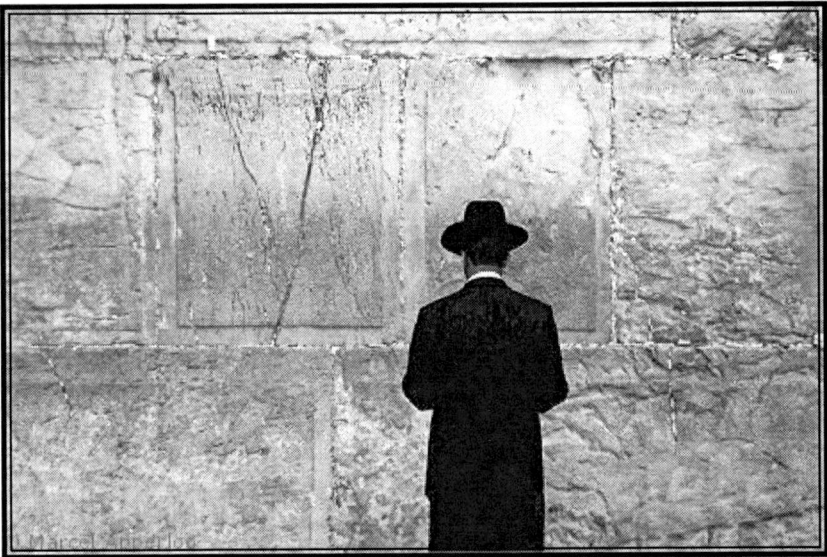

For example, some scientists say that religious people are wrong to insist that they know the truth about life based on their versions of what "God says." But religious people can say the same thing about scientists who elevate "chance" to the role of God. Even if religious people don't agree on who God is, they still all believe in a Creator. In fact, most people believe that the probability of life originating by chance is comparable to the probability of a dictionary popping out of an explosion in a printing press, or a monkey making a Rolex watch as a whim.[1]

But you can't blame scientists for rolling their eyes when

religious fundamentalists preach that the universe and all life on earth was created in six 24-hour days some ten thousand years ago. Though Richard Dawkins, the professed atheist scientist, sounds just as silly when he says, "There is, at bottom, no design, no purpose, no evil and no good, nothing but pitiless indifference."[2] Why he feels justified in saying this is surprising. Human expression rarely reflects indifference, especially in religious matters.

Paul Feyerabend, a philosopher of science, wrote to watch out for scientists who want to be the "new high priests" of our civilization. Perhaps he had personalities like Dawkins in mind when he wrote, "Science is neither a single tradition, nor the best tradition there is, except for people who have become accustomed to its presence...In a democracy science should be separated from the state just as churches are now separated from the state."[3]

Feyerabend intended to alert nonscientists to the fact that scientists tend to have an anarchistic streak because they make claims about truth that exceed their methods and their manners.[4]

Science has sent astronauts into space.

Science has changed the world.

So when scientists present the theory of evolution by natural selection as a fact, then uneducated people believe that it must have been proven. For example, the prominent evolutionary biologist Stephen Jay Gould wrote that "evolution is as well documented as any phenomenon in science, as strongly as the earth's revolution around the sun rather than vice versa. In this sense, we can call evolution a 'fact.'"[5] This sort of statement strongly suggests that everyone should believe what scientists say.

While Feyerabend's warning was probably forgotten as the crank expression of a puritanistic personality, Gould popularized evolution in the public eye through a few dozen books that he wrote, books like *Ever Since Darwin*, *The Panda's Thumb*, and *The Mismeasure of Man*.

Another famous evolutionary biologist by the name of Edward O. Wilson, who is more soft-spoken than Dawkins, and probably Gould too, was included in *Time* magazine's "America's 25 Most Influential People" in 1996. He was also dubbed the "new Darwin" by the journalist Tom Wolfe.[6] And, notably, Wilson has twice received the Pulitzer Prize for his books on ants and human nature.

As the "new Darwin," Wilson is not so reserved as Darwin was, or perhaps he is just more eagerly biased, thanks to the work of Dawkins, Gould, and others. For, though Darwin evidently devised his theory of evolution by natural selection in 1838, he waited more than twenty years to make it publicly known in 1859. But Wilson has no need to be reticent. Like his colleagues, he easily deifies scientific progress. He has no qualms in claiming that God is an artifact of the evolutionary process[7] and that "the greatest divide in humanity is not between races, religions, or the literate or illiterate. It is the chasm that separates scientific from prescientific cultures."[8]

But while Wilson's "chasm" is acclaimed by some, it is considered a deep misconception to others. An interesting contrast to the outlook of Wilson is that of Sri Aurobindo, who was educated at The University of Cambridge and died in 1950. He was as well known as Wilson in his own day, though Aurobindo was a philosopher, not a scientist. In one of his dozens of books, he wrote: "The average human being even now is in his inward existence as crude and undeveloped as was the bygone primitive man in his outward appearance."[9] To Aurobindo, then, the "inward" existence is the measure of the modern man, not technological or scientific advancements. In other words, cultivating qualities that are not expressions of the ego's drive to be prominent (selfish) defines the true capability of being human.

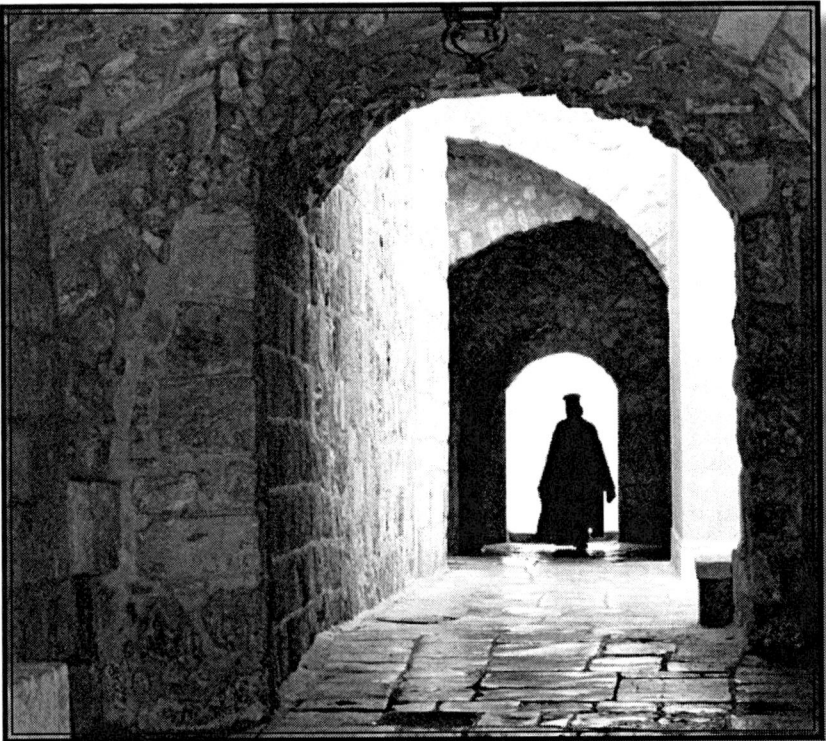

Whereas Wilson presents modern man as a technologically improving animal, Aurobindo presents him as a degraded spiritual creature because he is too much engrossed in the superfluous aspects of physical life. The outlooks of Wilson and Aurobindo are as different as land animals from water animals, or, more accurately, as different as the physical man from the spiritual man.

For even if Wilson appears to be a good-hearted intellect, he will still have to condone selfishness, greed, and war because he accepts that advancement, in evolutionary terms, proceeds by struggle. By this view, there can be no absolute standard for love for others because any standard will be considered relative to religion and culture. In the vision of the physical man, humans will create gods with different standards, even if they say their gods are absolute.

By contrast, Aurobindo believes humans have fallen into spiritual darkness by choosing ignorance over insight. He, and all who share some version of his view, exhorts us to focus on our own spiritual evolution and not on the theoretical physical kind in animals, because that distracts us from making meaningful spiritual changes in ourselves. For if we don't cultivate a will to change our selfishness, science certainly won't do it for us. He was aware that human consciousness goes from bad to worse because we continue to distract ourselves from the true work at hand.

Albert Einstein noticed this too, and so remarked, "All of our exalted technological progress, civilization for that matter, is comparable to an axe in the hand of a pathological criminal."[10] He also said, "To my mind, to kill in war is not a whit better than to commit ordinary murder."[11] In these comments, Einstein showed his understanding that too much focus on the physical world makes humans unbalanced and spiritually lost.

If we can separate ourselves from our beliefs for a moment, and from the indoctrinating influences that shaped them,
we can learn a lot about who we are. We can reflect on why we
want to believe like Wilson or like Aurobindo, as two extremes for
explaining our human situation.

If we are like Wilson, we will believe like he does. We
will accept that humans are only animals that struggle to outdo
each other because we are instinctively wired to be selfish. Indeed, if we are actually animalistic, the impending necessity to
try to save the planet from destruction, including already pre-
cariously-existing species, will never be realized as a large-scale
goal. Regardless of the urgency that humans work together to
save what is left from ruin, biological altruism as a motivating
force can't go very far. If selfishness is how we are supposedly
wired to be, then we will demonstrate that we refuse to share
adequately with others who are not related to us.

By contrast, if we are like Aurobindo, we will believe that
our selfish tendencies arose from a different source, from a choice
and not from instinct, from a spiritual decision and not an accidental outcome. But Aurobindo's understanding of human will
was much more sophisticated than Wilson's. And so, of course,
Aurobindo's role of God in human life would be more meaningful
than that of an evolutionist.

Aurobindo believed along the lines that we inherited more
than genetic information from our ancestors. Above all, we inherited the tendency to be selfish because we willfully forgot our
spiritual origins. That is why he claimed that the average man is
now inwardly "crude and undeveloped." The average man passes
along his imperfection, so to speak, but in a spiritual way. So the
history of spiritual degradation is like the history of congenital

disease, but spiritual degradation makes the whole world sick unlike the physical side of disease that affects far fewer.

Whether we choose to believe like Wilson or Aurobindo regarding our outlook on human imperfection, we should be clear about why we believe what we do. Otherwise, we will have to be counted among those who blindly accept their beliefs from others because we aren't capable of thinking things through for ourselves.

If it is our hearts that shape our way of believing, is this because we want to be loyal to the mainstream, to tradition, to our parents' way of understanding life? If we don't believe what they do, will it mean they won't love us the way we'd like to be loved?

If we believe that our minds, more than our hearts, determine what we consider to be true, then we should reflect on what influence most affects our thinking. Is it simply a matter of educational preference that becomes dogma and shapes our mental habits? Or a new fad in science, politics, or religion? Or is it just simple cultural prejudice? Or mathematical probability? Or logic, like the rule of parsimony?

The rule of parsimony is sometimes called the bread and butter of the scientific method, but that's just a playful oversimplification. This rule is also called Occam's razor, after a fourteenth century English philosopher and Franciscan friar named William of Ockham. But he himself never used the phrase. He simply suggested that when we search for an explanation for something, we should always avoid using unnecessary or complicated assumptions. Since the word "parsimony" means extreme or excessive frugality, it has a special connotation. It carries the warning that we should be cautious in formulating theories and explanations for what we believe to be true.

The expression "Occam's razor" actually occurred for the first time in 1852 in the writings of William Rowan Hamilton, an Irish mathematician who suggested that all things being equal (which they never are), the simplest theory or explanation for any phenomenon is more likely to be the right one. The word "razor" does refer to the implement used for shaving, though, in this context, as a metaphor for consciously cutting away useless complexity when our minds try to figure out how things work.

If we extend Occam's razor to a metaphysical inquiry (though scientists might think that is breaking the rules), then we can consider which is the simplest explanation regarding man's relationship with God: Man created God in his image as a device to improve his chances of survival as "the" glorified animal, or man was created in God's image because whatever humans decide to do is compelled by choice, not by chance. In other words, humans are humans because they reflect a capacity for intelligence if they choose to be wise.

But one can argue that neither of these statements are easy to assess by Occam's razor because they both contain assumptions. It's like what Einstein said: "Whether you can observe a thing or not depends on the theory which you use. It is the theory which decides what can be observed."[12] Of course, when Einstein uttered these words he was trying to understand quantum mechanics and not man's true relationship to God. But his point can still be well taken.

We can apply his reasoning to any aspect of life, even an empirical one, as Einstein argued to his colleagues, because our theories are usually translated as preconceptions that appear to shape our outlook regardless of what we learn to the contrary. And when it comes to assessing the truth about the relationship between humans and God, many people are so biased that they can't even reason. They are clamped to the workbench of their mental habits and too afraid to try to see the pieces of their life from any other angle.

For example, many who are stubbornly resolved to believe that God does not exist will dogmatically accept evolution to account for human life.[13] Why? Because dogmatic acceptance and stubborn refusal is the flip side of fear. When a person is afraid to reason on what he fears, he shows two truths about himself: first, that his preconceptions are emotionally based and not reason based, and second, that his preconceptions rule his outlook on life.

When it comes to God, reason doesn't have to be afraid. Even if things look bleak (like the history of religion with its brazen violent zealots) or confusing (like the multitude of ideas about God), there is still much to learn in an intelligent way from intelligent people about the truth of spiritual realities.

Of course, the relationship between God and man is historically complex and often tumultuous because God serves both the physical man and the spiritual man. The physical man, like

Edward Wilson, defines God as a human creation and uses him to define a specific cultural or "tribal" ego, which usually amounts to one group of people asserting themselves over another. Though Wilson doesn't use the word "ego" to describe the identity behind a commonly-held view about God among people in the model of a struggling evolutionary process, he does say that religious clash is an expression of bigotry. And bigotry, of course, is a major expression of the ego.

He writes about what happens when religious ideas and groups of people become mutually exclusive: "Then comes bigotry and the dehumanization of infidels. Our gods, the true believer asserts, stand against your false idols, our spiritual purity against your corruption, our divinely sanctioned knowledge against your errancy. In past ages the posture provided an advantage. It united each tribe during life-and-death struggles with other tribes."[14]

Wilson can justify religious clash in a positive way because he is an evolutionist and has a bias toward struggle, and he sees a functional advantage in loss of life. But what isn't easy to justify is his own religious stance, because it doesn't fit his evolutionary scheme. For he considers himself self-aware, unlike the poor blokes who are not privy to the knowledge that their beliefs about their theist or polytheist god or gods are just fulfilling the model of an evolving evolutionary role.

On the one hand, he considers himself the spokesman for most evolutionists who consider gods to be a dime a dozen. In an interview he said, "I'm fairly sure that there's not what I call a *biological* [Wilson's emphasis] god, that is, one that is guiding the origin of life on earth or our personal affairs. There's not a personal god. There's not a shred of evidence."[15] So here he denies the existence of God on the basis of lack of proof.

But then he contradicts himself. He denies his own argument that God is only a human creation when he says, "But there could be a cosmological god; there could...be something beyond our comprehension that started the universe. There are physicists who would say that's a naïve statement, but I can't personally throw out the idea of a god."[16] Surprisingly, Wilson admits that he isn't an atheist after all, and that God isn't necessarily a result of human ingenuity. But it doesn't make sense to assume that a cosmological god is more provable than a personal one. So why the discrepancy?

He doesn't give a reason. But he does admit that his allegiance is actually with believers when he says, "So I come down to being what I call a provisional deist. That is, I'm willing to have you label me a deist, in the sense that there's the possibility of a god who started it, but don't call me a theist, which is a person who believes in a personal god. I've never seen any evidence of [a god] influencing any human being or the fate of humanity."[17]

Why Wilson is comfortable with the idea of a cosmological god, but not a personal one, is strange indeed. Perhaps he prefers a cosmological god because such a god is far removed from his personal life and his conscience too. He seems to echo Aldous Huxley, the English writer, who wrote in "Confessions of a Professed Atheist:" I had motives for not wanting the world to have meaning; consequently, assumed it had none, and was able without any difficulty to find satisfying reasons for this assumption...The philosopher who finds no meaning in the world is not concerned exclusively with a problem in pure metaphysics; he is also concerned to prove there is no valid reason why he personally should not do as he wants to do...For myself, as no doubt for most of my contemporaries, the philosophy of meaninglessness was essentially an instrument of liberation. The liberation we desired was simultaneously liberation from a certain political and economic system and liberation from a certain system of morality. We objected to the morality because it interfered with our sexual freedom."[18]

Of course, Wilson probably isn't a deist for the same reason that Huxley was an atheist, but we may never know for sure. Even though Wilson wants to keep God on the far side of the universe and away from any personal encounter, he can still point out that atheists who believe in evolution are more religious than they realize. Why can this be said? An atheist does have a religious aspect and a built-in capacity for faith. For though he categorically denies the existence of God, he still has to believe that religious concepts are part of the evolutionary history of man, including himself. He has to, by virtue of the fact that he has faith in evolution by natural selection.

Religion is commonly defined as devotion or fidelity to various principles which includes faithful attachment to what is believed. In this way, even though evolution is presented in scientific language based on Darwin's ideas, it is still a religious doctrine. Why? Because to explain the diversity and complexity of life by chance requires faith in what seems impossible.

First, most genetic mutations, which are considered the raw material for evolution by natural selection, are known to be functionally harmful. They overwhelmingly result in disease and death. It isn't logical to attribute the building blocks for increasing complexity to a force akin to entropy. In other words, life can't be built up on what breaks down. Second, experiments show that mutations only cause variations in the traits of an existing organism, and never give rise to a new species. Third, DNA, which carries the blueprints for cell replication has a notable capacity to repair itself. This minimizes the occurrence of genetic mutation. The National Center for Biotechnology Information states: "The potential for DNA damage is counteracted by a vigorous surveillance and repair system. Within this system, there are a number of enzymes capable of repairing damage to DNA. Some of these enzymes are specific for a particular type of damage, whereas others can handle a range of mutation types."[19]

These three points can be examined in fruit fly experiments that have been conducted for nearly one hundred years. Though fruit flies have been exposed to radiation that causes mutations in their features like deformed wings and body parts, the fruit flies have always remained fruit flies. Norman Macbeth, who wrote about the geneticist Richard Goldschmidt and his classic fruit fly experiments, expressed that "after observing mutations in fruit flies for many years, Goldschmidt fell into despair. The changes, he lamented, were so hopelessly micro that if a thousand mutations were combined in one specimen, there would still be no new species."[20]

How can we buy the idea that a process like mutation, which is usually destructive to functioning systems (as demonstrated by the fruit fly experiments) could simultaneously construct them? By asking (and answering) the following questions, one can observe the difficult logic of believing that beneficial mutations could be the source for the increasing complexity of life in the midst of more overwhelming negative mutations: If a seamstress sewed thousands of pieces of ill-fitting clothes, would you hire her? Would the president hire her to make his clothes, believing she had the skill to make the most beautiful and functional suit in the competitive world of image? If your grandson made hundreds of wrong turns for every correct turn, would you believe he could get you to the airport on time? If your heart surgeon used hundreds of incorrect instruments for every correct instrument, would you believe that he could repair your heart? Would you give him the chance to try?

These questions show the illogic of assumptions that Darwinists hold. In the end, we have to recognize that believers in mutation, as the building material for life's astonishing complexity, have an established faith or an entrenched bias. Of course, such a statement makes scientists mad because they believe there is ample proof of selective processes in nature. And there is.

No one disputes the fact that certain physical variations that proved advantageous to an organism, or population of them, were inherited by succeeding generations. What is disputed, however, is that natural selection could so alter populations so as to create fundamentally different organisms, one from the other, species from species, amphibians from fish, birds from reptiles.

Natural selection is a real process and works well for explaining limited kinds of variations, like small-scale changes. But natural selection fails to explain the complexity of an organism. A minor change in the structure of an animal, like the beak or the feathers of a bird, for example, is an entirely different scale of phenomenon than the origin of that bird.

The next time I went to visit Swamiji, David, the fish salesman, was home preparing lunch for some Indian people who were soon to arrive. He was making proclamations about the spiritual blessings due to come to everyone. But I didn't like his comments. I had the feeling that David provided the swami with food and a room since he wanted a nicer car and a higher-paying job. He always seemed more concerned about his advancement in the outer world, not the inner one.

I didn't trust David's motives with Swamiji, or me either, for that matter. But at that time in my life, I disdained businessmen and their desire to be wealthy. I disliked everything they represented because I believed their attitude was part of what had made the world ugly. David told me to go find Swamiji in his room because I refused to banter with him.

"Good day, young seeker!" Swamiji smiled at me and was much friendlier because David was at home.

"How are you today, Swamiji?" I asked enthusiastically. I was relieved to find him open and expressive.

"As you see me!" he replied. He handed me a key ring crowded with keys.

It was a strange greeting.

He pointed to an old blue suitcase on his floor and asked me if I could find the key and open it.

The task seemed easy enough. I got down on my knees and studied the lock. I imagined Swamiji was watching me, but I didn't turn around to see. The curtains were open and sunshine poured in through the windows.

I looked carefully at all the keys to become familiar with their shapes and sizes. I didn't want to get caught trying to force a key that didn't fit the lock. It would be a metaphor for trying to force some spiritual belief that had no basis in reality.

I wondered if Swamjii was testing me in some special way. If I spent too much time trying to assess whether a key would fit the lock when it obviously wouldn't, then he would think me slow and unintelligent in discerning simple things. But if I didn't take enough time to check the keys in the locks, he might think me unfocused or impatient.

After going through all the keys twice, I found that none of them fit.

"None of the keys are the right size for your lock, Swamiji." I gave them back with certainty. I was about to ask him what was in the suitcase, but David called us to lunch. Nothing more was ever said about the mysterious missing key.

In the living room, David had set up a long table and at the end was Swamiji's place. Though two Indian couples came to share the meal, nobody ate what he did. His meal consisted of fruits, vegetables, and nuts. Arranged in little bowls around him were grapes, oranges, banana, papaya, kohlrabi cooked Indian-style, a baked potato, and some almonds. He used salt, but no butter.

During lunch, I sat on his left and felt privileged to be so near to him. I suppose nobody dared to get too close, but I didn't feel intimidated. There were multiple conversations going on at the table, so I took the opportunity to ask Swamiji what he modeled a good diet after, and how he felt food affected our ability to cultivate spiritual qualities.

He explained that he followed the Ayurvedic way of eating, which had been practiced for more than two thousand years in India. I noticed that he chewed only on the left side of his mouth as he popped the grapes over to that side with his fingers. He used a knife to cut his fruit and vegetables, but then ate them with his fingers.

He told me that "Ayurveda" roughly translates as the knowledge of life and healthy living, and that what you eat has an enormous influence on the quality of your mind. Therefore, it effects your ability to cultivate qualities like clarity, vivacity, and serenity, which give rise to more specific expressions of kindness, love, and self-control.

"What do you think a peaceful mind can do?" He grinned with his eyes.

"Well, lots of things," I stalled. "Maybe the most important aspect of having a peaceful mind is to understand the right relationship between knowledge and action."

"Don't be so mental," he rebuked me. "A peaceful mind is in control of a fit body. And a fit body comes from eating proper food in the proper way. It's very simple."

I knew what he meant about the importance of eating the right kind of food. My mother had always stressed that when I was growing up, and I respected her so much for her attention to the right way of eating. When we were not traveling, we usually grew vegetables and I loved to help her in the garden. She would relate how at work she'd bite into a big bell pepper for lunch like it was an apple, and everyone who saw her eat that way would shudder. She did the same thing with tomatoes and cucumbers too.

She taught my sisters and me to eat sensibly, with the result that we were fit to climb mountains and canoe rivers. So I knew what Swamiji meant by the importance of eating well. But he had much more to teach me about how food affected the mind and the ability to cultivate spiritual qualities.

"Have you heard of the *gunas*?" He dipped a piece of his banana into a little dish of salt.

"Sounds like the gunas wouldn't taste too good," I joked, imagining how awful his banana tasted.

"No, it has no taste at all because it isn't something to eat. The Western world doesn't know about the three gunas, and that is where their science of nutrition fails and why there are so many overweight people in the Western countries, besides there being too much food."

He explained that in nature, there are three qualities that express the range of the energetic vibration of matter, sometimes also called phases or modes of matter. The three gunas have Sanskrit names: called *sattva-guna, rajo-guna,* and *tamo-guna.* He described them in the following way.

Sattva-guna describes the quality of vitality in all its aspects, which manifests in an energetic body and understanding mind. This guna describes what is pure, clean, and happy.

Rajo-guna describes the quality of action which is experienced as craving, attachment, and willfulness. Of course, we need action and intensity to live in the world, in contrast to sitting in meditation in the mountains, but too much rajo-guna will make us restless. If we are restless, then we won't be able to cultivate spiritual qualities because we won't be able to exercise self-control with an unfocused mind and uncooperative body.

Tamo-guna describes the quality of lethargy and darkness, which is experienced as depression and dullness. This quality is dangerous to our spiritual lives as it creates the tendency in us to be stubborn and heavy in our thinking, feeling, and will to act. Tamo-guna creates serious obstacles to our spiritual growth.

Swamiji then told me how food is related to these gunas. I was fascinated and listened carefully, completely ignoring the other conversations around us. Sattvic foods contribute to vitality because they give the body energy without taxing it. And a vital body is the foundation for higher states of consciousness because it is the basis for spiritual growth and clarity. He emphasized that plants that grow above ground and that are eaten fresh and ripe are the most sattvic foods. This includes most fruits and vegetables. Included as sattvic foods are whole grains and fresh butter. I didn't know how butter could be sattvic when it is made from milk (not ripened in the sunshine), but I didn't ask him to explain.

He continued to say that rajasic food stimulates passion and activity and can make the body uncontrollable. Dry and hot foods, like chips and chilies, are good examples of rajasic foods as well as sour, bitter, and overly salty ones. Though he suggested that it would be good to avoid them, he strongly recommended avoiding all tamasic foods. They included old food, like canned and frozen food, and pickled or fermented things like wine and liquor of all types. Tamasic foods also included caffeine, chocolate, meats (including fish), and eggs. He highlighted that tamasic foods require lots of energy to digest, and so they have the tendency to exhaust the person who eats them. The result is that people who eat these foods feel heavy and sluggish. This causes them to gain weight because they don't want to move.

The two Indian couples who came to lunch had brought some curries, but they were too spicy for my taste. So I ate *chapati*, which is flat bread made only of wheat and water, and a dish of yogurt called *dahin*, with cucumber gratings and cardamom. In a deep platter was *sag*, prepared from "curd." I gathered curd was made from milk curdled by lemon juice where the whey was thrown out and the curd gathered in a ball until it became firm, somewhat like hard cream cheese. Then it was fried in dried cumin, coriander, and turmeric, and cooked with mustard greens.

I asked Swamiji why he didn't eat those dishes since they weren't tamasic, but he said they all had onions.

"Are you allergic to onions?" I asked him.

"Yes, but not in the way you think," he said.

"Is it because they aren't sattvic, and grow underground?" I queried, but I noticed he was eating potato which also grows in the dark.

A woman named Preeti heard what I asked and giggled. She ribbed her husband, who also was amused.

Preeti's bracelets jangled as she helped herself to more

curry, and she explained that swamis don't eat garlic or onions or leeks because they make their blood warm.

"But wouldn't you want warm blood in the Himalayas?" It made sense to me.

"No," she giggled again. "Not if you want to remain living like a monk."

"Oh," I said, not getting her point. Everyone laughed, including David. Later, Preeti told me that onions and garlic are considered to be aphrodisiacs and are avoided by those who practice celibacy.

The Swami began to tell us his story of how when he was eighteen years old, his father wanted him to marry. The custom in India in those days was to arrange marriages. So a beautiful girl from a wealthy family was selected for him. But he didn't want to get married, and so he ran away when the girl and her family came to meet him. Then, a couple of years later, his father again tried to arrange another girl without him knowing. Somehow he caught wind of it and disappeared. After that his father never tried to marry him.

Swamiji said he knew when he was young that he never wanted to marry because he wanted to devote his life to spiritual pursuits without having to provide for a family. So after he lived with Gandhi, he took to the life of a *brahmachari* and wore only yellow, which symbolizes growing knowledge. Also, according to Indian tradition, one who wears yellow signals to others that he doesn't want to marry.

But even when Swamiji studied with a spiritual teacher, he said that he still wore yellow for a few decades. He had to wait until his teacher told him that he had burnt his impurities in the fire of knowledge and was entitled to wear orange. Then he was elevated to a full-fledged swami and was given a new name, Swami Divyananda Saraswati. Roughly translated, it means "one who loves divine knowledge."

At first I thought it was strange that Swamiji only wore orange, the customary color of a swami, as he wasn't dogmatic or ritualistic in any tiring way. He always showed a flexible willingness to meet people and talk at their level wherever he met them. He was generally kind and playful with those who asked him questions. He easily rose above cultural differences, and was not biased racially or in any other way.

The only barrier that posed a problem for him was his Indian accent, which sometimes people couldn't understand at first. And sometimes Swamiji had a hard time learning English names that he had never heard before. Once he saw the name written down, he usually could remember how it was pronounced.

After the third talk of his that I attended, I watched nearby as a man named Greg went to meet Swamiji and shake his hand. I hadn't met Greg before, but I never forgot his name because Swamiji just couldn't get it right and Greg had to repeat it many times. Greg was not a name he had heard, and somehow he kept hearing "Grace."

"Grace?" he would ask.

And Greg would say, "No, it's Greg."

"You mean 'Grace'?" Swamiji asked again. The back and forth went on for a while until Greg gave up trying. But he was smiling and pleased that Swamiji insisted on calling him Grace. He must have liked the spiritual connotation and took it as a compliment. I wondered if Swamiji was playfully teasing Greg because it seemed so odd that he couldn't get his name straight after so much repetition. He wasn't hard of hearing, and spoke English very well.

Swamiji sometimes seemed like a child in the high-tech world of the West. He loved to ask questions about cars, trains, and David's color TV, something that he had never seen in India. But he called TV "the TB of the soul" and always made jokes about it. He also told us how when he first arrived in Vancouver, he saw people jogging along the streets, a sight he had never seen before. He laughed and said he thought they were running from the law. It was strange to him that people would run in a public place, as it was never done in India. Running was not considered dignified, especially as a form of exercise.

Swamiji was flexible and he adapted well to Western ways, at least the ones that didn't negatively affect his spiritual habits. He was resourceful in dealing with difficulties even though he was so old. He had told me that when the trekkers who found him in the Himalayas sent him a plane ticket to come to Canada, he found out that they didn't have good motives. They really weren't interested in learning spiritual truths or helping him to teach others. Instead they wanted to train him like an exotic circus animal and make money from the performance. They charged for admission to his public talks though Swamiji had made it clear that there should be no charge for sharing spiritual knowledge. He always accepted when people made a voluntary contribution for his food expenses since he had no source of income of his own. But he never asked for money.

He said the trekkers made him a prisoner and kept him locked in their basement except on the days he gave talks. They gave him little food and only one smelly blanket covered with cat hair to keep him warm though they knew cleanliness was so important to him. But one day, after a couple of months, they took him to a bookstore where he was scheduled to give a talk about Mahatma Gandhi. An Indian man in the audience came to meet him and they spoke in the Hindi language. Swamiji was able to explain his situation, and the two planned an escape for him. The man arranged for him to speak at a Hindu community center some days later, and after the talk an Indian family would tell the trekkers they were going to take him home. When the day came, there was nothing the trekkers could do to contain him, so he was finally freed. He told me nonchalantly that his difficulties were just a test for him to turn a stumbling block into a stepping stone.

Swamiji seemed so resilient at his age. He was also playful. David had a huge fat cat that would run and hide under Swamiji's bed when he saw him coming to his room. And Swamiji would call out loudly, "You little red monkey, get back here right now!" He could easily bend down on his knees and lift up the bedspread carefully and look for the cat, who would be waiting to swat him.

I watched when Swamiji would swat the cat back in his own special way. He'd fill up his lungs and his cheeks like he was playing the tuba and exhale with a huge "whoosh" right at the cat, which would take off terrified. But it was just an act, as the cat would be back for more and Swamiji would laugh until he cried. I enjoyed his antics with the cat, and it made me feel that he was a basically normal person in spite of his many disciplined ways.

He was also shrewd, like a poker game in a candy store. Though he was adored by many people who found him irresistibly sweet, he was also tough and cunningly perceptive. He knew when people tried to bluff him with seductive talk about spiritual things, and he always seemed to see through them. He could play a mean deck of cards and honestly win all your aces.

When word got around that a swami was staying in the West End, which was a wealthy neighborhood in Vancouver, Indians would come and try to cajole him into giving them miraculous blessings that they believed, for some strange reason, Swamiji would provide for them. But these were the greedy superstitious kind of people who came from India with lots of money, seeking even more.

Sometimes they wanted other kinds of blessings besides money. One day, when I happened to be visiting Swamiji along with a few others, a rich banker came to see him to request that Swamiji make his daughter two inches taller so she would be able to find a good husband. Another time, a Sikh woman brought her young balding son, who was only in his late teens, to ask Swamji if he would restore the young man's hair so that he would be more attractive and find a suitable wife. I was disgusted with what they requested, but Swamiji just made light of the situation. He simply told them that if they wanted magic, they should go to a magician. They looked at him in disbelief, like kids going away without their candy. I appreciated that he wasn't out to please people, and could easily say what needed to be said. He didn't cater to anyone.

About three months after I met him, Swamiji had to make arrangements to leave Canada for the United States because his visa would soon expire. He decided to head for Seattle. Since I had completed my graduate degree in philosophy, I asked him if I could travel with him for a while. I was intrigued by the idea of the many interesting people I could meet and what they knew about God. But Swamiji tried to dissuade me every time I asked him.

His first concern was that people might not trust him if he traveled with a woman, as his reputation was established as a monk. But I pointed out that Gandhi was well respected and he traveled with a young white woman to help him in various ways. His second concern was that I wouldn't be able to handle his constantly-shifting environment and the unknown rigors of travel. But I assured him I could, as I had traveled all my life. "I have slept on rocks in the desert," I earnestly told him. I begged him to let me go with him because I knew it was the best way for me to find out the real meaning of religion.

He finally agreed, but I had to make two promises. First, I would be required to follow a special diet much like his, though I could eat brown rice, beans, and milk. But I couldn't eat sugar, caffeine, wine, meat, eggs, onions, or garlic. Second, I would have to devote myself to spiritual practices, which meant I was to live a renunciate life and I would never go out socializing or be alone with men. He also made it clear that I shouldn't expect to be paid for my services.

O God, you are my God, I keep looking for you. My soul does thirst for you. For you my flesh has grown faint [with longing] in a land dry and exhausted, where there is no water.

Bible Book of Psalms 63:1

CHAPTER SEVEN

Dying of Thirst

I opened my eyes. I was stony cold with aching hips as I rolled over on my bed, a thin foam pad on the hardwood floor. Above me the shapes of oleander flowers pressed pink and white against my window. They were like the promise of truth that I could always perceive but not fully understand.

I was a renunciate in yellow, misery in a buttercup, seeking virtue in pain, love in denial, and meaning in contradiction. But I had aspired to live by an unshakable faith that one day I would find the true God.

I pulled up my blanket and whispered to myself, "Breathe deep, Sita, breathe deep. Go to sleeeeep." With my hand like a loving mother, I gently stroked my own head.

There was an animal, maybe a raccoon or an opossum, scratching out a nest beneath the floorboards. We were probably almost ear to ear, just a few inches between us.

Tonight my bed is a cave, I thought as I reflected on the various places I had slept in the past six years: in "regular beds" and in bedrooms in mansions, in kids' bedrooms (once in a bed frame shaped like a car), in laundry rooms, storage rooms, living rooms, behind couches, and on trains, planes, and at airports. But wherever I tried to sleep like a nomad, there was one thing that didn't change. I always had to be pleasant in the morning regardless of how well I had slept.

From San Diego, California, to Delhi, India, from the mountain towns of British Columbia to the deserts of Arizona, and from the tropics of Panama to the foothills of the Himalayas, there were cockroaches to fling off my face, bedbugs to squish, and black-faced monkeys to curse at as they peed on the thin metal roof of the Indian jungle hut, their urine sounding like rain falling from the trees and then, "thud," the sound of thunder as they jumped down and the roof buckled.

And the hairy spiders, with legs longer than my fingers, to search out with my flashlight as I, horrified, wondered where they moved from their usual motionless places. And the big black scorpion beneath my cot that would come out from under the wall that I'd try to catch with the fire tongs. And some kind of squirrel that chewed its way though the roof during the monsoon rains in spite of the rocks I wedged through the opening.

And in cities everywhere, the sounds of people like chaotic unwanted debris blowing into me and my exhausted brain hearing it all like chains dragging across metal, my nerves shredded and scattered, and then suddenly being awakened when it seemed I had barely gone to sleep though it was already morning.

In the San Francisco Bay Area, a disgruntled woman woke me up by vacuuming vigorously near my head where my bed was made of a few blankets in the corner of her living room. It was her way of announcing to me that her wishes for enlightenment, miraculous wealth, or whatever it was she wanted from Swamiji were not being granted in the way she expected.

Sometimes there were vibrating pipes, stinking drains, and wet trash smelling like rusty metal coming in through windows above dirty alleys in New York City where we stayed with poor Sikh and Hindu cab drivers. But they were often the most generous people in spite of their slum-like living quarters. And we weren't the only ones they fed. There were mice running in and out of the kitchen all night long with squealing and squeaking. And on the other side of the wall, the washing machines whooshed and whoomed before the sunrise.

Mansions were not that much better than slums. I felt claustrophobic and sucked dry in them. In state after state, especially Ohio, Rhode Island, Connecticut, Florida, New Jersey, and California, we were invited to stay with doctors, lawyers, and other rich folk. Their homes featured plastic flowers, locked windows, forced air, and dead hallways to lug our heavy suitcases down. They were like tombs above ground.

The rich Indian women often gave me grief. They had an enormous list of "do's and don'ts," and when I cooked Swamiji's food in their glowing granite kitchens I had to be exceedingly careful to use the right pans for cooking. I had to dry things with the "proper" towel, though some said that towels harbored germs so in that case I had to wait for the dishes to dry by themselves before I could put them away. And by then, sometimes I forgot where they went and had to muster the courage to ask again.

Besides the exhausting aspects of staying with the rich and the poor, I also experienced unique and noisy family members. Where we stayed in Panama with the ex-vice president and his family, their dogs barked for hours early in the morning and then the parrots joined them screeching when the sun rose. But Swamiji and I usually worked until 3:30 a.m. Late at night was the best time for writing letters because everyone had gone to bed and the phone never rang and we could work without interruptions.

Sometimes a crowd would start knocking at the front door like some impetuous flock of starlings, raucous and greedy to strip the morning of its silence, and me of all I could offer, while they waited for Swamiji to emerge from his room and talk to them. And often it would be a long wait while he showered and combed his long hair and people plied me with questions: "What's it like traveling with a swami? Are you enlightened yet?" And the Indians from India would often ask me: "Have you seen God?" It was such an irritating question. I was polite when I answered, but I often wanted to say: "No, you fool, God is a spirit, not any form that we can recognize."

Whenever I complained about not getting enough sleep, Swamiji always repeated that our changing environments didn't have to be a source of exhaustion to me. He said that I just had to learn the right mental attitude, which involved a willful detachment of my mind from any annoying objects of sense perception. Although he seemed to have succeeded in cultivating the habit, as he could fall asleep in the dentist chair when he was having a root canal, I constantly seemed to fail.

The scratching of the animal beneath me was a good example. The sound was just too loud to ignore. Maybe if I was up on a bed instead of the floor it wouldn't be so irritating. This was the struggle I often had with myself. One part of me justified why I couldn't succeed in overcoming whatever it was that kept me awake while the other part felt I just had to try harder.

"Yeah sure, what a stupid way to torture myself," I complained out loud, realizing the futility of my circumstances. For I was chronically tired and losing my will to keep trying to succeed at what seemed more and more impossible. There had to be an easier way.

"Be quiet, you creature!" I hit the floor with my heel a few times, though it didn't make a difference. I consoled myself knowing that at least the animal's efforts would serve some meaningful purpose, unlike my own efforts that seemed to scratch meaning from exhaustion and hope from what seemed hopeless.

I looked up at the dark outline of my ceiling. I thought, my life is like a Chinese box, holding many more boxes within it, like many mysteries, and the smallest and most hidden paradoxically the most evident. In it was my heartbeat like a bell clanging, like some Zen koan I couldn't solve and that made me panic. It had been pounding painfully for months, which seemed like years, and was especially loud when I was trying to sleep.

I wanted to open all the boxes and understand the order of them and how I had put them together and what it was that had gone wrong. But my mind was almost useless. I rolled over on my pad, positioned my hip on a rolled up sock for support, and shivered.

I had decided to take the unusual opportunity to travel with Swamiji because I wanted to be thoroughly exposed to the religious traditions of the world and also the various philosophies and psychologies of religion. I reasoned that staying with people of different religious backgrounds would give me the inside story about the real nature of religious experience besides what books could tell. Being a guest in strangers' homes would give me the perfect vantage point from which to observe people. It would be like a constant safari to see them in the tangled brush of their beliefs, which in some ways were more dangerous than lions.

I had seen the anger and ugliness in people, whether it was

professors, politicians, or preachers, when it came to defending their beliefs. History made it clear that war was the extreme manifest expression of the ego that would assert itself in spite of tragic consequences. In the extreme case of war, life to the ego meant that whatever didn't support it should be killed.

Amazingly, even well-traveled and educated people upheld the belief that they should support war (including the murder of innocent people), through the political ego that they chose to represent them. And regardless if these educated people were Democrats or Republicans, they were still the flip sides of the same coin, of the ideology that they were justified to support one ego over another. They couldn't see that human egos can never solve human problems except in the most patchwork kind of way that usually involves loss of life and detriment to the environment.

So when it came to me being in the intimate association of religious people in the private domain of their own homes, I knew I had to be exceedingly careful. Most believers, regardless of their brand of belief, supported war so I knew they would fight me to a finish if I confronted their ego in a way they didn't like on their own turf. I expressed a sort of professional politeness around most of our hosts as a way to protect myself. I was not convinced that all religions, like all religious people, had good intentions. I could see that most people were not logical and couldn't or wouldn't reason, especially on spiritual subjects.

Unlike me, Swamiji was surprisingly tolerant of the fact that different religions all claimed to know the truth about God. This conundrum of logic didn't seem to trouble him like it troubled me. Though he was set in his ways when it came to his diet, his lifestyle as a monk, and his belief in a Creator, he didn't mind what people called the Divine. In fact, the diverse cultural expressions about the nature of God simply confirmed to him that the primary human instinct (above wanting to have children) is the basic desire to worship an Absolute. For this reason, he considered the religious urge to be the defining characteristic of a person in contrast to an animal.

His respect for different religious traditions was reflected in a Sanskrit phrase from the Rigveda of ancient Hindu origin, that he often repeated and which sounded like *"Ekam sat vipra bahudha vadanti."*[1] When translated into English, it basically means that there is one Truth, or one God, that can be described in various ways by different names. The main principle that this phrase expressed is that the primary Truth, from which all life originates, cannot be adulterated by language in spite of the connotations of different designations.

This idea is the premise of the interfaith outlook which Swamiji upheld. He considered the one Truth, as expressed through different faiths, to be the indisputable recognition that God exists as the Creator of the physical world and laws of life. His main concern, then, was with the acknowledgement of the reality of God regardless of how a person approached or defined the Divine according to culture.

Not surprisingly, besides quoting from ancient Eastern spiritual sources like the Vedas, he also quoted from Western ones. As he had attended a Christian boarding school for many years, he claimed to be familiar with the Bible. So when we were in the Western world, he carried a pocket copy of the Bible to share with whoever would listen.

He liked to quote a scripture that pointed out that people who do not want to perceive the truth of God's existence are inexcusable. Why inexcusable? Because God is easily perceived through his creation. Swamiji's King James version of the scripture pointed out: "For the invisible things of him from the creation of the world are clearly seen, being understood by the things that are made, even his eternal power and Godhead; so that they are without excuse."[2]

Based on this scripture, Swamiji believed that the recognition of the existence of God is an immediate intuition and as much a part of our awareness as our need for oxygen. In other words, every person has this knowledge of God because the "invisible" qualities of God can be clearly perceived by us since we are made by God to perceive them. Simply stated, the intelligent design of life is known by us because our basic human intelligence reflects a supreme intelligence. So, as the scripture qualifies, those individuals who do not desire to acknowledge the existence of God though the creation are, for this reason, inexcusable.

Swamiji taught that people become "inexcusable" when they choose to turn away from knowing God because they'd rather worship their own minds and create gods in their own image; like gods of money, fame, or political ideals. He often read a scripture that explained: "Because, although they knew God, they did not glorify him as God nor did they thank him, but they became empty-headed in their reasonings and their unintelligent heart became darkened. Although asserting they were wise, they became foolish."[3]

I understood the meaning of these scriptures when he shared them with me. They helped me account for my own intuitive awareness of the truth of God's existence. Since I was raised in an atheist environment and had no indoctrination about God through any religion, I couldn't account for why I had such a strong spiritual awareness. But one thing I knew for sure. I couldn't chalk it up to genetics. No one in my family line, that I knew about anyway, was a seeker. Some of my relatives, whom I had never known except by name, were religious fanatics of a Christian sort, but I never considered fanatics to be seekers. To me they were spiritually asleep because they couldn't think for themselves or study religion on their own.

Though I tried to hide my spiritual need from my family because I knew it would be an embarrassment to them, except perhaps for my younger sister, I couldn't deny this need. That is why I had to search for answers in places and on paths where none of my family cared or dared to go. Of course, and not surprisingly, the belief that we should easily perceive at least the power and intelligence of God through creation, if not God's true name and other attributes, made most scientists mad, at least the ones I knew. They thought it a lousy argument that we could assure ourselves of God's existence just because we could see design in nature.

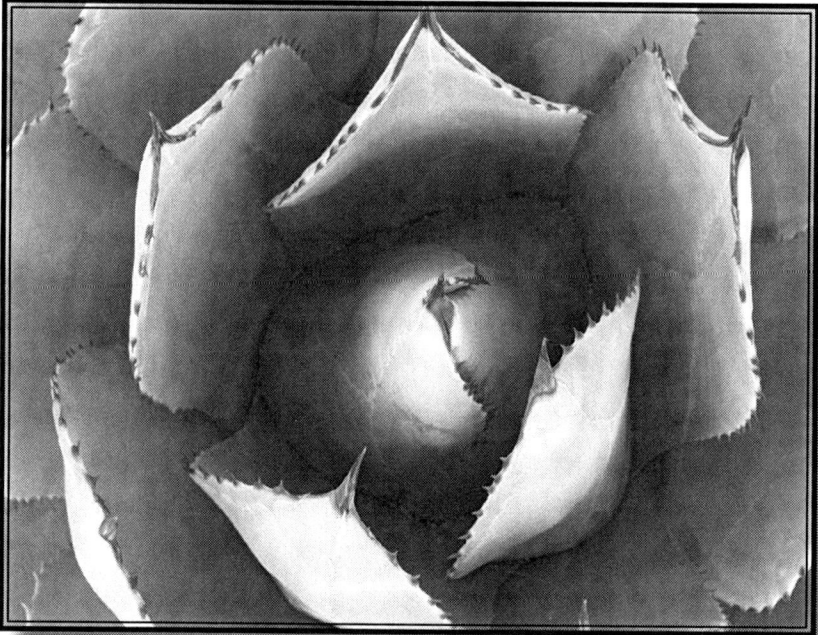

But it was easy for them to deny the existence of God based on intuition, which they must have equated with emotion. For they said they relied on reason, the same as scientific authority (the atheistic kind) that denied that reason could see beauty and order of a staggering degree as the product of intelligent design.

I liked a quote that I heard was attributed to Leonardo da Vinci which said: "Anyone who conducts an argument by appealing to authority is not using his intelligence; he is just using his memory."[4] These words became a motto for me.

Ironically, though my parents agreed to believe that chance is a more powerful creative force than the intelligence of a Creator for bringing about change in an organized way, they left nothing to chance in their personal lives. They were expert designers of what they would allow themselves to feel, know, and experience. They never let chance work its life-altering miracles on them because they believed it worked too slowly for them to be benefited by it in their own lives. Still, I couldn't accept the contradiction that chance alone could create a human being who consciously planned not to leave anything to chance when it came to the details of living life.

When I was studying philosophy at Memorial University in Newfoundland, I studied the word "God" to try to find out what it was about the word that scientists disliked so much. I asked my professor of ancient Greek philosophy to explain what the word "God" meant to the Greeks. The word "God," as he explained, though derived from the Greek *theos,* was never found in any of the ancient Hebrew manuscripts. Instead, God's name, called "YHWH" OR "JHWH," was used as preserved in the Hebrew Masoretic text where it appears almost seven thousand times.

Even from an academic point of view, my professor wanted to show me that the meaning of *theos* expressed what was essentially profound, magnificently awesome, and too far beyond the mind to comprehend in its entirety. He said that *theos* is derived from a deep exclamation and is more expressive of a feeling of awe than a mental conception of what is infinite.

"Now watch carefully," he smiled with his baby blue eyes. "I will demonstrate to you the meaning of the word."

He breathed deep down into his belly. "*Theos!*" he boomed.

"I get it!" I laughed, wiping the saliva off my face that had flown out on his utterance.

"Yes," he said, pleased with himself. He was a theatrical person. "The Greeks wanted to convey that the awareness of *theos* is deeper than knowledge. It is something immensely reverent that awakens the heart."

"I wholly share the sentiment," I agreed, wondering how I could find out the truth about God.

"Of course," he added, "people who have the intuition of *theos* as the Originator of life may still not know how best to conceptualize God for themselves in terms of a real identifying name, anthropomorphic images, or other attributes of religion."

That was exactly where I was when I first met Swamiji. I didn't know what concept of God pointed to an accurate knowledge of that reality, but I still believed I could find out. But the first step, as I thought back then, was to open my mind and heart and learn how to overcome my own ego as an obstacle to discovering what is actually real and not imagined. That way, too, I thought I could avoid being misled by others who claimed to know what was true, but who didn't actually know.

I was attracted to learning the Eastern ideas about how we can use our faculties of thinking and feeling to observe the motives that drive our actions. For the East seemed so much more sophisticated than the West in its articulation of the process of acquiring self-knowledge and how to dissolve the ego. Whereas the East taught one how to observe one's ego through self-awareness in an attempt to overcome its limitations, the West seemed to encourage people to identify with what their ego wanted.

I believed this happened in the Western world because science had established our sense of self as a measuring stick, as an objective instrument in relationship to other objects of our sense perception. And since science only focused on the physical aspects of our life, it taught us to be outwardly oriented. Our frame of reference was trained to project out onto the world instead of inwardly, as self-introspection.

As a result, the emotional and spiritual aspects of ourselves were subordinated to our mental capacities and physical interests. Spiritual matters and questions about the validity of religious experience could be easily ignored as inconsequential because technological advancement and manufactured output became the focus.

So, naturally, more and more scientists became atheists, and they deemed religion to be an outdated relic of a former stage in human evolution.

Though I was spoon-fed on science and the ideology that only the physical aspects of life were real, and basically all that mattered, I still had a spiritual need. I longed to know myself beyond the limits of science because I didn't trust scientists. They didn't seem to know themselves. They compartmentalized their consciousness and shut down their spiritual perceptions. As a result, they were too afraid of what they didn't know, so they simply denied, or ignored, what they couldn't explain.

Though I understood the value and utility of scientific advancements to society, and that they were intended to improve physical life and dispel superstition, I grieved the barriers they created to our knowing ourselves and also the natural world. I blamed our technological dependency on complacency.

I especially was unhappy with scientists who believed that scientific methodology was all that we needed to be wise. To me, they wouldn't or couldn't admit that a spiritual methodology could teach us what science didn't know, and wasn't equipped to understand. As seekers of knowledge, most scientists appeared to me to be missing something vital, something admittedly human, something relating to an awareness of themselves and their experiential presence in spite of their knowledge and practice of observation. I came to believe that most of them cared more about their own discoveries than anything else.

Though I studied the conceptual foundations of the scientific method for years and made it the special focus of my university studies, I felt unfulfilled. I knew I had to search for a new method for acquiring knowledge, one that could answer questions that were beyond the methods of scientists who had failed to admit they needed answering.

So I sought for a spiritual methodology that was more comprehensive, a methodology that could understand science in relation to metaphysical questions and realities. But I didn't want to adopt a spiritual method that corresponded to the narrow-minded people of most religions. I disliked religious dogma even more than its scientific counterpart.

When I met Swamiji, he intrigued me because he didn't fear emotion though he had a graduate degree in physics and was good at math. But, above all, he considered himself a spiritual man who had a spiritual explanation about life, its origins, and our human purpose and goals, though he still valued science and its discoveries.

He appeared to be unusually balanced. He was also disciplined. He took care of his body and paid attention to what and how he ate and drank. He also exercised by walking. He was physically strong for his age and seemed at least twenty years younger than he actually was.

One day I arranged to take him to the chiropractor because he had a pain in his shoulder that wouldn't go away. When the chiropractor asked if he could bend over, Swamiji replied, "You mean like this?" He stretched his legs out straight on the exam table and then leaned forward until his chest was resting flat on his knees.

"How old are you again?" asked the chiropractor, simply stunned.

When Swamiji replied that he was eighty-five years old, the chiropractor said he'd never seen such a flexible person over the age of fifty.

On another occasion, Swamiji was at a high school auditorium and, during the question and answer session after his talk, a student named Mark asked him if he practiced yoga. Swamiji replied that he had practiced yoga for many years, but that yoga involved much more than most people thought.

"Yoga is not just physical," Swamiji said. "It also involves cultivating healthy mental and emotional habits."

But Mark wasn't interested in any discussion. "Can you twist yourself up like a pretzel?" he laughed nervously.

"Oh my lord," Swamiji answered him playfully. "I will if you will."

"Okay," said Mark.

"Shall we try an elementary sitting posture?"

"Sure." Mark seemed pleased with the attention.

Swamiji pointed down at his own legs. "First, you take your right leg and cross it over your left, putting your right heel on the top of your left thigh. You see how this is done?" Swamiji made it look so easy.

"Yeah, I think I get it."

"Then, you cross your left leg and put it over the top of your right leg like this. Be sure to put your heel on the very top of your right thigh up where it connects to your hip. Can you do it?"

"Oh man, that's hard," Mark moaned. "I can't get my legs to bend like that."

The hundreds of kids watching Mark and Swamiji were impressed that a man who was about seventy years older than Mark was so much more flexible than he was.

After the kids clapped for Swamiji, he made a joke that kids in the Western world sat too much in front of the television and that was why they became so stiff. He said they shouldn't always try to be entertained by others, but instead learn to entertain themselves.

Once, Swamiji and I had to take a city bus when we were in Chicago. He easily climbed up onto the bus and sat down in the only empty seat up front reserved for the elderly. I stood nearby, amused at how everyone stared at him. He looked so exotic in his orange clothes with his long black hair and long grey beard. He explained to a teenage boy who inquired about his hair and beard that in India, swamis either shave off their beard and hair every few days or let it grow long and never cut it. He added that he chose to let his hair grow long because he lived where it was cold and it helped keep him warm.

Then the bus stopped to pick up a heavy older woman with stooped shoulders and white hair. She struggled up the steps one by one and paused to rest at the top. Seeing Swamiji sitting right in front of her made her mad. She snapped at him, saying that he shouldn't be sitting in the seats reserved for the elderly like her.

"Yes, ma'am," Swamiji smiled widely and stood up and helped her to sit down. He grasped the overhead bar beside me. I decided to ask the woman how old she thought Swamji was, and she said about sixty. I told her he was eighty-five years old and that he was entitled to sit where he had. She gasped, saying she was ten years younger than he was, but looked so much older than him.

I thought Swamiji's spiritual methodology must be exceptionally balanced between his inner and outer disciplines because his body was in such good shape, his mind was so clear, and he worked exceedingly hard for his age while keeping a good sense of humor. So I asked him about yoga. He said it was a method designed to discipline the mind, heart, and body so that one could be effective in whatever one wanted to accomplish. Swamiji defined yoga as the means to cultivate self-awareness through one's personal effort. Though the word "yoga" comes from the root word *yuj* which means to yoke, or unite, most people translate this to mean yoked with God or united with God. But Swamiji didn't mention God in his definition.

He said that yoga is primarily a method to unite "our self with our self" in the sense that our mind and emotions and our will to act are yoked together for a common purpose. I had never heard yoga explained like this before.

He mentioned that he first practiced yoga when he attended a Christian boarding school as a boy. He said they emphasized over and over that he should love God with his whole heart, his whole mind, and his whole strength. He said he took their counsel very seriously and stayed up late at night trying to figure out how he could learn to love God with his mind, heart, and strength all at the same time. Gradually, he understood that it meant to unite his faculties of thinking, feeling, and doing.

He realized as he grew up that the disciplines of yoga were meant to bring us an integrated outlook where we could be united in our different faculties even though they are defined in different ways as aspects and capabilities of human nature. His point was to indicate to me that these three aspects are usually never integrated in most people. For example, some people are overdeveloped in their minds and underdeveloped in their emotions, and vice versa, just like some people have more inertia than others when it comes to getting things done.

I thought it brilliant that Swamiji's spiritual methodology for gaining knowledge about ourselves included the self-awareness and self-study that academics usually ignored in their discussions of meaning and how to acquire understanding. He made it clear to me that if I was weak in one aspect of myself, another aspect would become out of balance. He said that if we don't really know what motivates our action, then we are governed by ego. If we don't understand what motivates our thinking, then we are governed by ego. If we don't understand what motivates our feelings, then we are governed by ego. So, then, yoga as a spiritual method sought first to dispel the ego from our minds and hearts and actions so that our consciousness would be able to perceive the truth about God and our relationship with him.

Swamiji practiced Raja yoga, a form of yoga that has eight progressive steps. The first two steps he called "the do's and the don'ts." He stressed that they were the foundation of a meaningful spiritual life because they taught us self-control. Interestingly, the first step is actually the "don'ts," not the "do's," and are collectively called the "Yamas."

There are five aspects of Yama: Aimsa (don't cause harm to anyone in thought, word, or deed), Satya (don't lie), Asteya (don't steal), Brahmacharya (don't have sexual relations outside marriage), and Aparigraha (don't hoard or acquire too many material possessions).

There are also five things to do, called the "Niyamas." They are Shaucha (keep yourself and your surroundings clean), Santosha (cultivate contentment), Tapas (show humbleness in your way of speaking and thinking), Svadhyaya (self-reflect), and Ishvara-pranidhana (come to know spiritual truths).

According to Swamiji, the Yamas and the Niyamas create the foundation for all spiritual practice because they teach us self-control. After learning the proper way to conduct our thinking and feeling, then we can learn the third step called "Asana." Asana is about learning how to become more aware of our body in the sense that proper postures, especially sitting postures, help us relax our minds and emotions, which he taught is essential for making spiritual progress. Also, connected with Asana is the idea that correct postures help us to be more physically fit and flexible.

The next step is called "Pranayama," or proper breathing. Deep breathing techniques allow proper oxygenation throughout the body's tissues and helps with concentration. Shallow breathing weakens our ability to think and focus, and causes us to have anxiety.

The final four steps, Swamiji called the four inner parts of Raja yoga: "Pratyahara" (detaching your mind from annoying or tempting objects of sense perception), "Dharana" (learning to concentrate your thoughts on a spiritual subject), "Dhyana" (being able to focus on specific thoughts without many interruptions), and "Samadhi" (deep inward focus).

I applied myself to practice Raja yoga for a few years, but it didn't satisfy me. At first I thought that maybe I just missed my family and the wilderness, and that thinking about them was a distraction to my progress. So I tried to concentrate more diligently and be more disciplined, but I felt pulled in two directions. I wanted to have more free time to spend alone and contemplate the truth about yoga, though Swamiji was getting busy with his programs and expected more and more of me.

Swamiji was asked to speak in Hindu temples, synagogues, gurdwaras, Sufi domes, Buddhist halls, Christian churches, in the homes of Quakers, and on radio and TV programs. He was also

asked to give public talks at bookstores, libraries, coffeehouses, parks, and at colleges, universities, and anywhere people wanted to hear about spiritual subjects. Once, he spoke in some old ruins in Mexico and people sat around on the walls while his translator shouted out what he spoke.

He was a vivacious and articulate orator and often told

humorous stories to illustrate his teaching points. Most people enjoyed his teaching style and found his energy uplifting and infectious. He talked on many spiritual subjects, including how to find happiness, the way to inner peace, how to overcome the ego, and about Mahatma Gandhi's teachings on nonviolence.

My daily work usually included taking dictation from him on my laptop (or by hand) for personal letters or for articles that he wrote for magazines and newspapers. I also cooked his meals, which wasn't ever easy in the constantly changing environments and rules associated with different peoples' kitchens. In India, I cooked over fire and the wood had be gathered from the forest where there were cobras, lone bull elephants, and the occasional tiger that ate the village dogs.

Besides making sure that the right kinds of foods were available for him, as he wouldn't eat grains of any kind, I had travel arrangements to make and things to pack and organize. There were also daily appointments that he had with many people who came to see him privately to ask his advice about personal problems involving meditation, yoga, illness, and family matters.

There was also helping him get ready for his public talks. I had to run the audio and video equipment, which meant I had to set up and organize the cords so nobody would trip on them, and sometimes there were hundreds of people who attended his talks. And I often introduced him to his audience and sometimes this required special preparation, especially if I had to speak in Hindi or recite something in Sanskrit.

In addition, I directed the question and answer sessions after his talks and helped him understand certain expressions, like idioms, that he hadn't heard in India. Though his English grammar was excellent, sometimes people didn't understand his accent and I had to repeat his answer to them. So I always had to pay attention to what everyone was saying.

We traveled by word of mouth. Some person in one place would tell a relative or friend in another place about him and so we'd hop from city to city, state to state, and country to country. Swamiji's conditions for accepting invitations to stay with people who wished to host him for any length of time was that they would pay for our transportation, arrange public talks for him, and provide us with food and two rooms to sleep in. In a joking way, Swamiji would often say, "I just need a roof supported by four walls."

Whenever a stranger, who was to be our new host for some

days or weeks, would meet us at the airport or train station, I tried to picture what their house looked like according to the way they dressed and wore their hair. I also tried to discern whether they would have more of a mental or emotional personality by the way they greeted us, and how much of a help or hindrance they would be to me. I learned so much about how to read people because I constantly had to assess them. I learned how to be shy around effusive people because they would exhaust me with constant conversation and they were also volatile with easy mood swings. Shy people made the best hosts. They followed their habits of daily living and didn't parade around us. Trying to get all of my chores done every day was infinitely more exhausting when I had to explain myself to people who asked a zillion questions.

Of course, Swamiji always got the guest room wherever we were and I had to make do with however I could be accommodated depending on how big the house was. Since he was a monk, I didn't sleep on his floor except on a few occasions when he was in the hospital. The only rule around my sleeping space was that I should be completely safe from the clutches of men. Swamiji protected me like a kitten from "the dogs," as he sometimes called them behind closed doors. He was exceedingly strict and often wouldn't even allow me to shake hands with men. He, too, would usually only touch me on the head.

Some men were jealous that Swamiji had me as his program director and assistant. They didn't realize why I traveled with him and that it was not Swamiji that I served, but my desire to find out the truth about God. Swamiji was just a means to find what I sought, but most people didn't know this and I didn't try to explain it to anyone.

Like a bird in a cage to a cat, I became a challenge to some men. They tried in various ways to seduce me and get me to leave my life with Swamiji so that they could claim me for their own, to serve them in whatever way they wanted. Many gave me money, special food items, clothing, jewelry, and one even bought me a house and a car. But I was never tempted by any of them, and I was disgusted that they thought they could buy me after all the hardships I'd endured.

Swamiji immediately knew their intentions when he saw what they offered to me (and not to him). But I had no need for jewelry or fancy clothes or expensive gifts. I had no room in my suitcase, anyway, for extra things to lug around. I wore only yellow Indian-style clothes called a *salwar-kameez* that identified me as a *brahmacharini* (one who is not married or looking to be married). But the concept of a brahmacharini was an entirely foreign concept to men in the West.

A salwar-kameez is a two-piece outfit made of loose drawstring pants with a matching collarless, long-sleeved, thigh-length shirt. Though Swamiji expected me to wear yellow cotton, just as he wore orange, the style of my salwar-kameez (which was mostly made for me by Indian women) could be as I wanted as long as my skin was covered and the shirt wasn't tight.

When I traveled with Swamiji, he was always alert that I didn't make myself a spectacle to men. He told me that it wasn't necessary for me to adorn myself outwardly as a way to appear attractive to people. He only insisted that I be clean and tidy in my personal habits and show a kind and willing attitude to learn my spiritual lessons. So while I was with him I never wore makeup, shaved my legs, or even wore earrings.

Men in India were more of a problem to me than men in the Western world because they viewed unmarried white women as fair game. Swamiji told me that most Indians had the impression that white women were whores because when the hippies went to India, their ideas about free love spread all around them. Western women had earned a degraded reputation for their scanty clothing and lascivious conduct.

Men on trains were always particularly interested in trying to touch me because in confined spaces it was easier for them. It was common to feel someone bump my arm or pinch my behind and I'd have to slap out and yell "Chalo!" [Move!] But one man, surprisingly, was much more polite. He asked Swamiji for permission to touch me on the face. Swamiji replied calmly that he would have to hit him first. The man backed off, knowing that it would be a sin to strike a swami.

Sometimes young men would sing filthy songs in Hindi when they saw me walking with Swamiji through the villages, carrying loads of vegetables and the lunch box and water jug, but Swamiji would always beat them down with his tongue. He had no fear of scolding them. He was fierce and intense even though he was so slender, and no one dared to defy him.

When we were in India, Swamiji told me never to tell anyone where I lived. But on one occasion somehow word got out that a Western woman was staying in Kadia Katan Garden above the Ganges River near Laxmanjhoola. Some men came to inquire about me because they assumed I had given Swamiji money, as Western people customarily give to swamis. They wanted money from me, but since I ran to hide in the storage room when I heard them coming, they threatened Swamiji instead. They warned him that if he didn't give them money, they'd kidnap me. I had to hide in the storage room every evening for a week because I was afraid they would find me. It was a terrible place to be confined because black scorpions lived in there, and I couldn't always have the flashlight on because batteries were hard to come by and we had no electricity. Though we had a neighbor close to us, named Swami Ganeshananda Giri, he couldn't help defend us from the gang. He was short, stocky, and looked fierce with his long matted hair, but he was over seventy years old and had some serious eye problems.

He did try to help in other ways, at least at first it seemed like help. He would bring me hot chapatis, Indian flatbread, that he cooked on his fire. Chapatis are made of wheat and water, and shaped like two tortillas joined at the edges. When you cook them, they puff up in the center and form a sort of cavity filled with air. But then they collapse and are flat when you eat them. He made

them big and thick, and I loved that they were chewy. He even had clarified butter, called *ghee,* that he spread on top.

Since Swamiji didn't eat wheat, I was usually underfed though occasionally I had *ram dana,* called "amaranth" in English. I wanted to eat the chapatis but Swamiji warned me that if I ate them, then Swami Ganeshananda would expect me to carry water for him from the spring, where we got our water too, and also ask me for money.

He was right. One day after accepting his chapatis, he called me to help him carry water from the spring and sweep the monkey droppings from around his hut. He also asked if I had any money hidden that I could share with him. My relationship with him changed and became strained. I realized I couldn't eat

his chapatis, no matter how hungry I was, because he didn't give them freely. From then on, I tried to avoid him.

When Swamiji went to the hospital at Haridwar, it was arranged that I would stay with a man named Bahadur Mahajan and his family, since Swamiji had known them all for many years. Since the hospital was run by monks of the Ramakrishna order, who were strictly Hindu, I wasn't allowed to spend the night there. But it was just as well. The hospital was very primitive by Western standards and in the bathroom was a pipe sticking out of the wall waist-high, which was meant to be the shower. In the rusty bucket beneath the pipe was someone's blood.

Fortunately, I didn't have to use that bathroom, but had my very own (a huge luxury in India) where I stayed at Mr. Mahajan's home. Bahadur was a professor at the local university in Haridwar, which is a famous Hindu pilgrimage town on the Ganges River about forty miles from Laxmanjhoola. Bahadur was curious about my university education in the Western world and was always asking me questions, but his wife, Urmila, was suspicious of me and locked me in my room at night. She was angry at me because her husband brought me sweets and gave me money when they came to visit us in Laxmanjhoola. But Swamiji never let me keep either, the sweets because they weren't part of my diet, and the money because I needed nothing for myself that he said he couldn't provide.

While I was staying with Bahadur and Urmila, I woke up one night and heard Bahadur outside my bedroom door complaining that he had a toothache. I was confused about what he wanted, and called out to him that he needed to speak to his wife and not to me. But Urmila heard my voice and came flying down the hall in a rage, yelling terrible names at me.

In the morning, when she unlocked my door, I managed to slip away without a word and never returned to her home. I decided I'd try to find my own way to the hospital to tell Swamiji what happened. But I had to be exceedingly careful. Single women, and even married ones who strayed out by themselves, could be killed for their kidneys, which were sold on the black market.

As I always wore traditional Indian clothes my white skin was not too noticeable. I pulled my scarf up high over my head. I tried to mix with women and children as I made my way through the markets and narrow brick alleys where vendors always stood and along the side roads where monkeys, cows, and pigs roamed free. Pilgrims wandered barefoot in bright-colored clothes carrying flowers to throw out to Mata Ganga, the Ganges River.

When I reached the hospital some hours later, there was Bahadur sitting beside Swamiji giving him a quart-sized jar of ghee and some fruit. The ghee was like gold, and a costly gift. Surprisingly, Swamiji didn't refuse to accept his gift as he normally would have done. He was too distracted. His face was worried, though when he saw me he looked relieved. Later he told me that Bahadur had told him that I had run away from his house, but that he didn't know the reason why. Of course Bahadur knew why, but couldn't admit what it was. Thankfully Swamiji didn't press me to answer any questions in front of Bahadur.

Sometimes, staying with strangers was even more difficult in the Western world because their lives were more complicated, and their houses were bigger. In the first year I traveled with Swamiji in the United States, we went down to San Francisco at the invitation of a wealthy Indian doctor and his crazy mixed-up wife. Dr. and Mrs. Gupta had a beautiful home with enormous windows that overlooked the San Francisco Bay. Though she had plenty of money to hire a maid, or many maids if she wanted them, she fancied me to be her servant.

She cornered me in the kitchen the morning after we arrived, and announced to me that in exchange for food she expected me to change all the linoleum in her enormous kitchen cupboards. They were so full that the bottoms sagged. She instructed me that I was to take everything out of these cupboards and stack it all in the backyard. Then I was to cut, with a pair of shears, a piece of linoleum to fit each cupboard. She emphasized that she wanted "a good job." I refused her on the grounds that I already had too much to do for Swamiji, but politely explained that I'd try to help her if I could. As a revenge, she gave me only bread to eat, but I nibbled on Swamiji's leftovers when she was gone from the kitchen.

Swamiji encouraged me to endure her treatment because he said that "worldly people" (as he often called people who worked and had families) were often mean to spiritual seekers and I had better get used to the persecution. They were mean, as he elaborated, simply because seekers had a different outlook on life that "worldly folk" dismissed as unimportant. But I didn't think this was the case with Mrs. Gupta. She was just jealous of Swamiji and wanted me to serve her ego as though she was entitled to have her own slave.

I tried to ignore her taunts, but it was harder for me not to get emotionally involved when she complained about me to others who came to visit Swamiji. She took a malicious delight in trying to cause me pain, but I learned how to hide my discomfort from her and pretended that I didn't notice her jabs. I hoped that enduring her meanness would help my spiritual goals come more clearly into focus.

One early evening when we were all in the car and on our way to a community center where Swamiji was scheduled to talk about his life in India with Mahatma Gandhi, we stopped at a drugstore so that Dr. Gupta could pick up some film for his camera. I realized I needed some batteries for the tape recorder and jumped out of the car and followed him into the store. As he was paying for his film, and I was in line behind him at the checkout counter, Mrs. Gupta came running into the store screaming, "I know what you are! You are a bitch for going after my husband!" Of course everyone at the front of the store stared at me, bewildered. Dr. Gupta shook his head and said to everyone, "She has a screw that is loose."

Some days before we left the Guptas' home, a woman at one of Swamiji's programs gave me a ten dollar bill so I decided to buy some flowers and give them to Mrs. Gupta as a way to kill her with kindness. I thanked her for teaching me so many things and told her that staying as a guest in her home for a few weeks had been a good spiritual experience for me because I had to practice so much self- control. For once she had nothing to say as I walked out the door with Swamiji, feeling overjoyed.

When we were in Calgary, Canada, our host named Roopa would ceremoniously enter Swamiji's room every day, but only when he was there to observe her. She would carry her "ritual items," including big yellow rubber gloves and a bleach bottle, and walk into the bathroom off of his room. Then she'd proceed to scrub his toilet and his bathtub with enough bleach to clean twenty bathrooms. I thought she wanted the suffocating fumes to be a potent reminder of her services to him, suggesting that she deserved some special favors for her efforts.

But Swamiji was oblivious to her designs or pretended that he didn't notice, and I know it made her mad. But since I was especially sensitive to bleach, I was the one that got sick. I was nauseated for days with a pounding head that made it hard for me to focus. I'd tell Roopa that I could clean the toilet for a change, but she insisted that it was her duty to get down on her hands and knees for a man as worthy as Swamiji. Her sanctimonious ways, I realized, were like so many so-called spiritual people who only pretended to be self-sacrificing. In fact, the more I observed, the more I realized that religion was a cloak for many dark and dirty dealings.

I appreciated that Swamiji never dangled occult mysteries in front of me like knowledge of some hidden mystical state that only he could tell me about, and which was essential for my spiritual progress. He recognized the deception of "spiritual teachers" who seduced others into thinking that they alone had the key to spiritual enlightenment, and so charged money to share them with others. He made it clear that involvement with the occult deals with two kinds of spiritual seduction. The first is on the part of the teacher who seduces others into thinking they have to be dependent on him for spiritual gains. The second, ironically, is on the part of the occult that seduces the teacher into being an agent of deceit to mislead other people.

To Swamiji, the occult was not a made-up world. It was not an imaginary place, but a spirit realm of demonic entities that attach themselves to people who are open to them. These entities specifically come through people when they try to be a channel to the spirit world through drug-induced or hypnotic trances to find out secret knowledge, or simply because they wanted to look important and have power in the eyes of others. Though dark forces do feed on ignorance, they especially target arrogance.

Traditionally, those who practice magic, seek for spirit guides, and want to have visions, are considered to be involved in the occult. But most don't realize that most religions contain occult mysteries at their base as a way to entrap people and mislead them in their way of worship.

I observed people from different religions who all claimed to be harassed by spirit entities. They came to ask Swamiji how to be rid of them. Some had succumbed to false teachers who wanted to enslave them. Some had made the mistake of trying to contact their dead loved ones. And some had called upon spirit guides that they thought would lead them to enlightenment, when in fact they led them into darkness and confusion. As a result, these people were stuck with troublesome nightmares, visions, and other disturbing problems.

Swamiji constantly emphasized to me that spiritual progress cannot involve the ego's drive to gain power over people, like evangelical preachers (whether Christian or Hindu) who claim to have God's spirit. To the contrary, he taught that spiritual progress has to be established on humility, but not the false humility that is a veil for pride. He always harped on the fact that spiritual attainments are not determined by how long you can hold your breath, if you can sleep on nails, or only eat every few days. He believed that our spiritual capacities can be seen in the fruits of our practice, in the open demonstration of true selflessness and the cultivation of the qualities of love, joy, peace, kindness, and self-control that show in our actions.

But, as he said, most people don't want to do the spiritual work for themselves and have a tendency to rely on occult ideas instead. We met many people who were like this.

When we stayed with a family in Aberdeen, Scotland, on the shores of the North Sea, our host Dena asked Swamiji a question as he finished his lunch on the porch one afternoon.

"Swamiji, what is the meaning of astral travel?"

He paused playfully before answering her. "What kind of travel?"

Dena explained that she had read a book about astral travel and how swamis know how to travel on astral projections.

"Do what?" He looked mischievous.

"Astral travel. You know, when your astral body goes out of you when you are in deep meditation or dreaming."

"Oh," he replied like he was interested, but then dismissed the question matter-of-factly by saying, "I have no time for astral travel. I'm too busy."

"What?" She sounded surprised.

Then he came on strong. "Astral travel is all nonsense. Don't get seduced by such ideas."

"But don't you think it could be beneficial?" She was insistent.

"How could it ever be beneficial?"

"Because when you go into an astral plane you can gain access to the past or the future so you could warn people about potential catastrophes and how to avoid them."

He replied that astral planes and astral projections are not at all a part of true spiritual discipline. "They will lead you astray." He was stern, though she looked incredulous.

"Really? Why, Swamiji?"

"Because, my dear Dena, they exist in the domain of dark things. There are forces in the universe that are evil, just like there are forces for good. You need to use your mind and heart to serve the good in this realm of waking. It is where your spiritual work is meant to be."

"But many spiritual seekers from the West have gone to India and learned to travel on astral projections." She couldn't get the meaning of his point.

"They are lying," Swamiji said. "Hardly anyone survives who ventures to learn such things. They belong to the occult world, and the occult is full of demons. Every religion shows the struggle between light and dark, between love and hate.

"What do you think, Sita?" Swamiji asked me for my opinion as he got up from the table to go to his room. But I knew he wasn't really interested in my ideas on the subject. It was just his cue to me to tell her that nothing he taught me about the spiritual life included involvement in the occult.

So I dutifully said, "The point Swamiji is making is that the occult is not the place to search for enlightenment."

"Where do you search for enlightenment then?" Dena balked.

"Mostly in observing my ego," I smiled. I was only partly joking.

"That's weird," Dena replied.

"It seems weird because no one wants to observe their ego. It's no fun, and not glamorous, like the idea of astral travel to a foreign country to catch the sunset. To face your ego and understand how it has a hold on you takes a lot of effort. But Swamiji teaches that the beginning of spiritual insight depends on renouncing your ego."

"Oh that sounds so boring," Dena shook her head. I wanted to agree with her, but Swamiji wouldn't take it as a joke from me and I'd probably get in trouble.

"Well, what about Jewish Kabbalah and Hindu theosophy?" Dena inquired of me. "Don't you think you can learn about your ego and overcome it through their mystical teachings? That is what they teach, after all."

"I don't," I said. "The thing is that the Kabbalah and theosophy are occult interpretations of Judaism and Hinduism. "

"Really?"

"Yes." I had figured it out before I met Swamiji. "Basically, the search for special hidden meaning only appeals to those who want to be viewed as special in the eyes of others. It just feeds their ego to think that they can have knowledge that others aren't capable of having because they are unique in a spiritual way."

But Dena argued that the Kabbalah defined the inner symbolic meaning of the Hebrew Bible.

"I follow what you are saying," I replied, "but the God of

the Bible is not a mystical God. He is a communicating God."

"But maybe that's just a trick to mislead us."

"Yes, but Dena, it doesn't take a mystical thinker to know what is meant when the Bible says that you must love God with your whole heart, mind, and strength. Does it?"

She changed the subject on me, like most people usually did when we got to this point in a conversation.

"Have you seen God in your meditations?" she asked.

"Are you crazy?" I wanted to laugh out loud but didn't want to sound cynical. I turned around to see if Swamiji was still standing behind us, but he had gone and so I felt freer to be more open.

"Just because I travel with Swamiji doesn't mean I know who God is. But I still want to know and investigate everywhere I can."

"Do you see blue lights or other mystical visions?" Dena wouldn't give up. She was drawn to the idea of the occult just like a horse craves carrots.

"Nope," I sighed. "That's not what you want to search for. I'd be scared if I saw blue lights or had strange visions."

"Well, what about the Hindus?" Dena wasn't listening. She didn't notice my efforts to change the direction of our conversation. She continued with the same line of thinking, not at all concerned about my warning to her. "They use mystical secrets to find God, you know."

"Well," I stood up to clear off Swamiji's lunch bowls, "Hinduism is totally bizarre and is based on strange ideas and strange-looking gods. They have deformed bodies, including many arms, and one wears a cobra around his neck. Another stands on skulls and sticks out her tongue at you, at least that is the way Kali is depicted in drawings and statues!"

"So what God do you pray to?" Dena's voice was getting hard.

"I pray to a God that I don't yet know, but want to know."

"What?" She was coming unglued.

"I don't believe in any concept of God that I've learned about so far."

"How can you say that, Sita?"

"For the simple reason that I don't believe a true conception of God is one that has an elephant head, like Ganesh, or a monkey head, like Hanuman. For Hindus, making up gods is like making up recipes, a little of this and a little of that and *voila*! there you have a new creation." I realized it wasn't kind for me to say that to her, but I couldn't help myself.

Dena started to scratch her foreheard. "But don't you believe that all these gods are part of the One God? Isn't that what Swamiji teaches you?"

"Well, how can all things be one thing? How can all gods with different attributes, powers, and personalities still be an expression of one God? It isn't logical, is it?"

"They are different versions of one Truth." Dena wouldn't budge from her ways.

"No, they're really not." I shouldn't have said it. I knew Swamiji would bust me when he found out that I had antagonized our host.

"How do you know?" Dena looked at me with suspicion. I could see her assessment of my spiritual attainment dropping like hail on a garden.

"Because it isn't possible. Common sense makes that clear," I said. "Mystical interpretations are dangerous because they get you to believe what seems so impossible. It creates worlds within worlds within worlds, and it all gets so jumbled and confusing. But the truth about God has to be simple, don't you think? If God is love, like many religions claim, then the truth about God has to be simple. A loving God wouldn't enable only a special few to know a mystical truth at the expense of all the other poor souls."

"Yeah, I can see what you mean," said Dena.

At that moment, Swamiji called me to his room and asked me what we were talking about. He cautioned me to be careful. He was always concerned that others would say things to discourage me or that I might discourage others, like he sensed I was doing to Dena.

Generally, he didn't like too much talking between me and our hosts. So though I tried to be superficial in my dealings with them, I didn't always succeed. I had nobody I could share my heart with, and sometimes it just overflowed.

I had learned the hard way not to openly question what Swamiji said to me or others. It was just too exhausting because most of the time he considered it to be my ego finding fault with him, instead of an honest desire on my part to understand and make sense of what he said.

Usually, when he wanted to point out my shortcomings and mistakes, he called me to his room after our work was done and everyone else was sleeping. It was almost always a painful process. After the long work of the day, and especially on program days (when he gave talks), I was so tired I had to fight to keep my eyes open. I was prone to be impatient after 2:00 a.m.

When he would say, "One thing more, please sit down," I knew I would be clobbered unless I easily admitted my mistake, whatever it was. For years, I worked with this scenario, and though I learned many ways to delay the inevitable, he would always find his way into my defenses. These late night encounters were difficult for many reasons, but especially because I longed for some appreciation from him instead of constant correction. I was dying for some affection and kindness. But Swamiji never praised me to my face, though I know he did behind my back, on occasion, because people sometimes told me what he had said.

The late night sessions never did get easy, only harder and harder as certain illusions about my spiritual self died, and others took their place. His "teaching me," as he called it, became more and more about how he wanted me to submit to what he said he knew for sure. But I always refused deep down to trust him entirely, though I tried to look for the good in him. He warned me over and over that I wouldn't succeed in renouncing my ego if I didn't completely accept what he said. So I tried hard not to challenge what he said by asking him questions, though I had an active questioning mind.

I took to using a plastic bottle cap from an empty spice container that I'd put in my mouth whenever he felt he needed to reprove me. Since it wasn't possible for me to speak with the cap in my mouth, I couldn't reply to the things that he said. As a result, I'd be able to get to bed at least an hour earlier than if I had tried to explain myself and why I had done whatever it was that I did that he questioned. Surprisingly, he never saw me put the cap inside my mouth, or maybe he just pretended that he didn't notice. It really worked like a charm unless he asked me a question that he expected me to answer. Then I had to get it out without him seeing and that was hard to do. I had to make some sort of coughing motion and take it out quickly.

Traveling with Swamiji was difficult, though most people thought it must be blissful. I was almost always outside my comfort zone. Not only did he expect much of me, but I didn't have any real time by myself except when I was trying to sleep. Even if I hid in the bathroom with a book for a while, he would find me and ask me what it was I was doing. I could never distract myself from the endless raids he made into my mind, taking thoughts I didn't even know were there and bringing them out in the open.

My sense of self was always changing as Swamiji pointed out how I could replace weaker habits with stronger ones. I thought it was what I wanted too, because I knew that a meaningful spiritual search was based on self-awareness and exerting effort to become more conscious, which involved change. But as time passed, I struggled to understand the difference between my ego's demands on my heart and mind, and my spiritual desire to drop the ego's attitude. The difficult part was that the better I got at observing my ego, the more subtle its expressions became. I seemed to play a perpetual cat and mouse game with myself.

I believed this was the real spiritual work that no one could see on the outside. But after years of intense self-observation in the exhausting circumstances of being overworked, I began to lose my strength. I didn't know if this weakening was a necessary stage of my spiritual journey that comes when the ego breaks down, or if it was that Swamiji's tutelage was leading to nowhere but weariness. I began to wonder if the spiritual part of our self that is supposed to renounce the ego, according to the Eastern traditions, wasn't really a spiritual part after all. It seemed it could be just another ruse of the ego. For if you tried to renounce what couldn't be renounced by your own efforts, then any attempt would be futile. It wouldn't matter how long you practiced.

Slowly I realized that the renunciate path relies too much on one's own effort, and not enough on divine help. There is too much ego involved in thinking that by renouncing certain needs and comforts one can find God. The renunciate traditions of the East believe that by avoiding things like tasty food, proper sexual relations, and material possessions, one can gain a clearer spiritual understanding. Though there is benefit to living a simple life, it can be carried to an extreme. Most renunciates we met seemed proud of their attainments, but we did meet one or two that seemed to me to be truly honest and humble.

One was a famous Indian yogi who invited us to Florida. He taught Hatha yoga, the physical forms of yoga. We stayed at his home for a few days where he talked openly to Swamiji. I heard their conversations as I followed behind them through the gardens. The yogi admitted that though he had practiced his spiritual disciplines diligently, he had not been blessed with spiritual insight. He said that he was in his twilight years, even though he was much younger than Swamiji. He felt his spiritual life was a huge disappointment. His confession was so meaningful to me because he affirmed what I was beginning to understand: The Eastern path seemed fruitless. Although Raja yoga taught the first steps to be an integrated person, it could not lead one to God. I began to think that the only way you could find out the truth about God is if God opened your eyes and personally led you to perceive him.

Even though I didn't know where my own spiritual future would lead me if I stayed with Swamiji, I was certain that I didn't want to return to the world. It taught people to be competitive in all areas of life, including academics, politics, and sports. The world of human affairs simply seemed to be organized by greed, including false religion that was used as a cloak to hide the real spiritual darkness that most people agreed to be trapped by and call "life."

Though I considered myself an enthusiastic person with a generally positive outlook and upbeat personality, I considered the pervading spirit of society to be governed by a deceptivity that ran so deep that even intelligent spiritual people couldn't see it. Why? Because they identified with the world's ways. They gained their spiritual sense of self through what they seemed to achieve for their egos. They had no reason to look beyond because they were already satisfied. I knew they didn't know the truth about God because they weren't humble, honest, or hungry for spiritual enlightenment.

It wasn't that I judged myself as being better than people who were enmeshed in religious practices that seemed so ridiculous. And I didn't judge my spiritual search to be better than people who used their time to make lots of money or pursue careers. But I did discern from what I observed that a full-time pursuit of material gain never made people happy. Also, by living a renunciate life with Swamiji, and living with very few belongings, I could see more and more clearly that the world taught superficiality. In everything, it seemed to appeal to the ego's desires for gratification and acknowledgement, as if a new piece of clothing, or a new and better car or office would bring a deep sense of satisfaction.

I saw that the world had infiltrated all the spiritual circles that I observed in my travels with Swamiji. They weren't separate from the world but were made by it. The egos that ran religion seemed to have the same desire for power as every politician. They

were just quietly veiled and made to look righteous and pure in a spiritual sense. Unsuspecting people, and especially people who wanted their ears tickled and their ego rubbed, were constantly seduced into believing the lies of spiritual leaders. I saw many power trips played out between the so-called spiritual folk that we met.

The renunciate types that Swamiji and I represented were just as bad as the rest. No one, hardly any one, seemed to be integrated and to demonstrate a true desire to help others in a real and loving way. They were too busy distracting themselves with their faulty spiritual practices that led them to nothing but a false sense of accomplishment, even if they had power over people.

But I wasn't easily jaded. For the more than six years that I traveled with Swamiji, I completely gave of myself and worked for no money. In my desire to be unselfish and to share with others in a spiritual way, I wanted to prove that it was possible to live for others as much as for myself, and especially others who were not related to me. I wanted to show the world that it was possible not to be selfish. I cherished the hope that my decision to go against the world, and swim up current, would qualify me to find out the truth about God.

Since I was about fifteen years old, I had performed a little ritual of hope that someday, somewhere, I would be rewarded for having the spiritual longing that I had, and so would gain the insight that I sought. My ritual was to feed ants, but only in the wilderness in some remote place where there was no chance that any other person would ever visit the same ant mound that I did.

My reasoning back then was that just like I fed the ants, which was really a miracle to them, as food was literally dropping on them from the heavens of my hand, I too would be fed with spiritual knowledge by a being greater than myself. Though I never fed ants when I was with Swamiji, the idea still persisted in me that someday God would feed me what is true. I just had to be patient.

Since I knew how to search for water in a desert canyon, I tried to visualize my search for spiritual meaning with Swamiji in a similar way. But little by little his teachings became arid to me, and where I once felt watered like a spring bloom in his presence, I was withering. But I wouldn't give up believing that someday, in some town somewhere, I would bump into someone who knew the truth and could point me where I needed to go.

I realized Swamiji didn't know the truth about God. Even though his teachings of yoga were a helpful foundation for my spiritual progress, I just couldn't make sense of how he could believe that all paths (like all religions) could lead to the truth about God. It was so obvious that different religions had contradictory teachings about the sort of relationship humans should have with God, besides other teachings like the condition of the dead, the means of salvation, and the essence of spiritual practice.

Though I could see the good that Swamiji did for others, the spiritual information that he shared with them didn't seem to change their lives. He hadn't changed mine, though he had taught me some disciplines I was grateful to learn. I had been exposed to many religions through him, but it was only a mental exercise. My heart ached all the time.

What troubled me most was that Swamiji's beliefs about God were constructed of different religious teachings from different religious traditions, and didn't feel solid to stand on. It was like his beliefs about God were narrow planks of wood that he wanted me to use as a bridge to the beyond. But I didn't feel secure and refused to walk on them because they were too wobbly.

The day I decided to leave Swamiji, I was in Long Beach, California. I was shaking from exhaustion and realized I had to go because my heart was giving out in a physical way. I told him that I was resigning my yellow clothes because I was tired of being a slave of weariness. I asked him to give me a little money, and I assured him I would keep in touch. He did not try to force me to stay, though I could see he was so sad.

I went to live with Julie, who was a friend of our host in Long Beach. She had a dozen cats and a dog. She said I could live for free in her studio apartment attached to her garage if I cooked her dinner in the evenings and fed her animals when she was out of town. I had nothing to my name but what I had learned. Though I was completely drained, I could see the value of my experiences with religion, and people who claimed to be religious.

I learned that, like most Christians of the Western world, the Eastern aspirants too, whether Hindu, Sikh, Jain, or Buddhist, didn't really study or understand their own scriptures. They based their beliefs only on a section of text that sounded good to them or gave them shivers. There seemed to be no spiritual comprehension in a broader way concerning what they knew about the history, or continuity, of their beliefs.

I also observed that most Jews hated Christ, who seemed an ideal man, but most Christians mysteriously called him "God" and couldn't explain why he should then have a Father.

The Buddhists were supposed to be *anatma* [without soul] as Siddartha Buddha, the founder of Buddhism, didn't believe in God. Buddha simply propounded a philosophy about how to minimize suffering based on specific rules of conduct in all areas of life. But though Buddhists pretend to be peaceful, the history of

Buddhism is full of spiritistic practices and fights between gods, goddesses, and demons. But when I pointed this out to Buddhists, they looked the other way. To them, being Buddhist was meant to be everything peaceful and nonjudgmental. It didn't seem to matter if there were contradictions at the base of their beliefs.

The Sikhs believe in Waheguru, their name for the infinite Creator, and their religion combines Hindu and Muslim teachings. Paradoxically, though, it is not Waheguru that they worship, but their holy book. It is a collection of six thousand hymns compiled in the seventeenth century called the *Guru Granth Sahib*. It was written by men, the ten Sikh Gurus, starting with Guru Nanak in 1469 and ending with Guru Gobind Singh in 1708. In their place of worship, called a *gurdwara*, people bow on their knees to this book which sits on a podium in a bed of white linen. It is ceremoniously fanned by a man with a white ostrich feather.

To the Hindus, God spectacularly morphs into every conceivable representation of power, wisdom, justice, and love, which are personified as gods and goddesses with their own different names. The interaction of these deities is the subject of many spiritual myths, and creates the religious sects in India.

But it gets more complicated. Though Christianity claims a monotheistic orientation because it teaches that there is only one God, Hinduism also claims a similar unity, though they believe that God is in all things, because God manifests in all ways, and so everything is united in God. This outlook is called monistic and is contrasted with the monotheistic belief that God, like the one in the Bible, is not omnipresent and is not governed by physical laws because he is the Creator of them. So, naturally, the nature of salvation according to Hindus will be very different than that of Christians.

There are enormous difficulties (and blatant contradictions) in believing that all paths, like all religions, lead to the same truth about God. According to Hindus, for example, the idea of salvation is not dualistic. This means that salvation is not found and attained by understanding and overcoming the fallen nature of man according to God's personalized prescription. The idea of enlightenment in Hinduism, which is variously called Moksha, Mukti, Samadhi, and Nirvana, is the opposite. It is somehow attained by becoming one with God, called God-Realization or Self-Realization. Of course, things get more complicated when it comes to sorting out how both reincarnation and resurrection could be valid, according to the purpose of one God, since reincarnation relies on the idea of an immortal soul while resurrection in based on the death of the soul.[5] Such entirely different systems for understanding the soul's relationship to God could not be contained in one absolute truth because such an absolute would never hold contradictions.

As I recovered for months at Julie's house and tried to still the intense pounding of my heart, I realized I had to go back to my roots to find out the truth about God. Not to the atheist mentality of my family, but to science. I decided that science would prevent me from getting lost in inconsistencies. For I believed that a true God, like a true religion, would not reveal truths that contradict the teachings of modern science.

I decided that scriptures from any religion of the world that talked nonsense about physical life and the origin of the earth in obvious mythical ways weren't likely to be spiritually correct. Of course, translation problems add to confusion about what is really expressed in scripture, because it often reflects the bias of the translator. But to me that was a minor issue.

The main scriptures of India belong to the religions of the Hindus (and its main sects of Saivism, Vaishnavism and Shaktism), Jains, Sikhs, and Buddhists. The scriptures of these four religions include thousands and thousands of pages, including the Vedas (the Rigveda, Yajurveda, Samaveda, and the Atharvaveda)[6] the Upanishads,[7] (over a hundred treatises that were composed about two thousand five hundred years ago), the Epics,[8] the Agamas,[9] the *Guru Granth Sahib*, plus those of the Buddhists.

Though many Hindus consider the Vedas to be God's word (*sruti*), meaning revealed by God and not inspired by men (*smriti*), they are full of contradictions. According to one hymn, the gods made the universe from the sacrifice of a cosmic man. "The moon was produced from his mind (manas), the sun (surya) from his eye...from his head the sky, from his feet the earth."[10] In another hymn, the composer asks, "What was the wood and what was the tree from which [the gods] carved the sky and the earth?"[11]

342

Later, in the Upanishads, the creation of the world was attributed to Brahman who, according to the Isa Upanishad, is a being that is separate from the universe. The Mundaka Upanishad, on the other hand, regards Brahman as the universe itself. But in the Svetasvatara Upanishad, Brahman is real, but the universe is an illusion (*maya*).

A creation account in the Chandogya Upanishad describes that the world was born from a giant egg. Conversely, the Brhadaranyaka Upanishad states that the Creator, feeling lonely and unhappy, "grew as large as a man and a woman entwined, and then divided himself in two, creating a husband and a wife. . . . In this way he created the male and female of all creatures—even down to the ants."[12]

In the Sikh scriptures, the idea of the creation being like a cracking egg was borrowed from Hindus' Chandogya Upanishad. God (called Waheguru) included all the energies of creation in a shell like an egg.[13]

In the Qur'an, the scriptures of the Islamic religion, there is no consolidated creation. But there are isolated verses that can be pieced together to show how Muslims believe the world came into existence. It is written that God created the heavens and the earth and made all the creatures that walk, swim, crawl, and fly on the face of the earth from a drop of water.[14]

I decided I had to read the Bible's account of the creation of the world and see if I could make sense of what it said.

In a time of universal deceit, telling the truth becomes a revolutionary act.

George Orwell (1903-1950), English Author

CHAPTER EIGHT

The Oasis

He meant to say "teacher." "No more teacha! No teacha!" Dr. Wu looked sharply at me as if he could use his eyes to cut through his heavy Chinese accent.

He had been taking my pulse and asked me how I came to have "an empty scattered heartbeat that was as erratic as an old person." So I had told him about my travels with Swamiji, the one he emphatically called "teacha."

"You will need a new heart soon if you don't rest now." He was adamant.

"I know," I admitted, "I overworked for a long time and didn't get enough sleep."

From a physical point of view my symptoms were serious, but not so painful as my feelings of disappointment. My heart bore the double brunt of my efforts to try and squeeze some spiritual essence from a path that was as hard and dry as stone.

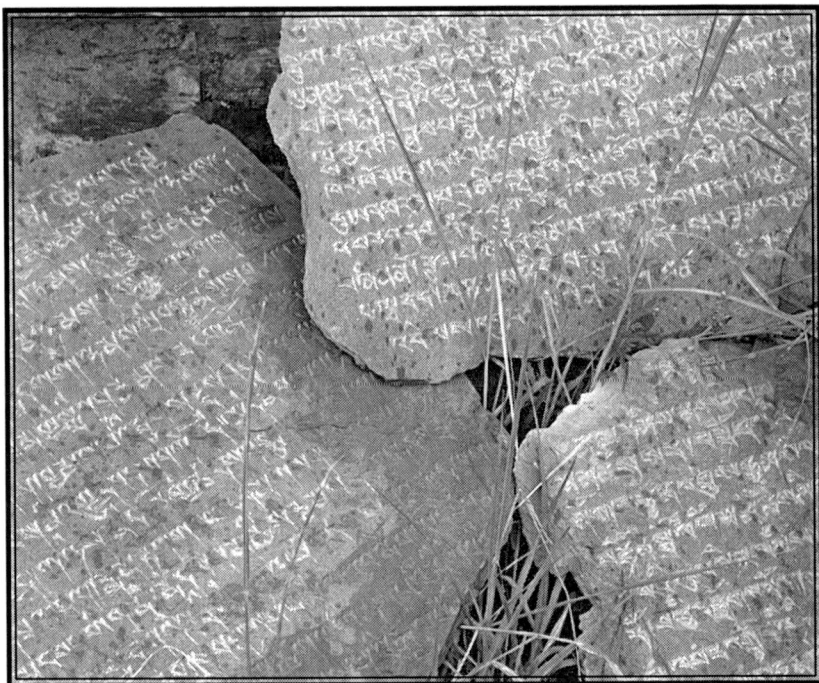

Dr. Wu's eyes softened. He, too, knew the ache of a broken heart, though outwardly he'd only acknowledge the futility of an impossible dream. He had told me that when he was a boy he watched his parents be murdered by Communist soldiers who marched into their peaceful Chinese village. Then they beat him and left him for dead. But somehow he had survived, though he was crippled and had to walk with two canes.

He hobbled with a seesaw-like gait, a disturbing up and down motion that made it easy to imagine how his legs had been broken in many places. I was horrified to learn what had happened to him, and I wanted to tell him how sorry I felt. But he cut me off with a shake of his head that meant he didn't want to be pitied.

"You see what happened to me," he spoke without emotion, "and all for my parent's dream that only led to their torture and death. Don't seek what you can't find because it will only make your heart sick." He rebuked me as if he knew the truth about life based on his own bitter experience.

Though he tried to couch his comments in the concern of the well-intended doctor, I knew why he wanted to discourage me. It was because he felt victimized by his parents' wish to show him a way of life not sold into the slavery of the Communist regime.

I could understand why Dr. Wu was jaded, but it didn't mean I was. Just because my search had not been fruitful in the way I wanted, I wouldn't deny my intuition that life had a divine source. I still believed I could find out and know that source in a personal way, and I didn't care if people told me I was crazy, especially those who knew what I had endured during my years traveling with Swamiji.

But then, most people were content like deer at the zoo eating out of the hands of the system of things, the whole un-enlightened world setup that created rulers and slaves, and high officials and lowly workers. Regardless of the country, the system would tell you what was real, what you had to believe. The Chinese government was just one extreme example.

Dr. Wu persisted in trying to convince me not to follow my heart and find out the answers to my spiritual questions. He needled me: "You didn't figure it out, did you? I wanted you to understand that my father and mother believed in a God that couldn't help them." He tapped me softly on the hand from across his desk where he sat. "They thought God would protect them from the soldiers."

When he said that, I realized that he was angry with God. By his thinking, God had abandoned his parents in their moment of need and so God was cast out of his heart for good, so it seemed. But then he surprised me by asking in almost a whisper as if one part of himself didn't want the other part to hear, "Is the search for truth, or what you call God, important enough to die for?"

"Definitely," I said without hesitating. "I would die to know the truth, or even trying to find it." Perhaps I sounded over-zealous, but I had always been a seeker. That was all my heart ever knew. "What about you?" I looked him in the eyes.

I didn't mean to suggest that I justified his parents' death because they resisted the rules of Communist politics. Perhaps they died making the point that was most meaningful to them. Maybe they wanted to boldly stand up for what they believed, in spite of the consequences. They must have known they would have to die.

But Dr. Wu didn't answer my question. He scribbled a few notes and then handed me a prescription written in Chinese. He explained that since I was too weak for acupuncture, I should continue to take herbs. He warned me not to wear anything tight around my chest, including bras. He said I should get to bed as early as I could, though he knew my internal clock was out of whack from going to bed after 3:00 a.m. every night for years and not sleeping enough in the morning.

After he finished playing the doctor, he half smiled and said, "You know, you were born in the Year of the Tiger! According to the Chinese horoscope, you have a drive to roam the wide open spaces of the earth pursuing what you seek, wandering where you must, hunting what you do. Most people are not so courageous as you. But you are brave like the tiger. And don't forget," he made an effort to end our appointment in an upbeat way, "tigers always land on their feet."

"Thanks," I smiled. "See you next week." I walked down the hall to the herb room.

I didn't question Dr. Wu about the contents of the herbs as I had studied Chinese medicine in one of my plant courses at the university years before. The dried, flat berries and chalky-dry plant parts were actually not magical charms, but an important source of minerals that would help revitalize my heart. But the dried scorpion-like creatures looked strange.

Every day I prepared a portion of my week's herbs in an electric cooking pot that came to a boil, and then simmered for a couple of hours. The resulting black sludge tasted awful, but it helped calm the pounding agitation and painful pricks in my chest, and the tingling that hummed in my arms and legs.

I thought about Dr. Wu's comments about my being born in the Year of the Tiger. I appreciated that he wanted to bring some fun to our conversation, but I wondered if he thought that our personal strengths or weaknesses are predestined.

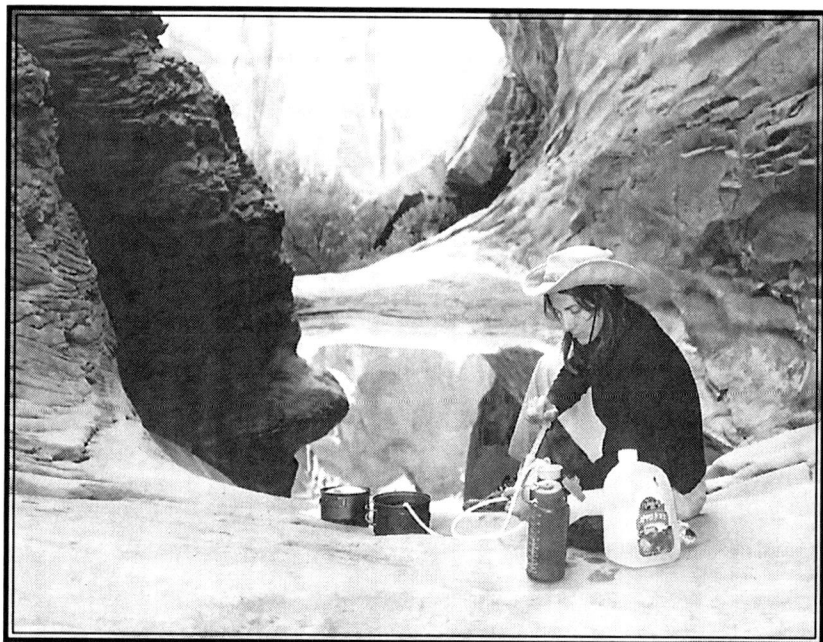

He might use my birth year, like astrologers use the stars, to justify my spiritual nature and my drive to find spiritual answers. It was a parallel to many scientists who believed that seekers had a peculiar brain chemistry that gave them a driven quality that others simply didn't possess.

I had been reading a couple of books like *Why God Won't Go Away: Brain Science and the Biology of Belief* and *Mystical Mind: Probing the Biology of Religious Experience*. I was amazed to find that scientists would go to such lengths to try and validate their atheistic outlook and overlook the spiritual decisions of people that stumbled the logic of scientific reasoning. I was one of those people. I didn't live to contribute to the gene pool, for example, because I had chosen not to have children. My purpose in life was not shackled to my physical needs, as I had tried to defy them. I didn't measure my success according to my bank account, my possessions, or my intellectual accomplishments.

Even though I lived in a little studio in the smoggy L.A. suburb of Downey, I refused to resign my spiritual search. From a worldly point of view, I had nothing to show for myself. No savings, no career label or high position in society. I didn't even get a Ph.D. degree for my study of the religions of the world, though I surely deserved more than one for all my work with Swamiji and the philosophy, religion, and language that I had studied. But academia doesn't recognize self-taught people, especially in the twenty-first century. Learning is political, outlined by committees and payment schemes.

I didn't have a car and so I rode the bus and shopped at a neighborhood store where I bought old vegetables for a lower price than fresh ones. I bought used clothes at a thrift store. But I wasn't unhappy just because of these things.

I had learned a great deal about human nature and discovered the pathetic truth about those who claimed to be spiritually enlightened. I had seen, too, that the essence of religion, East and West, was mostly a farce, a utopian disguise to cover dark and dirty dealings. Unsuspecting people were enslaved to doctrine and dogma by others for profit and power.

From my travels with Swamiji, I saw that religion seemed to have tucked within itself a dangerous tool that organized confusion. I decided that most people succumbed to ridiculous religious practices because they were afraid to stand alone.

Still, though I wasn't afraid to stand alone, I realized that I had to radically change my approach to searching for the truth about God. For I had wanted to be always on the outside of religion looking in, like a superhero that could jump a freight train without any harm to himself. I believed that if I was swift and careful, I wouldn't be snared by false organizations and have to ally myself with mischief makers. But maybe being strong and flexible to search where others couldn't wasn't the way to find what I sought.

By enduring life with Swamiji, I had missed something vital. The truth about God had to be available to anyone, and especially to those, too, who were not inclined to jump a train, or those who were uneducated or unhealthy. The discovery of the truth couldn't be the reward of either an intellectual privilege or an overzealous will to endure hardship. It seemed that it should be found by anyone with common sense and a humble heart.

I thought about the story of the woman who lost a needle in her house. Though, because she didn't have enough light at home, she went out to search for it under the light of a street lamp. When an old gentleman passed that way, he watched her carefully searching on the ground.

"What are you looking for?" He showed her kindness.

"My needle," she sighed.

The old guy got down on his knees to help her. "Now where exactly did you drop it?"

"Somewhere in my kitchen," the woman replied.

The old fellow must have rolled his eyes.

But that is the way it is with most of us. We get convinced that what we seek can be found in the wrong place, which means our search will never be fruitful, even if we convince ourselves that it will be.

I had run away from the West and sought enlightenment in the East because I thought that people would be less materialistic. I reasoned that people there lived closer to the land, and so they wouldn't be so greedy. They wouldn't be struck by the frenzy of those in technological societies who determined their worth by their gadgets, cars, and the number of bedrooms in their homes. I had also run away from priests and other costumed Christian characters, as well as the drab atheist mentality. I was drawn to the exotic land of spice and fragrance where every breathing thing could be openly considered an expression of divine life in a sort of inspired, festive indulgence. But I had come full circle.

Every week, for some months, I went to see Dr. Wu and he usually asked me the same questions. "Is your heartbeat calmer? Do you feel less tightness in your chest?" I had pushed myself to the breaking point exploring the path of the ascetic. I realized that it couldn't take me closer to the truth than those who pursued material things and comfort. But I always believed that without the hassles of too much stuff, the spiritual truth would be easier to find.

I called Swamiji once a week for the couple months he stayed in Long Beach. But then he left for India when he was almost eighty-nine years old. I knew he would never return because he had developed some serious health problems. Though Swamiji could never admit it to me, I knew he missed me terribly. But I had given him a chance to keep me as his helper.

I had told him, the day I left my spiritual search with him, that if he could admit that he wasn't perfect in a spiritual sense, then I would stay longer. But he couldn't admit that he wasn't perfect because he had believed for so long that anyone could become perfect, in a spiritual sense, if they followed the path of celibacy and discipline. It was evident to me that he wasn't spiritually perfect and nobody could be with an aging body, a mind that could be erratic, and emotions that could distort one's perception.

For him to believe that he had attained spiritual perfection was the biggest scam of the Hindu tradition upon him. That scam made him foolish, and he couldn't even see how he played the fool. I cried often for him the day I left, and also for myself. For I knew that he had so much potential, but he had chosen to be duped by tradition. He couldn't resist the temptation of being important in the eyes of others. Though he played the role of a simple spiritual man who had succeeded in renouncing his ego, and therefore was a qualified spiritual teacher, it was just a pretense on his part.

When I told him I was leaving, he said that he had planned to give me his "mantle," but only after he died. Then I would be elevated to a Swami, just like him. It would mean adoration from people and donations of food and money. It would mean spiritual authority over others and a place of honor in their hearts. But I wasn't tempted. I told him that I would never be a slave of my ego, and I would keep searching for the truth until I had no more strength.

The only place I had not searched for spiritual enlightenment was in the Bible. So I decided to look into it. I was amazed to learn that it didn't advocate the renunciate lifestyle at all, even though Catholic monks and nuns say they base their austere practices on its teachings. It actually denounced those practices as futile. In indisputable words it was written: "Those very things are, indeed, possessed of an appearance of wisdom in a self-imposed form of worship and mock humility, a severe treatment of the body, but they are of no value in combating the satisfying of the flesh."[1]

I had also read that in the fourth century, the Catholic Church mandated celibacy for priests though there was no basis for celibacy in the teachings of Christ or anywhere else in the scriptures. The Church was simply money hungry. The married priests, when they died, gave their inheritance to their oldest son. So the church leaders told the would-be priests that they had to marry "the Lord" so they wouldn't have an heir, but the Church could fill their coffers.

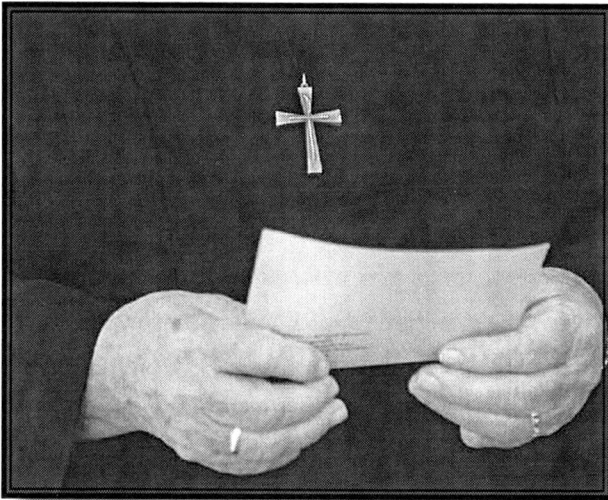

There was one scripture, though, that Swamiji had often used to justify his renunciate path, especially when he spoke to Christians in the Western world. It was the one where Jesus said that his kingdom was no part of this world.[2] In other words, as Swamiji interpreted it to mean, a true spiritual person would not rely on political leaders, fight wars, or be involved in amassing personal wealth as an expression of competitive rivalry.

I was like Swamiji in that I didn't want to try to be a productive member of a spiritually dead society. From the time I was very young, I wanted to mark my separation from such an entity, and the people attached to it. So Jesus' teaching that his kingdom was no part of the world was very appealing to me, and I longed to understand the context in which he said these words. But I couldn't understand what God's Kingdom was, and I didn't know who to ask. I sensed that the Bible had many layers of meaning and that there were both literal and metaphorical descriptions that conveyed spiritual teachings.

After six months of living in Downey, I felt well enough to move south a hundred miles to a beach town called Cardiff-by-the-Sea. I arranged to work there for a chiropractor in his office. He and his wife had hosted Swamiji and me in the years before, so I knew them well enough to make the move. I could only work 2 four-hour shifts a week because I was still so exhausted. But little by little, I increased my hours and my wages.

Some time later, I met Michael. He was a "Rolfer," a name for one who does a type of physical therapy designed to bring the body into alignment, into harmony with gravity. As my chest felt caved in after all my fruitless efforts to get spiritual enlightenment from Swamiji, I needed some bodywork. Michael had asked on his intake form what it was that I wanted to gain from his work. I had written that I wanted to become a more genuine person, taller and straighter. He must have liked that I said that because he commented on it some weeks later, in the context of telling me that I was an unusual person with unusual interests.

During the first session, he asked me to stand in my two-piece bathing suit in front of a symmetrical wall grid where a plumb bob hung down from the ceiling. That was where he checked his clients' postures as he could carefully observe them there. He said, "There are some areas on your left side that are tighter than your right side. And any time an area of your body has tension in it, it affects the rest of the body, some areas more than others."

"My chest feels tighter than anywhere else," I complained.

"Your shoulders are a bit high and forward, and you look a little hollow and collapsed in your chest."

"That makes sense," I sighed. "My heart feels down these days."

Michael offered some help. "If you decide to do the ten sessions that I recommend, we can see what layers unravel on both a physical and emotional level."

"Okay, I'm willing, but I don't have much money right now."

"Don't worry," he said, "I have a sliding scale and what matters is that you get your health and joy back." I felt so grateful that he was generous and good-hearted.

At the next session, one week later, he was working on my shoulders, ribs, and diaphragm to help my breathing and relieve the tension in my chest. He pointed out that shallow breathing is usually a reflection of the stress we've been under. "Have you had a lot of stress in your life lately?" he asked with hesitation and I knew it was because he didn't want to sound like a shrink.

"Have I? Yes," I nodded my head dramatically. "I worked so hard for so long at something that gave me nothing in return." I felt like crying as I realized the futility of my efforts with Swamiji.

He was the perfect gentleman and said in a calming voice, "It's okay to communicate your feelings because it will help your chest relax. When you talk about your feelings, it can help you get the pain out of your body."

"Well, it's a long story and most people aren't equipped to listen to me." I was lying on the table looking up at the ceiling while he worked on my shoulder. There was a colorful sign fixed to the ceiling that read "BREATHE!" So I took a deep breath and pondered how much I could tell him.

He must have known how I felt as he made a quick playfully quip. "So, it must have been med school, law school, or having triplets that exhausted you." He spoke in an upbeat, nonchalant way as if to tell me that he wouldn't be surprised by anything I'd say.

I wondered what he would think of me if I told him I was searching for spiritual truths. And if I mentioned my years with Swamiji and he didn't understand, I would have to feel defensive and defective. But I decided that I had nothing to lose by being open. After a few minutes, I told him that I had traveled with a swami for almost seven years because I was searching for spiritual truths and studying the religions of the world.

"You were searching for God?" He asked the question easily, without any negativity.

"Yes, that's the bottom line."

"Well, what did you find?"

"Nothing but heartache." I couldn't help but cry though I tried to hide it from him. I felt so disappointed.

"That hurts when you can't find what you're looking for." He consoled me simply, and patted my arm as if to say, "It's okay."

I managed to say, "I'm starting to feel like I'll never find what I'm looking for. Though I know it's out there, I don't know where to turn." I couldn't say anymore. My words were waylaid by frustration. I couldn't tell him that I felt like a failure, but he didn't seem to judge me as one.

He then asked me, "What's a swami? There's a famous surf break here in Encinitas called 'Swami's,' but I know you weren't referring to waves." I had seen an exotic, handmade surfboard hanging horizontally on the wall of his office and had commented about it the first time I had come in. He said he had made it out of rosewood, mahogony, and walnut. I liked that he was skilled and approached his work like art.

"No, a swami is a monk and spiritual teacher from India. The surf spot here called Swamis' is named after a Swami Yogananda who built a spiritual retreat on the cliffs above the ocean about fifty years ago."

"Really?" He sounded intrigued. "What kind of person was your swami?"

"He was tireless in promoting his truth about God. He was eighty-two years old when I met him, and he could work harder than anyone I knew. He had a good sense of humor and a huge commitment to his spiritual path. That impressed me about him, and I thought that maybe he could teach me about God." I didn't know how much he could understand about my ordeal with Swamiji, and why I would have taken up traveling with him in the first place, but he nodded his head as if he knew more than he let on.

"Seems like your swami made you work too hard for answers."

"That's an understatement," I choked out the words.

"So what do you do for a swami in order to get spiritual truths?"

"Kill yourself, basically." I spoke sarcastically.

"Oh, it was tough, huh?"

"More than you can even imagine!"

"Then why did you stay for so long if it was so hard?"

"Because I was in the habit of searching for meaning and purpose where it couldn't be found."

"You know, Sita," he said, "I'm not afraid to talk about God. It's actually one of my favorite subjects. Most people who come in here seem pretty confused about spiritual things, and rarely want to share their viewpoint."

The session had ended and I was preparing to leave. "Thanks," I said, shaking his hand, though I wanted to hug him for his words. Not only was he polite and professional, but kind-hearted and genuinely caring.

During the next two months of sessions, we covered many topics. One topic was about the way he said that I walked. It was part of his practice to show people how they walked so they could be aware of their posture. He said, "Do you notice how your heels strike down hard when you walk and that your head follows that pattern?" He exaggerated my walking style to help me get a sense of what he meant.

"Oh, so you think I'm a mope?" I tried to make a joke.

"Well, your energy naturally manifests in the way you

move, " he replied. He was matter-of-fact, not mean.

I remembered back to my junior high school days when I tried to befriend a depressed girl. She always moped down the hallways with her head down. That image of her was something that I didn't want to imitate.

Michael asked me unexpectedly, "How did you, a world traveler and explorer, arrive at your current state of heart?" It was an honest question, so I gave him an honest answer.

"I never have felt understood." He gave me space to explain myself. "I mean, I never really felt loved by anyone, including the swami who was supposed to know about spiritual love because he was always talking about it. But he was just a harsh taskmaster who wanted me to further his image. He said he was no part of the world, but he was just like everyone else even if his lifestyle was more eccentric."

"It's natural for us to seek love because we were made in the image of love."

"What did you say?" I didn't realize he was a spiritual person. He never talked much about himself.

"I mean, Sita, that God is love."

I must have looked at him like he was nuts because he added, "Does that sound odd to you?"

"No! But you've been holding out on me. What is your spiritual path?" I was excited to hear what he said.

He smiled quietly and didn't answer my question, but he told me that after the session he wanted to show me something. So when it was over, we walked down the stairs from his office and sat on a bench outside. He pulled a Bible out of his pocket and opened it.

He knew that I was cautious about anyone peddling their

spiritual wares, as I had told him about many things I had seen during my travels with Swamiji. He also knew that I wanted to know God, but that I wouldn't stand for any nonsense. For he knew that Swamiji had promised me that he would show me God's love, but he failed.

Michael also knew my background in sciences and so he just asked me a simple question. "Did you know long ago, around three thousand five hundred years ago, a remarkably accurate scientific statement was made in the Bible?"

My eyes must have widened. "Scientific?" I repeated.

"Yes," he responded seriously. "Look what is written here." He read to me, "'God is hanging the earth upon nothing.'"[3]

"Wow. How interesting," I remarked and then told him that even Aristotle, the Greek philosopher who influenced the Western world for two thousand years, rejected the concept of a void. Michael nodded.

"So who could have written such a statement?" Michael's eyes lit up.

"I don't know who wrote it," I replied.

"Moses did."

"Moses? But wasn't Moses a shepherd?" I inquired.

"Yes, he was. So," Michael appealed to my mind, " how could Moses come to believe that a heavy, solid object like the earth could stay suspended in space without any physical support?"

"Good question."

"After all," he continued, "Moses was raised in Egypt by the Pharaoh's daughter and he was probably tutored in Egyptian cosmology."

"What did the Egyptians believe, do you know?"

He told me that the Egyptians, like most ancient peoples, put themselves at the center of the universe. Their cosmology shaped the universe like a box, with Egypt at the center. But high mountains were thought to hold up the sky.

I was thinking fast as I listened to what he said. I was sure his intention was to get me to ask how Moses could have had such a completely different and notably accurate understanding of the earth's position in space. I had no answer for him, but just added some facts about ancient ideas about the earth.

I wanted him to know that I was no dummy. I told him that I had studied the ancient Greeks and that Thales, who died in 546 B.C.E., was hailed as one of the fathers of modern science. And Plato, in his dialogue called the *Protagoras,* even numbered Thales as one of the seven wise men of Greek culture. But Thales still believed that the earth floated on water!

I was so gratified to hear what Michael had read to me about the earth hanging in space. It gave me a feeling of hope that science could be used in a spiritual context to point out a spiritual purpose, and not just used by scientists to support their egos and atheism.

But what Michael showed me next, blew my mind. "Look what is written here. Read this!" He said that it was what King Solomon of ancient Israel had written about the water cycle some thousand years before the birth of Christ.

I read it out loud. "'All the rivers run into the sea, yet the sea is not full. To the place where the rivers flow, there they flow again.'"[4] When I finished reading, I paused for a moment and then raised my voice excitedly, "This is amazingly detailed and accurate!"

Michael smiled at my enthusiasm. The sunshine beat down on us and my heart felt so uplifted. He didn't hesitate to ask me: "So how could King Solomon be so scientifically accurate when the influence around him was nonsensical from a modern scientific point of view?"

I didn't want to give in to him too easily so I countered him with the question, "How do we know the influence on him was like the Egyptians on Moses?"

He then explained that the Canaanite cultures, adjacent to the Israelite one, believed something like the gods had made an egg that was full of creatures and when it hatched, the sky and heavenly bodies were formed. But, still, twin mountains had to hold up the sky. It was a lot like the Egyptian beliefs.

Before he went to lunch, Michael showed me another scripture. A Bible writer named Amos, who was a shepherd and a farmer, wrote two hundred years after Solomon about the water cycle from a different perspective. He said, God is "the One calling for the waters of the sea, that he may pour them out upon the surface of the earth."[5]

I was happily astonished. I loved what he was pointing out. Spiritual men wrote accurately about the physical world thousands of years before physical men, who had to figure it out on their own. The obvious implication of Michael's sharing the scriptures with me was that the Bible writers were inspired by God. They wrote what they couldn't have known for themselves.

Later, I did some research on the water cycle and found out that it was seven hundred years after Amos in the first century B.C.E., that a Roman engineer named Marcus Vitruvius, conceived the idea that rain falling in the mountains entered into the earth and created streams and springs at lower elevations. But throughout the Middle Ages, all the way from the fall of the Roman empire in the fifth century to the beginnings of the Italian Renaissance in the sixteenth century, the explanation for the continual flow of rivers was based on Homer's mythological ideas in his *Iliad*. Homer wrote some seven to eight hundred years before Marcus Vitruvius lived.

I remember reading Homer's *Iliad* in a university English course. Like all the ancient writings that I had read, natural phenomena was talked about in terms of the mood-driven actions of gods and goddesses. Homer's *Iliad* was no different when it came to account for the source of water on land. The water was apparently upwellings from a deep river god that circled the earth. His name was "Oceanus."[6]

Finally, at the end of the fifteenth century, one thousand four hundred years after Marcus Vitruvius, Leonardo da Vinci was recognized as making the first scientifically acceptable statements about the components of the water cycle.[7] They included: Water evaporates from the sea, forms clouds, precipitates onto the land, and flows back to the sea, just as King Solomon had accurately written some three thousand years before.

Not only did King Solomon describe the water cycle in accurate terms, but also in detail. I wondered if the spiritual oasis that I had been seeking was the Bible because it was special. No other book claimed what Moses and Solomon had said about the earth, and so long ago. The different religious books of the world that I had read couldn't come close. They were filled with myth and contradiction.

Another scripture Michael showed me, which he said was written about three thousand five hundred years ago, was that the earth was a circle: "There is One who is dwelling above the circle of the earth."[8] This was corroborated by Moses who wrote in another Bible book some seven hundred years later: "He [God] has described a circle upon the face of the waters."[9]

If the first scientifically-valid statements were Biblical, as seen in the writings about the water cycle and the earth being round and suspended in space, then this suggests that historians of science aren't accurate in their assessment that the ancient Greeks, who lived 500 to 600 years B.C.E., held out the first glimpses of the truth about the laws of nature and natural phenomena.[10]

For example, historians of science praise the Greek Anaximander (who was a younger contemporary of Thales) for being the first person to conceive of a mechanical model of the earth. But his earth was the shape of cylinder, not a circle! It had a height one-third of its diameter and was flat on top, where people lived. Nevertheless, his model is thought to be an improvement on Thales' cosmogony before him, because Thales believed that the earth floated on water. Anaximander's model allowed for celestial bodies to now pass under the earth and the sun, moon, and stars were located on concentric rotating circles. But Anaximander is especially praised as a revolutionary thinker because he decided that stars were rings of fire, and not gods.

Even Thales is regarded today as having searched for the cause of change in nature itself, as if he had some sense of natural laws apart from the mood-driven actions of the pantheon of Greek gods. But his cosmology still relied on some creative animating source that most scientists never seem to mention when they use Thales to support their atheistic outlook.

Thales didn't believe as Darwinists do, that change occurred by accident. To him, somewhere in the muddled relationship between the forces of the natural world and the gods, he determined that cause was always intentional. He couldn't conceive of being an atheist because, as Aristotle pointed out, "Thales thinks all things are full of gods."[11] Within his rationality was the idea that the force behind natural phenomena had a metaphysical source.

Though the gods Thales mentions are not those that appear in Homer's writings, they are more like powers stripped of personification. These gods or forces, however they were imagined, were also discussed by Aristotle who pointed out Thales' belief that a stone had a soul, as in the case of a magnet's pull on iron.[12] Whatever the specifics of Thales' thought in this regard, he did make a break from the traditional mythological interpretations of the workings of the natural world. For this reason he is celebrated as making a step in the right direction towards a meaningful scientific method.[13]

Ironically, most scientists today believe that Bible teachings, much more than Thales' earth floating on water and Anaximander's cylinder model of the flat-top world, have held back scientific advancement. But this isn't true, as seen by what the scriptures say about the round shape of the earth, its position in the sky, and the cyclical processes of the water cycle. So why the obvious bias?

In the case of the struggle between Galileo and the Roman Catholic Church in the seventeenth centuy, for example, it wasn't the Bible that was at issue. Galileo claimed that his scientific discoveries supported what the Bible said.[14] So what was the problem for Galileo? Simply, church politics. For Galileo had improved upon the telescope and consequently supported the findings of Copernicus, who showed that the sun, not the earth, was at the center of the solar system. But for nearly two thousand years, Aristotle's view of the earth-centered solar system was dominant. Aristotle's philosophy of the earth-centered model was based on his opinion that the earth couldn't move because it would grind to a halt due to friction. He also believed that the heavens were a complex series of spheres within spheres, with the earth at the center.

Thomas Aquinas, the ardent Catholic who lived in the thirteenth century, revered Aristotle and called him "The Philosopher." As a result, he worked for five years to fuse Aristotle's philosophy with Catholic doctrine. In his book *Galileo's Mistake: A New Look at the Epic Confrontation Between Galileo and the Church*, Wade Rowland showed that, through Aquinas, Aristotle's philosophy was wed to Church theology. The resulting theology was not Biblical.

By incorporating Aristotle's pre-Christian philosophy into their theology, the Church Fathers deviated from the teachings of the Bible. In so doing, Aristotle's earth-centered view became dogma of the Church of Rome. For his unwillingness to blindly accept this dogma, Galileo was sentenced by the Inquisition to life in prison, though the charge was dropped to house arrest because of his age.

Contemplating Galileo's situation made me realize that a true scientist wouldn't ever get stuck in bias or dogma. Galileo's case was so interesting because he proved that a wise scientist can both believe in a Creator, like he did, and also make immense scientific discoveries. In other words, spiritual and physical truths don't have to be mutually exclusive.

It occurred to me that most scientists had a negative reaction to the Bible, especially the creation account in Genesis, as a matter of bias because they hadn't read through it for themselves. In my university days, the Genesis account was often an object of mockery and abuse by my science professors because they blatantly called it myth. Of course, I couldn't blame them for calling Christians "stupid" who spouted out that the creative days of Genesis were six periods of 24 hours each. But I couldn't help but think that maybe they were just as stupid for not having studied what they had already judged.

I decided that I would study the creation account and see what I could find out for myself. The Bible, after all, had proved to be accurate with regards to the shape of the earth, how it was suspended in space, and also in the details of the water cycle. Prior to my study of the creation account, I compiled a list of the order of events that I knew scientists believed occurred with regards to the creation of the earth and how life began.

First, the universe was thought to have a beginning called the "big bang." Then, according to what scientists say the fossil record shows, life first appeared in the sea as single-celled organisms, and then gradually became multi-celled and complex, and crawled onto land as fish with lungs. Finally, humans appeared millions of years later. So what exactly does the creation account say, and how does it measure up to what scientists describe as the successive events in the emergence of life as we know it? And, more importantly, how does the account stand in relation to the findings of the fossil record?

To begin with, I learned that the creation account allows for the earth to be billions of years old. The word "day" in the Hebrew language means various periods of time, not a day based on a cycle of the sun. And, after all, if you read the Genesis account, you find that the sun wasn't discernible from the earth until the fourth creative day and so the cycle of the sun couldn't be logically established as the measure of time for a creative day.

Specifically, the Genesis account shows that the creation events occurred in the following order: (1) a beginning, (2) a primitive earth in darkness, and covered by water and gases, (3) light, (4) an atmosphere, (5) large areas of dry land, (6) land plants, (7) sun, moon, and stars discernible in the atmosphere, (8) sea animals and birds (9) mammals (10) humans.[15]

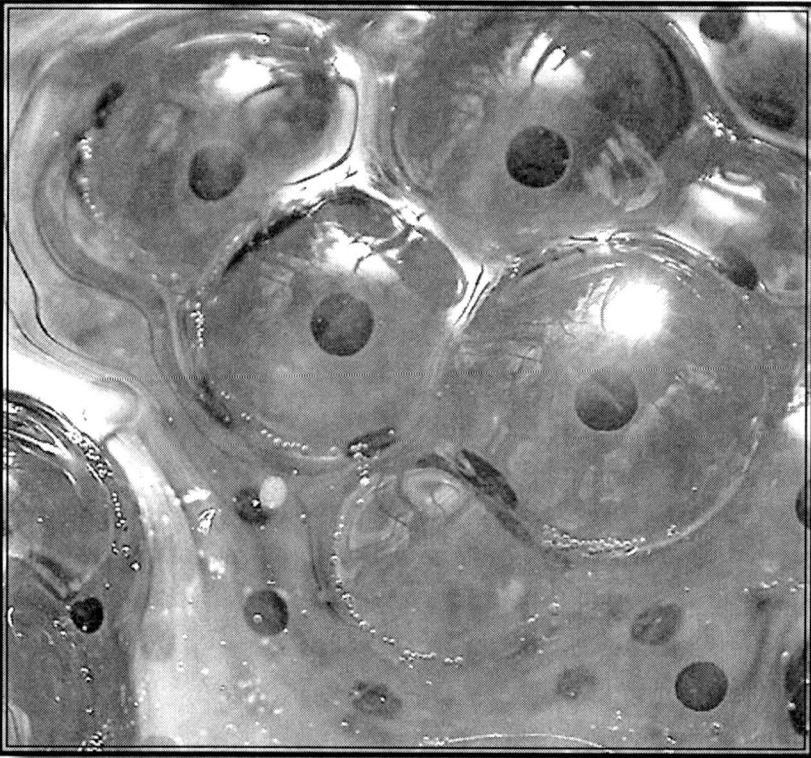

The creation account is remarkably similar to what scientists agree are the stages that gave rise to life on earth, but the creation account is thousands of years older. Of course, the major difference between them is that the creation account calls for a Creator as the force behind the progressive development of life from simple to complex forms. By contrast, most scientists believe that the sequence of events to establish life happened by accident.

Speaking of accidents, what are the chances that a Bible writer could make up the order of ten events so similar to what scientists claim to be the right sequence of events? What are the chances that a person could get the sequence right on the very first try? These are rational questions that set a logical precedence or accountability upon which we can determine the accuracy of our beliefs, either that life arose by accident or was an expression of willed purpose.

In terms of numbers, just what is the probability that someone could pick out ten numbers, one through ten, in the right order on the first try? Not very likely. It is only 1 in 3,628,800. So was it just a lucky guess that the Bible writer stated the steps of creation in accordance with scientific ideas? But what about scientific ideas? Does the fossil record support what scientists say occurred in the long stretch of time from the creation of the earth until now?

Fossils are considered to give a valid history of life because they are the remains of ancient life-forms and their habits. The difficulty of accurately dating fossils, and the rocks they are found in, causes disagreements between scientists. But the general trend in the fossil record is widely recognized: Older rocks show less complex fossils and younger rocks shows more complex fossils.

Where single-celled organisms, like microscopic bacteria, are considered to have originated on earth more than 3.5 billion years ago, multi-celled organisms don't appear spectacularly in the fossil record (in terms of numbers and diversity) before about 550 million years, before the Cambrian period in earth history. Scientists believe that the Cambrian period lasted roughly 55 million years and was marked by the sudden appearance of a vast variety of hard-bodied, complex creatures. For this reason, the Cambrian period is often called "the Cambrian explosion." The fossil record shows that major groups of invertebrate sea animals including trilobites, snails, starfish, sponges, and jellyfish all appeared on earth simultaneously.

The immense diversity of Cambrian fossils, in contrast to the lack of diversity of fossils before them, was a remarkable discovery. Even Charles Darwin was painfully aware that this sudden proliferation of so many new complex life-forms, which are recorded in the fossil record, did not support his theory that life-forms evolved gradually. He acknowledged this blow when he wrote: "Geology assuredly does not reveal any such finely-graduated organic chain; and this, perhaps, is the most obvious and serious objection which can be urged against the theory [of evolution]."[16]

In addition, the complicated physiological structures of the Cambrian fossils must have perplexed Darwin. They showed that ancient life-forms had a circulatory system, gills, and eyes, which weren't all that different from their modern relatives. The eye of the trilobite, for example, was so complex that paleontologist David M. Raup wrote: "The trilobites used an optimal design which would require a well trained and imaginative optical engineer to develop today."[17]

According to the creation account, the fossil record should and does contain complex life-forms suddenly appearing and then multiplying without notable change in their body structures. In other words, fossils show regular distinctness over time. This consistency is in harmony with the creation account, which is based on the idea that life-forms did not evolve from a common ancestor.

Certainly, many of the Cambrian life-forms went extinct. But what about those that didn't? Sponges, jellyfish, starfish, and snails, for example, remain identifiable today in the same form. Why didn't they mutate? On this subject one evolutionist wrote: "The bony-finned coelacanth, thought to be long extinct but rediscovered in 1938, has been approximately static some 450 million years."[18]

He also pointed out that "the nearly timeless species are not exempt from the changes of proteins that go on in all living beings, and they could surely vary in many ways without loss of adaptiveness, but their patterns have become somehow frozen... From the point of view of conventional evolutionary theory, long-term stasis is hard to explain. Rapid evolution is comprehensive as species adapt to new conditions or opportunities but it is incongruous that species remain unchanged through changing conditions over many million years."[19]

So what is the consensus about the fossil record? What does it show with regards to change in animal structure or behavior? Have missing links or transitional fossils been found to support Darwin's theory?

Darwin pointed out his belief that parallel to the processes of extinction of species would be their mutation into new life-forms. He wrote that "just in proportion as this process of extermination has acted on an enormous scale, so must the number of intermediate varieties, which have formerly existed, be truly enormous. Why then is not every geological formation and every stratum full of such intermediate links?"[20]

The lack of occurrence of transitional links in the fossil record is not disputed by acclaimed scientists in our day. Even Stephen Jay Gould, paleontologist, admitted this when he said, "The extreme rarity of transitional forms in the fossil record persists as the trade secret of paleontology. The evolutionary trees that adorn our textbooks have data only at the tips and nodes of their branches; the rest is inference, however reasonable, not the evidence of fossils."[21] Not the evidence of fossils? What does Gould mean by "extreme rarity"? Extreme rarity means probably nonexistent.

And Ernst Mayr, one of the twentieth century's leading evolutionary biologists, notably wrote: "Paleontologists had long been aware of a seeming contradiction between Darwin's postulate of gradualism, confirmed by the work of population genetics, and the actual findings of paleontology. Following phyletic lines through time seemed to reveal only minimal gradual changes but no clear evidence for any change of a species into a different genus or for the gradual origin of an evolutionary novelty. Anything truly novel always seemed to appear quite abruptly in the fossil record."[22] From these statements, it appears Mayr's conclusions are more in accord with the Bible account of the sudden appearance of distinct forms than they are with evolutionary ideas.

Niles Eldredge, the renowned palentologist who proposed the evolutionary theory of punctuated equilibrium with Stephen Jay Gould in 1972, surprisingly said: "No wonder paleontologists shied away from evolution for so long. It seems never to happen. Assiduous collecting up cliff faces yields zigzags, minor oscillations, and the very occasional slight accumulation of change over millions of years, at a rate too slow to really account for all the prodigious change that has occurred in evolutionary history."[23] This is an extraordinary remark for an evolutionist to make because it defies the accuracy of the idea that evolution proceeds by slow change over time.

Eldredge continued to say, "When we do see the introduction of evolutionary novelty, it usually shows up with a bang, and often with no firm evidence that the organisms did not evolve elsewhere! Evolution cannot forever be going on someplace else. Yet that's how the fossil record has struck many a forlorn paleontologist looking to learn something about evolution."[24] So Eldredge, too, admits that paleontologists can't find the physical evidence to support the idea of transitional links.

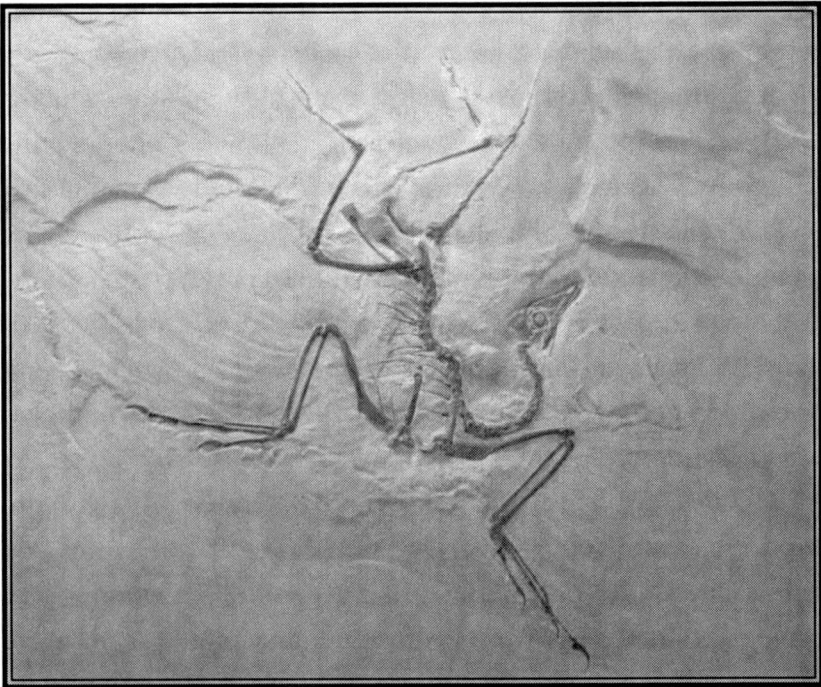

Regarding bird evolution, Alan Feduccia, former head of biology at the University of North Carolina, Chapel Hill, expressed that the missing link from reptiles to birds really was a bird after all. He said, "Archaeopteryx probably cannot tell us much about the early origins of feathers and flight in true protobirds because Archaeopteryx was, in the modern sense, a bird."[25]

When it comes to the evolution of reptiles in relation to mammals, Tom Kemp, the curator of the zoological collections at the University Museum at Oxford, has this to say: "Each species of mammal-like reptile that has been found appears suddenly in the fossil record and is not preceded by the species that is directly ancestral to it. It disappears some time later, equally abruptly, without leaving a directly descended species although we usually find that it has been replaced by some new, related species."[26]

According to Robert Bruce Knox, elected Fellow of the Australian Academy of Science, the fossil record simply does not give scientists a way to create lines of relatedness between species. He wrote, "People suppose that phylogeny can be discovered directly from the fossil record by studying a graded series of old to young fossils and by discovering ancestors, but this is not true. The fossil record supplies evidence of the geological ages of the forms of life, but not of their direct ancestor-descendant relationships. There is no way of knowing whether a fossil is a direct ancestor of a more recent species or represents a related line of descent (lineage) that simply became extinct."[27]

James Marden, professor of biology at the Pennsylvania State University, had this to say about insects: "Certain modern species are reasonably similar, in their anatomy, to fossils of winged insects dating back 325 million years. The problem is, wings appear in the fossil record already full formed...So miraculous a thing is insect flight that nearly all insect biologists believe it would have evolved only once."[28] Insect wings appear fully formed! No transitional links have ever been found, and insects have been around a long time.

Others have acknowledged the same phenomenon. David Kitts, professor of geology at the University of Oklahoma, wrote: "Despite the bright promise that paleontology provides a means of `seeing' evolution, it has presented some nasty difficulties for evolutionists the most notorious of which is the presence of `gaps' in the fossil record. Evolution requires intermediate forms between species and paleontology does not provide them."[29]

Because factual evidence cannot be found today for missing links, though millions of fossils have been found and catalogued, it is logical to assume that they will never be found. J. Francis Hitching, the British author, points out that sometimes fossils are made to appear as transitional links to support Darwin and his followers, but he writes that he isn't one to be duped. "It takes a while to realize that the 'thousands' of intermediates being referred to have no obvious relevance to the origin of lions and jellyfish and things. Most of them are simply varieties of a particular kind of creature, artificially arranged in a certain order to demonstrate Darwinism at work, and then rearranged every time a new discovery casts doubt upon the arrangement."[30]

Finally, with regards to the evolution of the horse, Gerald A. Kerkut, former Head of the Department of Neurophysiology at the University of Southampton, admits: "It would not be fitting in discussing the implications of evolution to leave the evolution of the horse out of the discussion. The evolution of the horse provides one of the keystones in the teaching of evolutionary doctrine, though the actual story depends to a large extent upon who is telling it and when the story is being told. In fact one could easily discuss the evolution of the story of the evolution of the horse."[31]

It is surprising that, in spite of the fact that evolutionary scientists themselves admit that the fossil record does not show evidence of transitional links, they still persist in believing in evolution. Why is this the case? Richard Lewontin, a Darwin fundamentalist, gives an answer. He says that scientists don't have to be logical. In his words, "We take the side of science in spite of the patent absurdity of some of its constructs...because we have a prior commitment, a commitment to materialism." He added, speaking for scientists in general: "It is not that the methods and institutions of science somehow compel us to accept a material explanation of the phenomenal world, but, on the contrary, that we are forced by our a priori adherence to material causes to create an apparatus of investigation and a set of concepts that produce material explanations, no matter how counter-intuitive…that materialism is absolute, for we cannot allow a Divine Foot in the door."[32]

So what can one say to Lewontin and all who agree with him? That his dogmatism is too emotional? That the greatest tragedy of his life is his unwillingness to consider what is greater than his own ego? That he would rather be hit by a train than step outside his comfort zone?

Lewontin demonstrates that, in the end, what we all believe is directly determined by our emotional maturity. For free will is essentially an expression of our personal inclination, an honest reflection of our wisdom. Perhaps the most telling aspect of Lewontin's psyche being exposed here is that he is afraid to confront himself, and the possibility that there is a God after all. His not allowing "a Divine Foot in the door," regardless of the consequences, smacks of an unwillingness to use his mind in an open way to explore the meaning and purpose of life. For, as he says, science does not compel him, and all whom he represents, to accept a material explanation of the phenomenal world.

One would think that he, as a scientist, would have a serious analyzing mind and a rational commitment to unlocking the mysteries of life. But by limiting his awareness to a solely empirical outlook, and by making science his Savior, he seems to take up company with those who create false gods. For Lewontin has admitted that he, and all who believe like he does, will accept the constructs of science as the altar for worship in spite of the "patent absurdity of some of its constructs."

This sort of thinking is akin to the Christian fundamentalists, who, regardless of the evidence to the contrary, adamantly claim that the six days of creation are composed of 24-hour intervals. So Lewontin's dogmatic adherence to the materialistic outlook is, in essence, no different than the Catholic Church leaders who rejected Galileo's discovery that the earth orbited the sun. They preferred to believe Aristotle's idea that the earth was the center of the universe, in spite of Galileo's evidence to the contrary. Of course, in the sense that they wanted to make the earth, like their egos, the center of attention, they were true to the forces of dogma.

Though Lewontin exposes his lack of intellect to others, he still tries to hide behind it. Real intelligence, though, does not arise from the ego's perceptions, but from a progressive willingness to strip them off and see things in a broader context. A wise person will not compartmentalize his consciousness, as Lewontin does. He won't divide his capacity for thinking from feeling as a justification for avoiding the fear of what he doesn't know.

One who searches for the spiritual oasis, for the meaning and purpose of life, knows that life is about relationships and about motivations based on feelings; feelings like denial, fear, rejection, acceptance, courage, and love. To understand life, then, is to understand these feelings and how we are driven by them.

My search for the spiritual oasis was a simple metaphor for my desire to understand emotion and its relationship to the mind. I wanted to know how to balance my capacity to feel, which was enormous, with my capacity to think, which was also huge. I knew that if I could find true spiritual principles, I could live with both abundant feelings of gratitude and with clarity of mind. My feelings wouldn't contradict my thinking, and my thinking wouldn't override my feelings.

Though it may seem like there are many reliable answers about how to live in harmony with one's own faculties, I couldn't find a balanced person to explain these things to me. But I knew that a balanced person would have to be shaped by spiritual principles that taught him or her how to appreciate and learn from feelings, as well as how to cultivate the mind and understanding.

Based on the scientific accuracy of the Bible with regards to the creation account, the round earth hanging in space, and the details of the water cycle, which were written some three thousand years ago when the rest of the world was writing myth, I began to discern that the Bible could relate the truth about God. But first you had to demonstrate the right heart condition before you could build an intellectually accurate knowledge.

You had to cross the desert of your own self, wandering in a lonely and windy desolation regardless of your social standing. You know, when you set off by yourself, that your ego can't teach you the truth because the ego always wants to be the creator of truth. For this reason, the ego creates and follows worldly wisdom because it finds no delight in submission to higher spiritual laws.

As I started to read and study the Bible, I walked away from the desert of myself and entered a valley that was hidden from the outside world. In that valley was an oasis rich in color, textures, and shapes that I had never seen before. I experienced sensations and feelings that I had only somehow imagined. What I read had a dazzling effect on me, and I couldn't explain it to anyone. I felt full, as if a spring of recognition flowed, bubbling out of me. I couldn't make sense of where it came from. I only knew that it was beyond me, but connected to me, flowing from a deep place.

The Bible told me, in a language of date palms and fragrant jasmine, that the essence of human life is not death and finality, but an open-ended outflowing potentiality. This potentiality is an expression of God's will. These things are hard to understand unless you read the Bible's words, though most people are unwilling. But the Bible is an oasis. When you arrive there, you find out that its waters hold the secret of life. Of course, it is not a secret that only a few are allowed to know. It is available to anyone and everyone who wants to know what it is. But first you have to pass the tests of honesty and humility before you can drink the water.

Noticeably, not many people have been willing to pass these tests; hence, many so-called Christians are violent, egotistical people who use their beliefs as political tools. The world wars were instigated and fought by Christian countries who believed that God was on their side. Clearly these people did not have God's spirit or backing because they practiced murder and hatred.

I discovered an intriguing scripture that read, "For the word of God is alive and exerts power and is sharper than any two-edged sword...and is able to discern thoughts and intentions of the heart."[33] I had seen nothing like this written in the other scriptures of the world's religions. This scripture basically means that if you read the Bible, then it will act like a mirror in which you can see your true heart motives in relation to your ego.

For example, some read the Bible in order to refute it, while others read to gain spiritual knowledge. In the latter case, the desire to read would be a spiritual motivation, not an egotistical one. The inner motivation is the impelling force which reveals the true person, as represented by the heart's condition to open and not close, to learn and not resist, to love and not push away.

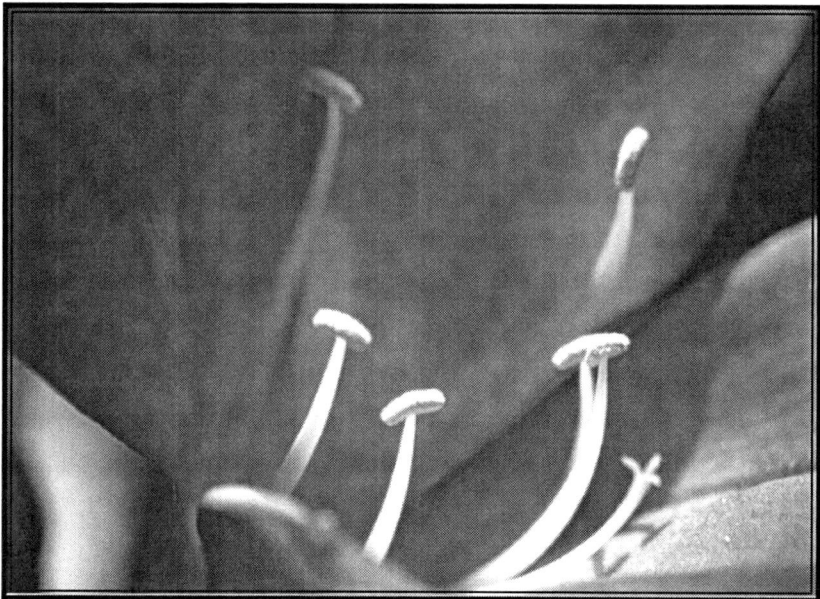

The more I read the Bible, the more I felt compelled to read. It wasn't like anything I had ever set my eyes upon. I discovered that the Bible told a love story of immense proportions. In fact, it seemed to be the greatest love story ever told. Most people can't realize this simply because for so long controlling people have used the Bible as a club. Perhaps it makes sense, though, that in this world of division, the greatest love will be masked by the greatest absence of love. Why such a polarity exists is explained in the Bible. But to understand it you have to be humble enough to examine how and why this polarity came to be in the first place.

I saw that the Bible teaches us how to equip our minds with knowledge of what love is and how it acts. For love can be known only from the action that it prompts. The Bible holds out an invitation to understand the truth about love. It makes clear how the source of love is divine. We are made to reflect this love, and will feel it more and more, as we make the effort to strip off our selfish inclinations, both conscious and unconscious.

I began to notice the basic theme of the Bible, which is that God is love. If you want to learn to love in a selfless way, then you can know God. In contrast, it is written, "He that does not love has not come to know God because God is love."[34] The idea of God as love is a difficult concept for many people who are accustomed to believing that there is no conscious force in the universe besides their human will. But the Bible teaches that God is love, so love is not distinct from God. This means that God does not possess love as an attribute the way he possesses power, wisdom, and justice. In other words, the essence of God is love, though love as an abstract quality is not God.

God is not abstract. He is not an impersonal force but an entity, though a spiritual being and not a physical one. The Bible is about the love that emanates from God and was modeled by Jesus. Of course, it sounds bizarre to scientists, especially atheists, to think in terms of love as God's essential nature. They do not consider love to be a compelling creative force in the same way they regard chance to be a compelling force for change. Similarly, it is probably impossible for them to think of themselves, even in terms of a mental exercise, as being created. Their egos simply won't allow it. Notably, in the Bible book of Psalms it is written that the "supercilious one" makes no search for God. "All his ideas are: 'There is no God.'"[35]

But love for the idea of an absolute love can stir the heart. A personal relationship with absolute love is appealing. Though in order to begin to develop this relationship with love, we have to expand our understanding. A foundational principle in the Bible is that love has a universal nature. It is much more than a limited personal emotion.

When I read about the man Jesus in the books of the Greek scriptures, I learned that he could perfectly reflect God's love. There was a reason that he could do what the rest of us could not. There are a lot of stages involved in understanding why that was possible for him, but the point here is that Jesus was a model of love for us. He could be trusted because of his intimate relationship with God. The night before he died, he told his disciples he was giving them a new teaching. It was a commandment for them to love each other just as he had loved them.[36]

Why did Jesus say this? Because love was to serve as an identifying mark of the people who applied his teachings in their lives. Jesus explained, "By this all will know that you are my disciples, if you have love among yourselves."[37] Certainly, then, it is confusing to see that people who call themselves Christians are among the most violent people on earth. But it is because they don't have the motivation to love, and they use the idea of love to dominate others by force. These people are not disciples of Jesus, even if they say they are, because based on what he taught we know that he would not approve of their violent behavior.

This actuality doesn't have to be a stumbling block. It just means that if you want to know God and his purpose for mankind, then you have to be willing to listen and learn. There are rewards to knowing these truths, but it doesn't mean you can earn them. It isn't like the world's ways, where so many earn a position of power through domination, bribery, and nepotism.

Another possible stumbling block for people is that they can't understand why a God of love would allow so many to suffer throughout the ages. But it isn't God who causes suffering, but people who have chosen to live independently of an accurate knowledge of God. This statement isn't as simplistic as it sounds, but serves as a starting point for a discussion of evil in the world. Through historic and prophetic patterns, the Bible shows that love will always win over hatred and violence. But this can only be understood by those who cultivate the qualities of love, joy, peace, patience, kindness, faith, mildness, and self-control.[38]

Many people who haven't read the Bible will say that it contradicts itself, that it wasn't God-inspired, that everyone has his own interpretation, which then renders it useless as a universal teaching tool. They also say that God is partial, that the Bible is a white man's book, and that it is not practical for our modern day. But perhaps such people don't want to understand what it says because they can't admit that they aren't spiritually thirsty. They have no interest in enlightenment.

The Bible was written by some forty people over a period of sixteen centuries and contains sixty-six books, but I still noticed its significant internal harmony. For even though it was written by people from all walks of life, its themes continued unhampered and coherent from the Hebrew scriptures (Old Testament) through the Greek scriptures (New Testament). It is exceptional that people with different levels of education, wealth, and cultural experience could not only write compatibly about God, but also continue to reveal God's purpose for humans and the earth. For a herdsman, an orchard harvester, a tax collector, a physician, a prophet, and a king all wrote books of the Bible, and yet remained true to the same line of reasoning, even in the smallest details. Though it would seem likely there would be ample opportunity for collusion in the Bible's writings, because it took 1,610 years to be compiled, there remarkably is none.

P. Marion Simms explained in 1929 that the Bible, though much older than other classical writings like Homer and Plato, has a special category all its own: "In the number of ancient MSS. [manuscripts] attesting a writing, and in the number of years that had elapsed between the original and the attesting MSS., the Bible enjoys a decided advantage over classical writings...Altogether classical MSS. are but a handful compared with Biblical. No ancient book is so well attested as the Bible."[39]

This means that the Bible has been well-preserved and studied. There are more than one thousand seven hundred ancient manuscripts of the Hebrew Scriptures, which exist in entirety or as fragments. They date back to the first or second century B.C.E. Not surprisingly, there are more than five thousand manuscripts of the Greek Scriptures, the oldest having been written in the second century C.E. Additionally, there are some ten thousand copies of early translations in other languages.

The well-known Chester Beatty Biblical Papyri contains both Old and New Testament texts that were written in Greek and date back to the second and third centuries C.E. In the introduction to his volumes on these papyri, Sir Frederic Kenyon stated that the papyri were sound in comparison with existing Biblical texts. He wrote, "There are no important omissions or additions of passages, and no variations which affect vital facts or doctrines. The variations of text affect minor matters, such as the order of words or the precise words used...But their essential importance is their confirmation, by evidence of an earlier date than was hitherto available, of the integrity of our existing texts."[40]

Sir Kenyon's experience with the ancient Biblical texts indicates that though modern translations may vary, the variations are minor. Due to the fact that so many ancient manuscripts exist, it is possible to determine an accurate meaning of the original languages. Even if some translators take the liberty to alter the original meaning of the text, these deviations can be identified by comparing translations.

Initially, what I appreciated most about the Bible was that it supported my belief that only an integrated person could have an accurate spiritual comprehension. It pointed out that only an integrated mind, heart, and will to act can understand what it means to know God. In other words, the development of all the human faculties can support a balanced understanding and satisfy one's emotion, intellect, and ability to act upon their direction. Jesus showed that we must strive to be integrated in order to know the fullness of love. He said, "You must love your God with your whole heart, your whole mind, and your whole strength."[41]

So what does it mean to love God with your whole heart? It means, first of all, that you recognize that you have a spiritual need, a need to know what is true about life and the purpose of your existence. It means that the fulfillment of this need will satisfy your potential as a feeling, thinking, and action-oriented being. And second, it means that you yearn for a relationship with love, a love of the highest kind. This means that you want to know who God is. God is capable of a loving intelligent relationship through means of real communication, which, from our side, involves prayer.

A scripture points to an appealing invitation: "Draw close to God and he will draw close to you."[42] But, to start out with, knowing God means knowing his name. For it is not possible to have a close relationship with someone whose personal name you don't know. Many people, though, balk at the idea of God personified because they don't like that God is traditionally called a "he." The use of this personal pronoun, however, doesn't mean that God is male. No, God is neither a misogynist, nor created by one. "He," even like the word "God," is an anthropomorphic term of reference.

Though God is also called Lord, Adonai, or Father, it doesn't mean that God is literally these things as we know them to be in human terms. Just like these designations that refer to God's identity, the words "madam," "boss," "mother," and "grandma," can all label the same woman. Though labels provide a frame of reference and give a name, in a sense, to some entity, they don't identify the personal nature of that entity. In the case of the woman, to know her is to know her personal name. For only her name, after all, reminds us of everything we have learned about her. The name of a person is, indeed, the key to our relationship with him or her. For if we refer to someone as "that man" or "that woman," we are pointing out that we don't know who he or she is. The same is true about our relationship with God.

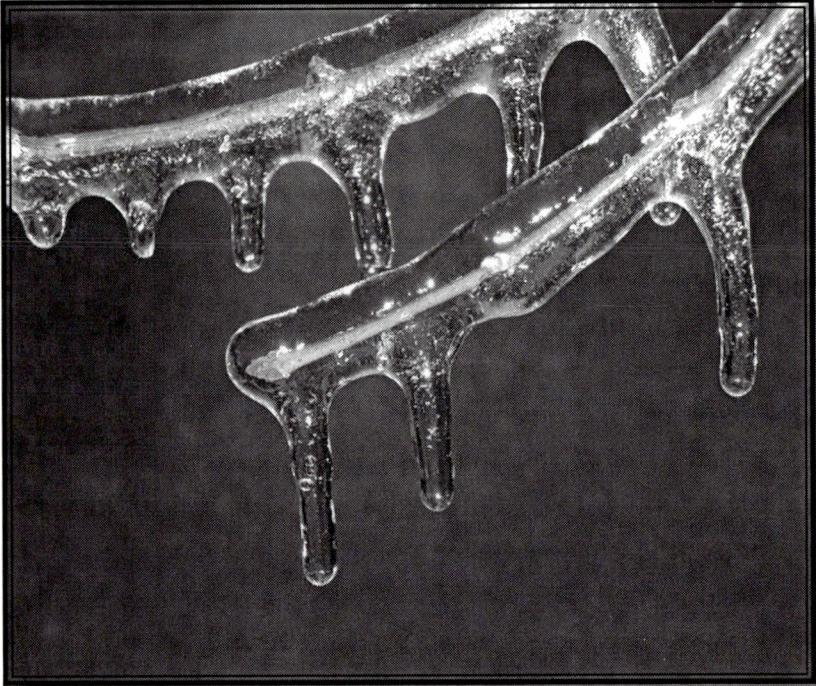

Most people don't know that God has a name, though God tells us his name in the Bible on many occasions. The reason is that Bible translations these days say that God's name is "Lord." But that is equivalent to saying, for example, that your mother's name is "Mom," or your daughter's name is "girl." Why, then, when it comes to the important matter of knowing God's personal name, do most modern Bible translations leave it out of the Bible and substitute "Lord" instead?

For example, in Isaiah 42:8 it is written in the *Living Bible,* "I am the Lord! That is my name." In the *New American Bible,* the same title is given, but the letters are capitalized. The same is true for the *Revised Standard Bible*, the *Scofield Reference Bible*, and the *King James Version*, plus others. By contrast, the translation by James Moffat reads, "I am the Eternal, the true God; that is my name." But the *Jerusalem Bible* translates the same scripture as "My name is Yahweh," and the *New World Translation*, translates it as "I am Jehovah. That is my name."

So why the discrepancy? What is accurate? "Lord," Yahweh," or "Jehovah"? With some simple study, one can find out that God's name in ancient Hebrew comes from the verb *hawah*, which means "He Causes to Become." This name occurs 6,828 times in the Hebrew as YHWH or JHVH. But since ancient Hebrew did not use vowels, the exact pronunciation of YHWH or JHVH could not be preserved.

The practice of substituting titles for God's name developed among Jews, who were afraid of using God's name in vain. This practice was applied in later copies of the Greek *Septuagint* (the Greek version of the Hebrew Bible, translated between the first and third centuries B.C.E.), the Latin *Vulgate* (the fifth-century Bible in Latin), and many other translations. The name Jehovah was first restored to the English Bible in 1530 by William Tyndale. In a note to this edition he wrote: "Jehovah is God's name...Moreover, as oft as though seeist LORD in great letters (except there be any error in the printing) it is in Hebrew Jehovah."

Tyndale's influence caused translators to use Jehovah's name in just a few scriptures, but to write "LORD" or "GOD" in most places where JHVH originally occurred in the Hebrew. The translators of the *King James Version* in 1611, for example, kept Jehovah's name in four places, one being Psalms 83:18 which reads, "That men may know that thou, whose name is JEHOVAH, art the Most High over all the earth."

The issue of God's name is closely linked to the concept of salvation that is developed in the Bible. Salvation is dependent on the understanding that humans, who were made in the image of God, unlike animals who cannot choose to cultivate love in a conscious way, were created to have a relationship with him. In other words, humans cannot fulfill their potential and purpose without the recognition of God and his direction in their lives. Essentially, this means knowing what God's will is for mankind. Of course, this idea does not sit well with those who cringe over the concept of submission, because of all that it implies. But for those who choose to have a personal relationship with God, it is not felt as a burden for two main reasons.

The first is that when you develop a relationship with God, you feel the effects of this relationship in your personal life. You feel, though not as a made-up whimsical sentimentality, the effects of a pure and clean love on your heart and mind. You change your outlook because you raise your own standards of feeling and thinking. You practice loving more selflessly and practice thinking more objectively. Second, you rely on God's spirit, which is tenderly compassionate. In fact, the Bible uses the metaphor of a nursing mother to teach us about the depths of Jehovah's feelings for us. It is written, "Can a woman forget her nursing child, that she should not have compassion on the son of her womb? Yes, they may forget, yet I will not forget you."[43]

Salvation, then, is based on choosing to love in spite of the influence of the opposing, dark and angry world upon you. There is a reason that choice becomes a pivotal principle in the Bible. Choice sets up the basis for judgment, both in our personal lives and on the part of God. For the Bible teaches that there is a distinction between good and bad, love and hate, life and death. As a scripture in the Hebrew scriptures point out, "I have put life and death before you, the blessing and the malediction; and you must choose life in order that you may keep alive."[44] Though this may sound ominous, it really isn't scarey. What it means is that we have the freedom to choose what we want to do. Jehovah is not compelling us to do what we don't want to do, but he does point out that there are consequences to our actions. Everyone knows this applies on a physical level, but it especially applies on a spiritual level, where the repercussions of our choices are more serious because they are far-reaching.

If we can admit there is a right and a wrong in principle (though this is disputed by the philosophers of the world), then there is an indisputable result. Choice separates those who wish to love God and each other from those who don't. There isn't a middle ground or a fence to sit on. Though there are naturally various degrees of love that we display to one another and to God, the reality is that love will never stop growing.

As we gain more understanding about what love is in principle and practice, we can continue to cultivate its qualities. By contrast, the consequence of not loving each other means that we cannot get to know or love the divine. For the divine is the basis of love. In the Greek scriptures of the Bible it is written, "If anyone makes the statement: 'I love God,' and yet is hating his brother, he is a liar. For he who does not love his brother, whom he has seen, cannot be loving God, whom he has not seen."[45] Another scripture reads, "If we continue loving one another, God remains in us and his love is made perfect in us."[46]

When I read these scriptures, I recognized that I always wanted to be connected to others through the spirit of love, as much as or more than through the physical expression of love. Though I knew that love as a spiritual quality was best expressed among people, because they could consciously relate to love, I could ironically feel the spirit of love when I was in nature. I could hear it whispering, though not as a sound in my ears. It was more like a constant awareness that everything beautiful around me was willed and intentional, a purposeful expression of connectedness. Nature was so rich, vast, and intricate that I could never take it all in; it constantly kept me in wonder and in a state of heightened awe. I naturally felt this way, even though others, and especially my parents, wanted me to believe that life was not

an expression of willed intelligence. Still, though I always tried to share my feelings with them, they refused to take me seriously.

Once, when I was hiking with my family in the mountains for a day, I was telling my father how I loved to walk by and brush the pines that overhung the trail. I liked to touch them with a loving gratitude for their beauty. But when I showed my father how I touched them, he rebuked me. He told me that I was taking my sentiments too far because plants are not sentient and I shouldn't get carried away. I must have looked so strange to him out there on the trail, loving the pines as if I knew them personally. But at that point in time, I had been living and working outside for so long that I felt the spirit of life in such a strong way.

It always hurt me that I couldn't find anyone to understand how I felt, and how much I cared about beauty, though I always did try. A big part of my search for the spiritual oasis, then, was the search for an acknowledgment from someone, for some sort of clear recognition that what I felt was real. When I found the oasis, as the teachings of truth in the Bible, I made an extraordinary find. There were others like me who had also found the way to the same oasis. These were people who had made the same search as I had, and so were much like me.

Truly, it is crucial to understand why some people, like the ones who find the oasis, choose to love God while others refuse. When I first began to discern the basis of this distinction, and why it exists in the first place, I found an interesting scripture. It supported how I had always felt, and so validated my intuition. The scripture was expressed in the form of a question: "Do you not know that friendship with the world is enmity with God?"[47] Oh, how my heart leapt with gladness when I read this! I understood immediately what it meant. I had never trusted the world as meant by the Greek word *kosmos*, the world of human beings who are alienated from God. That is why I always searched for meaning away from the world, in the wilderness. It was also the reason I took up traveling with Swamiji. But I didn't initially realize that his teachings were actually a part of the world, though so concealed in such a clever way that he didn't even see it for himself. For though he thought he was separate from the world because he lived like a renunciate, his teachings were not distinct from the ways of the world.

The nature of the world can be seen most clearly in the fact that Jesus was murdered because what he taught went against the world's ambition. In a spiritual sense, the world hated him. Many people object to the use of the word "hatred" because it is so strong. But who can deny that hatred exists? As the world's condition deteriorates, there are more and more expressions of hatred, especially between groups of people that have different religious beliefs.

Jesus, who was the model of love, could still call a spade a spade when it came to denouncing those who showed hatred to God through hypocrisy. To the Jewish religious leaders of his day, who were called Pharisees and claimed to love God, he said, "Woe to you, scribes and Pharisees, hypocrites! because you resemble whitewashed graves, which outwardly indeed appear beautiful but inside are full of dead men's bones and of every sort of uncleanness. In that way you also, outwardly indeed, appear righteous to men, but inside you are full of hypocrisy and lawlessness."[48] Jesus also exclaimed, as a way to point out their selfishness, that "the greatest one among you must be your minister. Whoever exalts himself will be humbled, and whoever humbles himself will be exalted."[49]

So Jesus was killed because those who hated God did not obey his teachings about how to love God. On this basis, Jesus told his disciples that all who loved him, like he loved God, would be persecuted. In the days before he died, he said to them: "If they have persecuted me, they will persecute you also; if they have observed my word, they will observe yours also."[50] On another occasion Jesus informed his disciples: "People will deliver you up to tribulation and will kill you, and you will be objects of hatred by all the nations on account of my name."[51] So I realized that loving what Jesus represented meant that, when push came to shove, the world would hate me for it. Why?

For one thing, loving God means understanding what will happen to those who choose to know and love God versus those who choose not to know and love God. This dichotomy points to something essential: The alienation from God was originally a willful turning away. Salvation, therefore, is also applied to those who are persecuted, even killed, by those who don't want to know or love God. For death, according to the Bible, was not an original part of human life, as it is with animals. And part of humans being made in God's image meant that they wouldn't die. Though not immortal, humans were originally perfect in a physical way. They knew right from wrong. So when the first humans willfully decided that they wanted to live independently of God, they chose to be self-ruling. Eventually this led to their downfall and death. Though there are many details that must be understood in the unfolding of their decision and the repercussions that it involved, what is important to point out here is that earth was meant to be a place of peace, not a place of increasing insecurity and desperation.

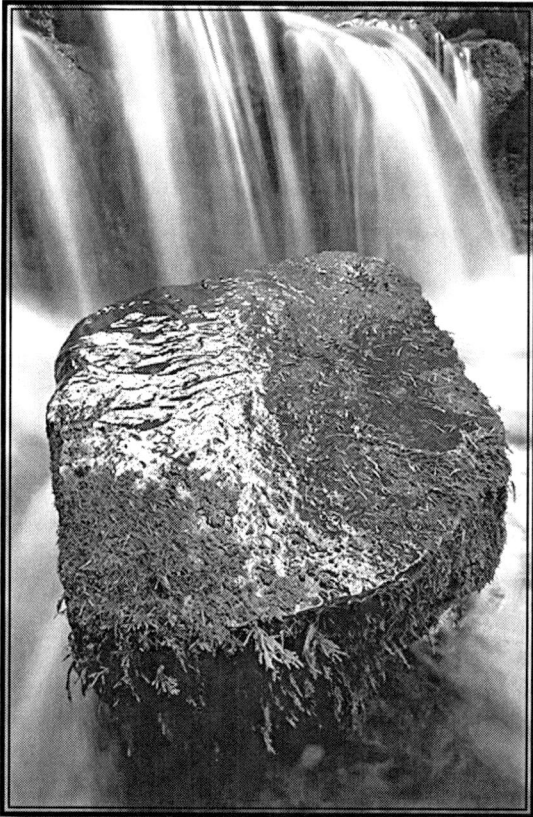

From the first century until today, people who have followed Christ's teachings have been killed for it. But they died with a hope for the future. They knew that by keeping their integrity to God, and not being turned away from him by the world's influence, they would be given the provision of a resurrection. This meant that they knew they would return to life on a peaceful earth that had been restored to a garden-like condition.

Those who were not persecuted to the point of death could still practice the peaceful way of life regardless of their culture. For all these people were united in the same spirit. Towards each other they practiced love because God taught them: "Clothe yourselves with the tender affections of compassion, kindness, lowliness of mind, mildness, and long-suffering. Continue putting up with one another and forgiving one another freely if anyone has a cause for complaint against another."[52] In another place I read, "Now that you have purified your souls by your obedience to the truth with unhypocritical brotherly affection as the result, love one another intensely from the heart."[53]

But even when they were persecuted for their beliefs by those outside of the oasis, so to speak, Jesus said to pray for them to have a change of heart. It is a powerful thought to raise your consciousness to the level of praying for those who persecute you. Though many people might find this a strange way to deal with adversaries, I didn't. In fact, I wanted to be identified with a group of people who all wanted to participate in imitating the love of Jesus, who taught that "Jehovah is very tender in affection and merciful."[54]

But those who wish to participate in this sharing of love, and to live in peace with each other, need to understand what is required. It means having an accurate knowledge of God's will. For Jesus warned, "Be on the watch for the false prophets that come to you in sheep's covering, but inside they are ravenous wolves."[55] Here, false prophets are equated with wolves in contrast with docile sheep. The comparison is meant to emphasize the difference between crafty machinations used to mislead others through ego from God, and a humble willingness to go where one is spiritually led. But humbleness here does not mean weakness or stupidity. To the contrary.

Only a shrewd and spiritual mind, based on a loving heart, can understand what Jesus meant when he said, "Go in through the narrow gate, because broad and spacious is the road leading off into destruction, and many are the ones going in through it; whereas narrow is the gate and cramped the road leading off into life, and few are the ones finding it."[56] Even most people who call themselves Christians don't appear to know what the narrow gate means and where it leads. Neither do they understand what Jesus meant by "God's Kingdom," in opposition to the world's kingdoms or governments. The reason is that they are part of the world's governments and don't understand how God's Kingdom, which is a theocratic government, will bring an end to violence, and those who practice violence.[57]

One can clearly see what it means when Jesus said that his followers must love God with their whole mind in addition to their whole heart. It means that one comprehends what will be the outcome of his or her personal choices. Free will is the basis of love and truth because one must choose to love and act accordingly. To use one's mind in an accurate way, then, means one lives in harmony with one's heart. As a consequence, a person will be known by the things that he does, regardless of what he says he believes. The Bible explains that "love is long-suffering and kind. Love is not jealous, it does not brag, does not get puffed up, does not behave indecently, does not look for its own interests, does not become provoked. It does not keep account of the injury. It does not rejoice over unrighteousness, but rejoices with the truth."[58]

As I studied prophecy and the different levels of meaning in the Bible, I found out that those who drink of the water of life and keep drinking that water have a promise made to them: "He [God] will wipe out every tear from their eyes, and death will be no more, neither will mourning nor outcry nor pain be anymore. The former things have passed away."[59]

When I read this, I knew that divine love can never be diminished. I had the strong realization that nothing could take this love away from me unless I turned away by myself. "For I am convinced that neither death nor life nor...governments nor things now here nor things to come nor powers nor height nor depth nor any other creation will be able to separate us from God's love."[60] I knew that the water of life was God's love. I also knew that it would flow forever and never run dry.

Notes

Persian poet, Jelaluddin Rumi, *The Essential Rumi*, translations by Coleman Barks (San Francisco: HarperCollins, 1995), p. 50.

A night full of talking that hurts,
My worst held-back secrets.
Everything has to do with loving and not loving.
This night will pass.
Then we have work to do.

CHAPTER TWO: SEARCHING FOR SPRINGS

1 Hubert H. Humphrey (1911–1978), U.S. Democratic vice president and politician, speech, March 26, 1966, Washington, D.C.

2 "At that time Jesus exclaimed, 'I bless you, Father, Lord of heaven and of earth, for hiding these things from the learned and the clever and revealing them to mere children.'" Matthew 11:25, *Jerusalem Bible, Eight Translation New Testament* (Illinois: Tyndale House Publishers, Inc., 1987), p. 81.

3 Matt was probably taught to use the watch analogy by his L.D.S. church leaders as an argument for God's existence. The analogy was used in the seventeenth and eighteenth centuries as a way to explain the order of the natural world and God's relationship to it. In recent years the argument is used in the same way to support the idea that there is intelligent design manifest in all life-forms.

4 A theist believes in the existence of God or gods. An atheist denies the existence of God or gods. A deist believes in one God who created, but who does not intervene in, the universe. A monotheist stresses belief in only one God. A monist believes that there is only one supreme being, as opposed to a belief in good and evil as conflicting powers. A polytheist believes that there is more than one god.

5 Thomas Barloon and Russell Noyes, Jr., "Charles Darwin and Panic Disorder" *Journal of the American Medical Association* 277 (1997): 139. Clifford A. Picover, *Strange Brains and Genius: The Secret Lives of Eccentric Scientists and Madmen* (New York: Quill William Morrow, 1998), p.290. Ralph Colp, Jr., *To Be an Invalid: The Illness of Charles Darwin* (Chicago: University of Chicago, 1977), p. 97. W. B. Bean, "The Illness of Charles Darwin," *The American Journal of Medicine* 65 (1978): 573.

6 Abdullah Yusufali, *Meaning of the Holy Qur'an*, Sura 4:163; 5:44-48. February 23, 2009 from http://www.islamicity.com/mosque/QURAN/4.htm.

7 Abdullah Yusufali, *Meaning of the Holy Qur'an*, Sura 4:157. February 23, 2009 from http://www.islamicity.com/mosque/QURAN/4.htm.

8 In the Hebrew Scriptures (Old Testament) is recorded the Mosaic Law Covenant that the nation of Israel was under. When Jesus died, the Mosaic Law covenant was ended. Referring to its cancellation, Paul pointed out that God took the Law out of the way "by nailing it to the torture stake." (Colossians 2:13, 14). *New World Translation of the Holy Scriptures,* with references (New York: Watchtower Bible and Tract Society of New York, Inc., 1961), p. 1417.

9 Luke 16:16, *Today's English Version, Eight Translation New Testament* (Illinois: Tyndale House Publishers, Inc., 1987), p. 550.

10 Revelation 19:10, *The Living Bible, Eight Translation New Testament* (Illinois: Tyndale House Publishers, Inc., 1987), p. 1876.

11 The apostle Paul explained that the gift of prophesying would pass away once it was no longer needed. "Whether there are gifts of prophesying, they will be done away with...For we have partial knowledge and we prophesy partially; but when that which is complete arrives, that which is partial will be done away with." 1 Corinthians 13:8-10, *New World Translation of the Holy Scriptures,* p. 1383.

12 The phrase "Ten Lost Tribes of Israel" refers to the time after the ten-tribe kingdom of Samaria was conquered by the Assyrian Empire in 740 B.C.E. The account given at 2 Chronicles 34:6-9 (Compare 2 Kings 23:19, 20) implies that during King Josiah's reign there were Israelites still in the land. But Joseph Smith wanted the *Book of Mormon* to link a migration of Hebrews to the ten-tribe Israelite nation of Samaria. That

is, he wanted the Hebrews that he claimed to migrate to the Americas to be the conquered Israelites of Samaria. In fact, official Mormon literature states that the *Book of Mormon* is a description of "the ancient history of this people, telling of their wars, movements, kings, and their religion–which was the religion of Israel, for these people were Israelites and practiced the law of Moses." See the missionary pamphlet published by the Church of Jesus Christ of Latter-day Saints, 1982, p.3.

13 In 1650, Thomas Thorowgood published his bestseller *Jews in America, Or, Probabilities that those Indians are Judaical, made more probable by some additionals to the former conjectures."* David Koffman in "Native Americans & Jews: The Lost Tribes Episode" writes, "The Lost Tribe idea found favor among early American notables, including Cotton Mather (the influential English minister), Elias Boudinot (the New Jersey lawyer who was one of the leaders of the American Revolution), and the Quaker leader William Penn." February 23, 2009 from http://jewish.goodnewseverybody.com/american.html.

14 Charles Darwin, *The Autobiography of Charles Darwin 1809–1882*, with the original omissions restored, edited and with appendix and notes by his grand-daughter Nora Barlow (London: Collins, 1958), p. 59.

15 Janet E. Browne, *Charles Darwin: Voyaging (Vol.1)* (London: Jonathan Cape, 1995), p. 97.

16 Darwin explained natural selection: "As many more individuals of each species are born than can possibly survive; and as, consequently, there is a frequently recurring struggle for existence, it follows that any being, if it vary however slightly in any manner profitable to itself, under the complex and sometimes varying conditions of life, will have a better chance of surviving, and thus be naturally selected. From the strong principle of inheritance, any selected variety will tend to propagate its new and modified form." *Charles Darwin, The Origin of Species by Means of Natural Selection, or the Preservation of Favoured Races in the Struggle for Life* (London: John Murray, 1872), p. 3.

17 Charles Darwin, *The Origin of Species*, p. 429.

18 Charles Darwin, *The Origin of Species*, p. 143.

19 Charles Darwin, *The Origin of Species*, p. 205.

20 Charles Darwin, *The Origin of Species*, p. 205.

21 Charles Darwin, *The Origin of Species*, p. 2.

22 Francis Darwin, ed., *Charles Darwin: His Life Told in an Autobiographical Chapter, and in a Selected Series of his Published Letters* (London: John Murray, 1892), p. 61.

23 Francis Darwin, *The Life and Letters of Charles Darwin, including an Autobiographical Chapter, Volume 1* (London: John Murray,1887), p. 304.

24 Charles Darwin, *The Origin of Species*, p. 265.

25 Charles Darwin, *The Origin of Species*, p. 282.

26 Charles Darwin, *The Origin of Species*, pp. 285-287.

27 Charles Darwin, *The Origin of Species*, p. 282.

28 Charles Darwin, *The Origin of Species*, pp. 289, 417.

29 Charles Darwin, *The Origin of Species*, p. 264.

30 Ralph Colp, Jr., *To Be an Invalid: The Illness of Charles Darwin* (Illinois: University of Chicago, 1977), p. 136.

31 John Bowlby, *Charles Darwin: A New Life* (New York: Norton, 1990), p. 240.

32 Lybi Ma, "On the Origin of Darwin's Ills," *Discover* magazine, Health & Medicine/Infectious Diseases, September 1, 1997. February 23, 2009 from http://discovermagazine.com/1997/sep/ontheoriginofdar1225. "One explanation of his ills, suggested by many scholars, is Chagas' disease, which is transmitted by the bite of the benchuca beetle. Apparently Darwin was bitten in 1835 while in Argentina, and his gastrointestinal complaints are typical Chagas symptoms...As for the Chagas diagnosis, Barloon points out that even if Darwin did suffer from the disease, it doesn't explain his many other problems."

33 Adrian Desmond and James Moore, *Darwin: The Life of a Tormented Evolutionist* (NY: Warner Books, 1991), p. 456.

34 Charles Darwin, *The Autobiography of Charles Darwin, 1809-82*, p. 115.

35 L. Croft, *The Life and Death of Charles Darwin* (UK: Elmwood, 1989), p. 104.

36 Francis Darwin & A.C. Seward, eds., *More Letters of Charles Darwin: A Record of His Work in a Series of Hitherto Unpublished Letters* Volume 1 (London: John Murray, 1903), p. 98.

37 Charles Darwin, *The Autobiography of Charles Darwin 1809-1882*, p. 115.

38 Richard Dawkins, *The Blind Watchmaker: Why the Evidence of Evolution Reveals a Universe Without Design* (New York: Norton, 1986), p. 6.

CHAPTER THREE: RUINS IN THE SAND

1 The complete poem, "Ozymandias" by Percy Shelley:

I met a traveller from an antique land
Who said: Two vast and trunkless legs of stone
Stand in the desert. Near them on the sand,
Half sunk, a shatter'd visage lies, whose frown
And wrinkled lip and sneer of cold command
Tell that its sculptor well those passions read
Which yet survive, stamp'd on these lifeless things,
The hand that mock'd them and the heart that fed.
And on the pedestal these words appear:
"My name is Ozymandias, king of kings:
Look on my works, ye mighty, and despair!"
Nothing beside remains: round the decay
Of that colossal wreck, boundless and bare,
The lone and level sands stretch far away.

February 23, 2009 from http://en.wikipedia.org/wiki/Ozymandias.

2 Galatians 5:19-22, *New World Translation of the Holy Scriptures*, with references, pp. 1403,1404.

3 James 4:4, *Revised Standard Version, Eight Translation New Testament* (Illinois: Tyndale House Publishers, Inc., 1987), pp. 1673,1675.

4   Lao Tzu, *The Way of Life*, translated by Witter Bynner (New York: G.P. Putnam and Sons, 1980), p.25.

5   Lao Tzu, *The Way of Life*, pp. 38-39.

CHAPTER FOUR: RUMORS OF A WELL

1   In Darwin's words, "Natural selection acts only by taking advantage of slight, successive variations. She can never take a great and sudden leap, but must advance by short and sure, though slow steps." *The Origin of Species* (London, John Murray, 1882), p. 156.

2   Loren Eiseley, *The Immense Journey* (New York: Random House, 1957), p. 200.

3   "Religion is the opium of the people" is one of the most frequently quoted statements of Karl Marx. It was translated from the German original, "Die Religion...ist das Opium des Volkes" and is often referred to as "religion is the opiate of the masses." The quote originates from the introduction of his 1843 work *Contribution to Critique of Hegel's Philosophy of Right* which was released one year later in Marx's own journal *Deutsch-Französische Jahrbücher*, a collaboration with Arnold Ruge." February 23, 2009 from http://en.wikipedia.org/wiki/Opium_of_the_People.

4   Karl Marx, Introduction to *A Contribution to the Critique of Hegel's Philosophy of Right, Collected Works, V. 3* (New York, 1976). February 23, 2009 from http://en.wikipedia.org/wiki/Opium_of_the_People.

5   Alen Woods and Ted Grant, *Reason in Revolt - Dialectical Philosophy and Modern Science, Vol. 2* (New York: Algora Publishing, 2003), p.107.

6   Herbert George Wells, *The Outline of History: Being a Plain History of Life and Mankind, Vol. 4*, 4th edition (New York: Macmillan, 1923), p. 1113. February 23, 2009 from: http://books.google.com/books?id=FGg MAAAAIAAJ&pg=PA1113&dq=%22prevalent+peoples+at+the+close +of+the+nineteenth+century%22#PPA1067,M1.

7   Francis Wheen, *Karl Marx: A Life* (New York: W.W. Norton & Company, 2000), pp. 179-180.

8 Wheen, *Karl Marx: A Life*, p. 180.

9 David McLellan, *Karl Marx: His Life and Thought* (New York: Harper & Row, 1974), p. 280.

10 Henry Crabb Robinson, *Diary, Reminiscences and Correspondence of Henry Crabb Robinson* (Boston: The Riverside Press, 1898), p.371. February 23, 2009 from http://books.google.com/books?id=MLC2bvDoU-4C&printsec=frontcover&dq=Henry+Crabb+Robinson#PPR1,M1.

11 Walt Whitman, *Specimen Days and Collect* (Philadelphia: David McKay, 1882), p. 197.

12 Louisia May Alcott, Joel Myerson, Daniel Shealy, Madeleine B. Stern, *The Selected Letters of Louisa May Alcott* (Georgia: University of Georgia Press, 1995), p. 277.

13 Ralph Waldo Emerson, *Essays and Poems* (New York: Harcourt, Brace and Company, 1921), p.133. February 23, 2009 from http://books.google.com/books?id=500hAAAAMAAJ&printsec=frontcover&dq=Ralph+waldo+Emerson,+essay+on+spiritual+laws#PPR1,M1.

14 Emerson, *Essays and Poems*, p.133.

15 Ralph Waldo Emerson, *The Prose Works of Ralph Waldo Emerson* (Boston: James R. Osgood and Company, 1875), p. 509. February 23, 2009 from http://books.google.com/books?id=NFMRAAAAYAAJ&pg=PA509&dq=%22the+multitude+of+false+churches%22#PPP9,M1.

16 Emerson, *The Prose Works of Ralph Waldo Emerson*, p. 241.

17 Emerson, *The Prose Works of Ralph Waldo Emerson*, p. 243.

18 Emerson, *The Prose Works of Ralph Waldo Emerson*, p. 243.

19 Emerson, *The Prose Works of Ralph Waldo Emerson*, p. 245.

20 Rabindranath Tagore, *Gitanjali* (London: Macmillan & Co., Ltd., 1942), pp. 29-30.

21 Tagore, *Gitanjali*, pp. 25-26.

22 Tagore, Gitanjali, pp. 30-31.

CHAPTER FIVE: IN PARCHED PLACES

1 Charles Darwin, *The Origin of Species*, p. 429. In the conclusion of his book, Darwin wrote about the magnificence of "the view of life, with its several powers, having been originally breathed by the Creator into a few forms or into one."

2 George Johnson, science writer, wrote an article called "Designing Life: Proteins 1, Computer 0," in *The New York Times* (March 25, 1997). In the article he discussed a contest which occupied scientists in the year 1996. He wrote that scientists "armed with their best computer programs, competed to solve one of the most complex problems in biology: how a single protein, made from a long string of amino acids, folds itself into the intricate shape that determines the role it plays in life...The result, succinctly put, was this: the computers lost and the proteins won...Scientists have estimated that for an average-sized protein, made from 100 amino acids, solving the folding problem by trying every possibility would take 10^{27} (a billion billion billion) years." February 23, 2009 from: http://query.nytimes.com/gst/fullpage.html?r es=9407E6DA103BF936A15750C0A961958260.

3 Jelaluddin Rumi, translated by Coleman Barks, *Feeling the Shoulder of the Lion: Selected Poetry and Teaching Stories from the Mathnawi* (New York: Threshold Books, 1991), from the poem called "The Thicket."

CHAPTER SIX: MORE MIRAGES

1 Edwin Conklin, biologist, wrote: "The probability of life originating from accident is comparable to the probability of the unabridged dictionary resulting from an explosion in a printing shop." *Reader's Digest* (1963): 92.

British astronomer Sir Fred Hoyle wrote: "The chance that higher life forms might have emerged in this way [by chance] is comparable with the chance that a tornado sweeping through a junk-yard might assemble a Boeing 747 from the materials therein...I am at a loss to understand biologists' widespread compulsion to deny what seems to me to be obvious." "Hoyle on Evolution," *Nature* 294 (1981): 105.

Hoyle also remarked that scientific challenges to evolution have "never had a fair hearing" because "the developing system of popular education [from Darwin's day to the present] provided an ideal opportunity...for awkward arguments not to be discussed and for discrepant facts to be suppressed." "The Universe: Past and Present Reflections." *Engineering and Science* (1981): 8-12.

Dr. Harold Morowitz of George Mason University is currently the principle investigator on a National Science Foundation grant to study the molecular processes of how life emerged on earth. See *The Mason Gazette*, August 14, 2006: "Mason Students Have Access to One of the World's Foremost Researchers on the Origins of Life." Dr. Morowitz expressed, "Life is too intricate to have random origins. There are laws of physics and chemistry at work that governed the process. We may not yet know all of the laws, but for a scientist, answering these questions is a continuum of discoveries." February 23, 2009 from http://gazette.gmu.edu/articles/8808.

2   According to Richard Dawkins: "The universe that we observe has precisely the properties we should expect if there is, at bottom, no design, no purpose, no evil, no good, nothing but pitiless indifference." God's Utility Function," *Scientific American* (1995): 85.

3   Paul Feyerabend, *Against Method: Outline of an Anarchistic Theory of Knowledge* (New York: Verso, 1993), p. 238.

4   Feyerabend, *Against Method: Outline of an Anarchistic Theory of Knowledge*, p. 238.

5   Stephen Jay Gould, "Dorothy, It's Really Oz," *Time* magazine 154 (1999): 59.

6   Tom Wolfe, "Sorry, But Your Soul Just Died," *Forbes* magazine, 158 (1996): 210. He states: "Neuroscience, the science of the brain and the central nervous system, is on the threshold of a unified theory that will have an impact as powerful as that of Darwinism a hundred years ago. Already there is a new Darwin, or perhaps I should say an updated Darwin, since no one ever believed more religiously in Darwin than he does. His name is Edward O. Wilson."

7   E.O. Wilson also claims that science is neither a philosophy nor a belief system. He calls it "a combination of mental operations that has become increasingly the habit of educated peoples, a culture of illuminations hit upon by a fortunate turn of history that yielded the most effective way of learning about the real world ever conceived."

Edward Wilson, *Consilience: The Unity of Knowledge* (New York: Alfred A. Knopf, 1998), p. 45.

Assuming Wilson knows what the "real world" is, which is debatable outside scientific circles, he still does not explain what the "culture of illuminations" (above) means. In any case, he does define what is REAL by his following criteria. He writes: "(1) repeatability--seeing the same phenomena occur under the same manipulations or natural sequence of events (2) economy--managing resources in an organized methodical way (3) mensuration--using universally accepted scales for measurement to avoid ambiguity, (4) heuristics--the project stimulates further discovery often in unpredictable new directions, (5) consilience--the explanations of different phenomena most likely to survive are those that can be connected and proved consistent with one another." *Consilience* pg. 53.

Wilson's work deals with a slice of life, a narrow brick wall, something hard like the outside of the skull or some other outer structure of appearance. What is real to him, and those who follow him, lies in the category of the externalizing outwardly-oriented mind. The externalizing mind weighs and judges and pronounces. But strangely the question of what is real, does not question who it is that knows what is real. He doesn't include self-knowledge in his criteria.

8 Wilson, *Consilience: The Unity of Knowledge*, p.45.

9 Sri Aurobindo, *Synthesis of Yoga* (M. Himatsinghaka, 1970), p. 69.

10 In Einstein's letter to Heinrich Zangger, December 6, 1917. The collected papers of Albert Einstein. March 2, 2009 from http://press.princeton.edu/catalogs/series/cpe.html.

11 Alice Calaprice, *The Quotable Einstein* (New Jersey: Princeton University Press, 1996), p. 129.

12 Objecting to the placing of observables at the heart of the new quantum mechanics, during Heisenberg's 1926 lecture at Berlin.

13 Professor D.M.S. Watson, who held the position of the Chair of Evolution at the University of London for more than twenty years, wrote: "The theory of evolution (is) a theory universally accepted not because it can be proved by logically coherent evidence to be true but because the only alternative, special creation, is clearly incredible." D.M.S. Watson, "Adaptation," *Nature* 123 (1929): 233.

14 Edward O. Wilson, "Intelligent Evolution: The consequences of Charles Darwin's 'one long argument,'" *Harvard Magazine* 108 (2005): 33. He continues, "It buoyed the devotees with a sense of superiority. It sacralized tribal laws and mores, and encouraged altruistic behaviors. Through sacred rites it lent solemnity to the passages of life. And it comforted the anxious and afflicted. For all this and more it gave people an identity and purpose, and vouchsafed tribal fitness — yet, unfortunately, at the expense of less united or otherwise less fortunate tribes."

15 David Roberts, "EOphilia," Grist: Environmental News and Commentary, Oct 17, 2006. February 23, 2009 from http://www.grist.org/news/maindish/2006/10/17/wilson/index.html.

16 Roberts, Grist: Environmental News and Commentary, Oct 17, 2006.

17 Roberts, Grist: Environmental News and Commentary, Oct 17, 2006.

18 Aldous Huxley, "Confessions of a Professed Atheist," Report: Perspective on the News 3 (1966): 19. Aldous Huxley (the grandson of evolutionist Thomas Huxley) was an influential writer of the twentieth century.

19 See the website for The National Center for Biotechnology Information. February 23, 2009 from http.//www.ncbi.nlm.nih.gov.

20 Norman Macbeth, *Darwin Retried: An Appeal to Reason* (Boston: Gambit, 1971), p. 33.

CHAPTER SEVEN: DYING OF THIRST

1 This phrase comes from the *Rigveda* which is a group of songs composed around three thousand years ago in praise of thirty-three deities, many of which are deified natural elements. In the *Upanishads*, which were composed about five hundred years later and were not songs, but more like philosophical treatises about the nature of existence, there is found the similar idea that truth can have different names, just like cows of different colors still give the same color milk.

2 Romans 1:20, *King James Version, Eight Translation New Testament* (Illinois: Tyndale House Publishers, Inc., 1987), p. 1076.

3 Romans 1:21, 22, *Kings James Version, Eight Translation New Testament* (Illinois: Tyndale House Publishers, Inc., 1987), pp. 1076, 1078.

4 The Notebooks of Leonardo da Vinci. February 23, 2009 from http:en. wikiquote.org/wiki/Leonardo_da_Vinci. See notebook XIX.

5 The concept of reincarnation depends on the idea that the human soul is immortal and lives on after the death of the body. By contrast, the concept of resurrection is based on the idea that there is no immortal soul and that when a person dies, he ceases to exist.

6 The Vedas were composed nearly three thousand years ago and were transmitted orally from teacher to pupil until the fourteenth century when they were written down. They are grouped into four sections with four names: *Rigveda* (songs in praise of the thirty-three Vedic deities); *Samaveda* (contains the songs sung by priests during the offering of various plant juice and milk mixtures to the various 33 deities named in the *Rigveda*); *Yajurveda* (the manual for priests of the Vedic religion); *Atharvaveda* (contains remedies to heal illness, including magic and spells). February 23, 2009 from http://en.wikipedia.org/wiki/Vedas.

7 R.C. Majumdar, *The History and Culture of the Indian people, Vol. 1: The Vedic Age* (Bombay: Bharatiya Vidyan Bhavan, 1971), p. 502. He wrote: "All the philosophical systems and religions of India, heretical or orthodox, have sprung up from the Uphanishads."

8 The Indian Epics included The *Ramayana* of Valmiki and the *Mahabharata* of Vyasa. They were written sometime between 500 B.C.E. and 200 C.E. according to K.A. Nilakanta Sastri and G. Srinivasachari. See *The Advanced History of India* (New Delhi: Allied Publishers, 1982), p. 59.

9 *Agama* basically means "scripture" in the Hindu, Jain, and Budhist religions, but they are more like are popularized "manuals" for how to worship God through the use of idols and temples. They also give details about mantras, mystic diagrams, charms, spells, domestic observances, social rules, and public festivals. February 23, 2009 from http://www.dlshq.org/religions/agamas.htm.

10 Maurice Phillips, *The Teaching of the Vedas: What Light Does It Throw on the Origin and Development of Religion?* (London: Longmans, Green &

Co., 1895), p. 129.

11 Wendy Doniger O'Flaherty, *The Rig Veda: an Anthology: One Hundred and Eight Hymns* (London: Penguin, 1981), p. 103.

12 Alisstair Shearer and Peter Russell, translators, *The Upanishads* (London: Wildwood House Ltd., 1978), p. 46.

13 *Sri Guru Granth Sahib*, p.839. February 23, 2009 from http://www.sikhs. org/english/frame.html.

14 Abdullah Yusufali, *Meaning of the Holy Qur'an*, Sura 21:30. "Do the unbelievers not realize that the heaven and the earth used to be one solid mass that we exploded into existence? And from water we made all living things. Would they believe?" February 23, 2009 from http:// www.islamicity.com/Mosque/QURAN/21.htm.

CHAPTER EIGHT: THE OASIS

1 Colossians 2:23, *New World Translation of the Holy Scriptures*, with references (New York: Watchtower Bible and Tract Society of New York, Inc., 1961), p. 1418. All future Bible references for this chapter will be to the New World Translation unless otherwise noted.

2 John 18:36, p. 1308.

3 Job 26:7, p. 666.

4 Ecclesiastes 1:7, *World English Bible*, Feb.23, 09, http://ebible.org/web/.

5 Amos 5:8, p. 1132.

6 Homer wrote about "the mighty deep-circling Oceanus, stream from whom all seas and rivers rise, all springs and bottomless wells." Homer, *Iliad* (Indianapolis: Bobbs-Merrill Educational Publishing, 1977), p. 429.

7 S.M. Karterakis, B.W. Karney, B. Singh and A. Guergachi, "The hydrologic cycle: a complex history with continuing pedagogical implications," *Water Science & Technology: Water Supply 7* (2007): 23-31.

8 Isaiah 40:22, p. 901.

9 Job 26:10, p. 665.

10 The Mosaic Law (that was binding upon the Israelites until Jesus died in 29 C.E.) helped the Israelites to distinguish between what was clean and unclean. This Law code involved physical hygiene, diet, and even waste disposal. Notably, laws that required the burying of human waste, the quarantining of the sick, and washing after touching a dead body were many centuries ahead of their times. For examples of laws regarding these things see: Leviticus 13:4-8; Numbers 19:11-13, 17-19; Deuteronomy 23:13, 14.

11 Aristotle, "On the Soul," translated by Hippocrates, G. Apostle (Iowa: Peripatetic Press, 1981), 405a19. Aristotle's "On the Soul" is a treatise about the nature of living things and how he accounted for the animating spirit of life. In this treatise, Aristotle discusses the different kinds of souls possessed by different things, which gives them life and their special characteristics. Also, see James A. Arieti and David M. Gibson, *Philosophy in the Ancient World* (Maryland: Rowman & Littlefield, 2004), p. 45. They write: "Perhaps Thales believed that the soul is a god because it causes things to move and that movement is the essence of being alive."

12 Aristotle, "On the Soul," 411a7.

13 Though Thales thought that the *arche* (principle matter) was water, Anaximander called it *apeiron*. But apeiron is much more difficult to conceptualize than water. According to Anaximander, apeiron held a mystery but was also supposed to be without mystery. He explained it as an infinite, ageless substance which still could somehow hold opposites like heat and cold, wet and dry and which, in some hidden way, could give rise to the various shapes and colors of life.

Aristotle referred to Anaximander's apeiron as a kind of primal chaos, an idea which appeals to evolutionists today who claim that life evolved in a primeval soup. This soup, like a primal chaos, had to miraculously conceal within itself the power to create life by accident. In fact, some evolutionists believe that Anaximander coined two important concepts that justify a meaningful beginning to evolutionary theory: the idea that all things are related, and the idea that all things change over time.

The idea that all things are related is not new with Anaximander, though, because Thales before him believed that all things were made from water and so were related through their origins. Regardless of Thales' beliefs, the idea that living things change over time is not hard to find in ancient times. Also, since no physical mechanism was ever known to identify the processes of change, everyone offered his own ideas much like they do today. So even if one mythical tradition was discarded, it only meant that another would be invented to take its place. The third-century Roman writer Censorinus wrote about the natural history of man and included this comment: "Anaximander believed that there arose from heated water and earth either fish or animals very much like fish. In these, humans grew and were kept inside as embryos up to puberty. Then finally they burst and men and women came forth already able to nourish theselves." Scientists today suggest that Anaximander was highlighting that human infancy is an extended and vulnerable period of time, so the idea of being safely tucked in the mouth of a fish would protect an infant nicely.

14 Galileo defended heliocentrism (the claim that the sun and not the earth was at the center of the universe), and that this discovery did not refute the Bible's teachings. Church authorities believed that Galileo's findings did refute the Bible teachings and cited Psalm 93:1, 96:10, and 1 Chronicles 16:30, which all stated that the world is "firmly established, it cannot be moved." They believed that these verses supported Aristotle's view that the earth literally couldn't move. Aristotle had taught that it would grind to a halt due to friction. February 23, 2009 from http://en.wikipedia.org/wiki/Galileo_Galilei.

15 The Genesis creation account shows that there was an indefinite period of time that passed before light and life was created at the start of the six creative days. "In the beginning God created the heavens and the earth" (Genesis 1:1). Then there was darkness upon the surface of the water until the first day began. The creative days included:
Day 1: light, the separation between day and night as we know it (Genesis 1:3-5).
Day 2: the atmosphere (called the "expanse") was formed as a division between the water below it and water vapor above it (Genesis 1:6-8).
Day 3: Dry land emerged and vegetation appeared (Genesis 1:9-13).
Day 4: The sun, moon and stars became visible from earth (Genesis 1:14-19).
Day 5: Aquatic and flying creatures appeared (Genesis 1:20-23).
Day 6: Land animals and man appeared. (Genesis 1:24-31).

16 Darwin, *The Origin of the Species* (London: John Murray, 1869), p. 265.

17 David M. Raup, "Conflicts Between Darwin and Paleontology," *Bulletin, Field Museum of Natural History* 50 (1979): 24.

18 Robert G. Wesson, *Beyond Natural Selection* (Massachusetts: MIT Press, 1991), pp. 207-208.

19 Wesson, *Beyond Natural Selection*, pp. 207-208.

20 Darwin, *The Origin of the Species*, p. 408.

21 Stephen Jay Gould, "Evolution's Erratic Pace," *Natural History* 8 (1977): 14.

22 Ernst Mayr, *Toward a New Philosophy of Biology: Observations of an Evolutionist* (Massachusetts: Harvard University Press, 1988), pp. 529-530.

23 Niles Eldredge, *Reinventing Darwin: Great Evolutionary Debate* (London: Phoenix, 1995), p. 95.

24 Eldredge, *Reinventing Darwin: Great Evolutionary Debate*, p. 95.

25 Alan Feduccia, "Evidence from claw geometry indicating arboreal habits of Archaeopteryx," *Science* 259 (1993): 792.

26 Tom Kemp, "The reptiles that became mammals," *New Scientist* 92 (1982): 583.

27 B. Knox, P. Ladiges & B. Evans, *Biology* (Sidney: McGraw-Hill, 1994), p.663.

28 James H. Marden, "How insects learned to fly," *The Sciences* 35 (1995): 27-28.

29 David B. Kitts, "Paleontology and Evolutionary Theory," *Evolution* 28 (1974):467.

30 J. Francis Hitching, *The Neck of the Giraffe: Or Where Darwin Went Wrong* (London: Pan, 1982), p. 27.

31 Gerald A. Kerkut, *Implications of Evolution* (*International Series of Mono-*

graphs on Pure and Applied Biology, Division: Zoology, Volume 4) (New York: Pergamon Press, 1960), pp. 144-145.

32 "Billions and Billions of Demons" is the title of Richard Lewontin's *New York Times* book review of Carl Sagan's book *The Demon-Haunted World: Science as a Candle in the Dark*, Volume 44, January 9, 1997.

33 Hebrews 4:12, p. 1441.

34 1 John 4:8, p. 1468.

35 Psalm 10:4, p. 693.

36 "I am giving you a new commandment, that you love one another; just as I have loved you, that you also love one another" John 13:34, p. 1302.

37 John 13:35, p. 1302.

38 Galatians 5:22, p. 1404.

39 P. Marion Simms, *The Bible from the Beginning* (New York: McMillian, 1929), pp. 74, 76.

40 Sir Frederic Kenyon, *The Chester Beatty Biblical Papyri: Descriptions and Texts of Twelve Manuscripts on Papyrus of the Greek Bible* (London: Emery Walker Ltd., 1933), p. 15.

41 Matthew 22:37, p. 1204.

42 James 4:8, p. 1455.

43 Isaiah 49:15, p. 913.

44 Deuteronomy 30:19, p. 274.

45 1 John 4:20, p. 1468.

46 1 John 4:12, p. 1468.

47 James 4:4, p. 1455.

48 Matthew 23:27,28, p. 1205.

Notes

49 Matthew 23:11,12, pp. 1204, 1205.

50 John 15:20, p. 1304.

51 Matthew 24:9, p. 1206.

52 Colossians 3:13, p. 1418.

53 1 Peter 1:22, p. 1457.

54 James 5:11, p. 1456.

55 Matthew 7:15,16, p. 1183.

56 Matthew 7:13,14, p. 1183.

57 Jesus said in his Sermon on the Mountain that his disciples should pray for God's Kingdom: "Let your kingdom come" (Matthew 6:10), p. 1182. "The righteous themselves will possess the earth, and they will reside forever upon it" (Psalm 37:29), p. 716.

58 1 Corinthians 13:4-6, p. 1383.

59 Revelation 21:4, p. 1492.

60 Romans 8:39,39, p. 1363.

Photography Credits

Written permission has been granted to the author to publish the photographs that appear in this book. Photographs that are not listed belong to the author or were retrieved from stock photo or other free Internet sites.

CHAPTER EIGHT

Acknowledgments

I am grateful to have the opportunity to publicly thank my husband, Michael Mitchell, for helping me so much on this book, and for encouraging me every step of the way. His computer and design skills helped to make this book a piece of art. Most importantly, I appreciate that he understands the relevance of this book's subject matter on our lives.

I also want to thank my father and mother, Del and Carol Wiens, for giving me a colorful upbringing, full of adventure, travel, and education. I have always been proud of their ability to seek out new lands and keep their bodies fit for exploration. Special thanks to my mother for sharing her journal with me regarding the details about what we ate and the food available as we traveled across Africa.

I also want to thank my sisters, Paula and Alison, for the adventures we have shared in foreign lands. Our shared memories of the places we have seen, and the people we have met, are precious to me.

Annie Krug has been a wonderful editor for this book; it has been a great experience to work with her. I am grateful for her dedication, stamina, and commitment to thoroughness and excellence. Her good humor has brought me so much joy and I have loved sharing my passion for writing with her. It seems only once in a lifetime that I could expect to find such a compatible person as her to work with me on this project, to which I've given my whole heart.

How can I ever thank Jim and Pattie Manglis for their constant expressions of loving kindness and friendship. Their support has meant so much to me. Jim has been a father-like mentor and has supplied the right encouragement to keep me going and see the writing in a balanced way.

Joe and Susan Elmer have contributed to this book by sharing knowledge and support. Thanks to Susan for her help in proofreading and finding things that only she could see. She also tirelessly listened to me talk about my ideas for this book and made valuable suggestions.

Also, many thanks to Jordan Mitchell for his help with computer graphics. As a professional graphic artist, he contributed to the creative process involved in designing the book cover. His assistance has been invaluable.

Finally, I could never have written this book without the support and friendship of so many people who understand my point of view and love me for it.

ABOUT THE AUTHOR

SITA MITCHELL is a writer and teacher living on the coast of San Diego with her husband Michael and chow chow Remy. Her passion is to get the most out of life and to help others to do the same. Sita would like to hear your thoughts about her book. Write to her at **Searchingforlifeswater.com**. And if you liked what you read - tell a friend.

This book can be ordered from:

your local bookstore

or

from Sita Mitchell

by sending a check payable to

Sita Mitchell for $20.00 U.S. to

699 North Vulcan Ave. # 84

Encinitas, California

92024

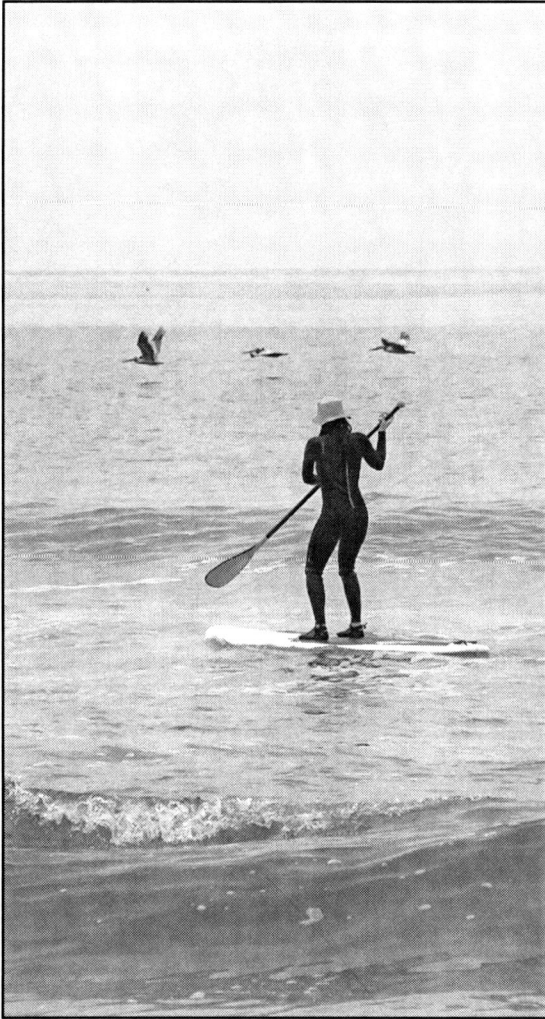

Printed in the United States
149158LV00004B/59/P